INFORMED WORSHIP

Informed worship leads to deep worship

GW00708323

SOTIRIOS CHRISTOU

Books by Sotirios Christou

The Priest & The People Of God - 2003
Revised as: Images Of Formation - 2009
Evangelism & Collaborative Ministry - 2004
Anglican & Beyond Repair - 2005
Paul & The Unsearchable Riches Of Christ - 2006
Revised as: The Unsearchable Riches Of Christ & Paul
- 2007, 2008, 2009 x 2
Worship As You Like It - 2006 Revised as:
Informed Worship - 2007, 2008, 2009 x 3, 2010
The Psalms - Intimacy, Doxology & Theology - 2010

First published in Great Britain by Phoenix Books.
18 Bullen Close Cambridge CB1 8YU
TEL 01223 246349
The right of Sotirios Christou to be identified as the author
Of this work has been asserted to him in accordance with the
Copyright, Designs and Patents Acts 1988.

We pray to You, O God, who are the supreme Truth,
        and all truth is from You.
We beseech You, O God, who are the highest Wisdom,
        and all the wise depend on You for their wisdom.
You are the supreme Joy, and all who are joyful owe it to You.
You are the greatest Good, and all goodness comes from You.
You are the Light of minds, and all receive their understanding
        from You.
We love You – indeed, we love You above all things.
We seek You, follow You and are prepared to serve You.

Alfred The Great King Of England   849-899

The spirituality of presiding is I think all in your voice. Your tone, words, cadence, timing, timbre, your sounds, your voice's pauses and silences - all conspire to make the voice the most versatile and most powerful tool you have to lead others. Be loud and you'll scare. Be soft and you'll entice. Use too many clever words and you'll block...No jazz at all and the words fall flat. You proclaim, invite, dedicate, pray, teach, sing, lead, chant, dream, lament, challenge, cry - and all with your voice. What is in your voice is your presence. And what is in your presence as you preside can be God's Spirit or not.

Siobhan Garrigan The Spirituality Of Presiding 2007

Almighty God
to whom all hearts are open
all desires known
and from whom no secrets are hidden:
cleanse the thoughts of our hearts
by the inspiration of your Holy Spiri,
that we may perfectly love you
and worthily magnify your holy name:
through Jesus Christ our Lord. Amen

The Collect For Purity Thomas Cranmer   1489-1556

CONTENTS

CHAPTER ONE
WORSHIP IN THE OLD TESTAMENT

CHAPTER TWO
COUNTERFEIT WORSHIP

CHAPTER THREE
THE PSALMS AND WORSHIP

CHAPTER FOUR
CHRIST AND WORSHIP

CHAPTER FIVE
WORSHIP AT THE THRONE OF GOD

FOREWORD

Worship is the first calling of the church. Both personal and corporate worship lie at the heart of Christian discipleship. Worship is to, for, and about God. Its primary purpose is to honour Him. To achieve that purpose it needs to combine passion with intelligence, and the worship of the heart with a thoroughly informed understanding of the greatness of God.

Sotirios has written this book with passion, to enrich our understanding of the worship of God. The later chapters have a particular focus on sung worship in the Christian tradition, but Christians of all traditions would benefit from what he has to say.

By drawing together insights from a wide variety of authors and perspectives he has opened windows from different traditions of worship, which throw light on one another. Decades ago JB Phillips wrote 'Your God Is Too Small.' This book could be subtitled 'Your Worship Is Too Narrow.'

None of us can claim that our practice of worship adequately honours God who has revealed himself in Jesus Christ. 'Informed Worship' provides a splendid collection of insights to equip us to think about the way we worship, and to engage with God with greater integrity.

Don't use this book to criticize others' worship. Use it to enrich your own.

+ Graham Cray Advent 2007

PREFACE

As I was hesitant about whether to embark on a new project about worship I laid a fleece before the Lord. I decided to start writing at the beginning of September 2006 and my prayer during this month was that the Lord would confirm whether or not I should continue. As I studied the book of Exodus and gained fresh insights about worship, and as the month progressed, I was much aware of God's presence and believe it was right to continue. I focused on worship from the Old Testament and the New Testament, as I wanted to see what the Lord had to say: and because I wanted to see how relevant insights from Scripture could be to our worship today and to avoid coming with my own agenda. The first five of the seven chapters are expositions from Scripture about worship. I believe many of these insights are important because they can enhance our corporate worship. The other two chapters contain insights from authors and songwriters who are knowledgeable about worship.

I am grateful for feedback on ch. 6 from Richard Rhodes-James, Guy Brandon, Andy Irons (a talented songwriter) and Lizzie Pridmore, all from St. Barnabas Church, Cambridge. I considered what Lizzie had to say was both challenging and significant as she is relatively young. So I responded by revising the order of the contents, renaming one or two sections and also amalgamating one or two others. Graham Cray also gave me feedback on ch. 6 which led to some revision. In the January 2009 edition, as a result of my ongoing research on contemporary and charismatic worship, Ch. 6 and 7 have continued to be revised and expanded. The new topics now included 'Alternative Worship,' 'All-Age Worship' 'Creative liturgical Worship' and 'Pentecostal Worship.' In ch. 3 The Psalms & Worship, included Psalm 119 – 'Intimacy with the Lord.' In this latest revised edition in April 2009, in ch. 7, there is new material on 'Transcendence & Immanence' and 'Biblical Or Romantic Intimacy?' The original version was 58,580 words and the latest is 88,624 words. I have over 150 books on worship and am inclined to think the average Christian has read very little about this topic. My heartfelt concern is for Christians to learn more about worship and broaden their horizon - rather than think 'sung worship' is the essence of Christian worship - and to remain content with what they know, and ignorant of what they don't know: and for Christians to aim for a deep level of learning and understanding, to inform and shape their corporate worship.

INTRODUCTION

When I had my call for ministry tested in the Church of England a number of years ago, I went with a simple trust that this was what the Lord was calling me to. During a Selection Conference over two days I was interviewed by three selectors, who had the authority to recommend to my bishop whether or not I should train for the ordained ministry. One of the most constructive and helpful comments the selectors made, was that they wanted me to show an *'intellectual curiosity.'* *'Intellectual curiosity'* cultivates an enquiring mind and invites us to ask searching questions about the Christian faith – that can deepen our faith.

The inspiration behind this book reflects an enquiring mind that seeks to identify biblical principles of worship and also sets out to explore contemporary and charismatic worship. Many churches have members who go on Christian holidays which have large scale celebrations and like many other churches their model of worship is likely to consist of preaching, sung worship and prayer ministry. My instinct is that Christians would value learning more about worship. So I trust that my biblical studies along with my research will enable us to be more informed about worship from Scripture and about the dynamics, the history and theology of contemporary and charismatic worship.

Bob Kauflin a pastor and worship leader for 30 years says: 'The church music landscape has changed dramatically over the years. In many churches singing now occupies up to half the meeting, led by a musician who may or may not have theological training or pastoral gifts. People often choose churches more for the music than for the preaching or doctrine. It's been suggested that music is the new sacrament that mediates God's presence to us. Obviously there are reasons for great concern.'[1]

He believes a pastor can ensure the worship leader chooses songs that have theologically balanced lyrics, rather than ones that are popular. Songs can be chosen that remind us of God's promises and faithfulness in the midst of our trials, especially revealed to us in the gospel. The pastor can also help people to understand what biblical worship entails. And while it is easy to overlook, Kauflin reminds us that the biblical picture of worship is far richer, more complex, deeper, more fulfilling, more comprehensive than our present 'worship' culture suggests. That's why pastors need to study the theology of worship.[2]

John Leach in 'Liturgy and Liberty,' believes there is so much more of God to encounter in our corporate worship. He highlights one of the fundamental aspects of Christian worship, namely that this is always a response to something God has done. But, he also touches on a dynamic aspect that can easily be overlooked. Namely, that on occasions, worship in the Old Testament in the Tabernacle and The temple, resulted in a greater manifestation of God's glory and presence.

> The people worshipped in order that God would come among them in power, to be enthroned on their praises and to manifest his glory. This left me in a dilemma. Which way round was it? Where did God fit in – at the beginning or at the end? Did we worship God because he was there, or was he there because we worshipped?[3]

Leach concludes both could be true. This is an important reminder that God is not only present as we begin our worship, but that he can also come and manifest his glory and presence among his people more intensely. This model of worship is evident in 2 Chron. ch. 5 – 7 where Solomon calls upon God to come among his people as he consecrates the Temple. In response the Lord comes in his 'overpowering glory and overwhelming presence.' In 'Living Liturgy,' Leach reminds us that at times in the Old Testament individuals or groups experienced the Holy Spirit coming upon them. For example, the elders in Num. 25, Saul in 1 Sam. 10 and his soldiers in 1 Sam. 19. He also points out, 'The primitive church had a theology and experience of God coming among them. This is seen in Acts 4: 31 as God comes among his people in response to their prayer and in ch. 10: 44 when he interrupts Peter's sermon when the Holy Spirit came down on Cornelius and his household.'[4] It is also seen on the Day of Pentecost at the coming of the Holy Spirit on the disciples.

In Anglican worship one of the Communion prayers (B) calls on the Lord to: 'Send the Holy Spirit on your people.' A similar prayer is used by the bishop for the candidates in the Confirmation and Ordination Services. 'The theology of God coming among his people is also clearly seen in well known hymns such as: Come

Holy Ghost Our Souls Inspire, Come Down O Love Divine and Come Gracious Spirit Heavenly Dove.'[5] In charismatic worship the prayer that is often used, 'Come Holy Spirit' is perfectly valid. This is a challenge not to remain static in our corporate worship, but to be open to the divine promptings of God by his Spirit.

When thinking about Christian worship we can forget that it is not primarily about what pleases us and we should take care not to subtly make ourselves its central focus. John Pritchard, Bishop of Oxford, reminds us of the essence of worship.

> Worship is fundamentally for God, to God and of God. Worship is offering all of ourselves, to all that God has revealed himself to be…Worship is the means by which we interrupt our preoccupation with ourselves and attend to God. We are endlessly absorbed and fascinated with ourselves, our image and appeal. Worship is the great corrective to all this.[6]

And Jonathan Gledhill, Bishop of Litchfield sums up the wonder of Christian worship.

> Worship is the response of the creature to the Creator: to worship is the desire to give true worth to what is beyond our powers of appreciation. To worship is to be aware of the heavens declaring the glory of God: to worship is to be aware of the transcendence of God: the infinite distance between the Maker and the made: and at the same time His immanence: to be part of a creation that longs to respond more properly to God at work within it.[7]

We are probably aware that the origin in English of the word worship is 'worthship' which expresses value – the worth placed on someone or something. Graham Kendrick refers to the word '*proskuneo*' as the most commonly used word to describe worship in the New Testament, which means 'to come forward to kiss' (the hand). '*Proskuneo*' denotes both the external act of prostrating oneself in worship and the corresponding inward act of reverence and humility.'[8] The weakness of the derivation 'worthship' is that it depends on making a subjective assessment of God's worth. David Peterson, a former Principal of Oakhill Theological College, echoes this when he says: 'Worship means by derivation to "attribute worth" which suggests that to worship God is to ascribe him supreme worth…But, worship interpreted and understood in this way may not have anything to do at all with the particularity of biblical revelation.'[9]

Peterson's understanding of what constitutes worship leads him to say: 'While worship is often broadly defined as our response to God, there is an important theological context to be considered when worship is presented in such terms…At one level we must discover from God's own self-revelation in Scripture what pleases him. We cannot determine for ourselves what is honouring to him. In particular we need to take seriously the extraordinary biblical perspective that acceptable worship is something made possible for us by God.'[10] We come to worship God according to the biblical principles he has given us and these should reflect the essence of our different styles of worship. Peterson echoes this: 'The worship of the true and living God is essentially an engagement with him on the terms that he proposes and in the way he alone makes possible.'[11]

Archbishop William Temple, has a definition of worship that captures how every aspect of our being is involved in it.

> Worship is the submission of all our nature to God. It is the quickening of the conscience by his holiness: the nourishment of the mind with his truth: the purifying of the imagination by his beauty: the opening of the heart to his love: the surrender of the will to his purpose, and all this gathered up in adoration, the most selfless emotion of which our nature is capable.[12]

But, a definition of Christian worship also has to include Christ or it would be incomplete. Christopher Cocksworth, Bishop of Coventry, shares how during his ordination training each member in his tutorial group was asked to give a definition of worship in one sentence. He was working for a research degree in the area of Christian worship and gave a suitably sophisticated answer. 'It was something on the lines of offering our whole lives to God in grateful self-giving. But, along with others in the group, I was much more moved by the answer of a young Church of Scotland ordinand on an exchange visit to the college. "For me" he said "worship is joining with Jesus as he praises his Father." He made the reality of Christian existence and the nature of Christian prayer and worship startlingly clear and simple. To be a Christian is to be in Christ through his Spirit. To relate to God in prayer and worship is to do so *in, through* and even *with* Christ.'[13]

Professor Hoon emphasises the Christological centre of Christian worship, which by definition is Christological. He also points to the analysis of the meaning of worship, which likewise must be fundamentally Christological.

> Such worship is profoundly incarnational being governed by the whole event of Jesus Christ. Christian worship is bound directly to the events of salvation history while bridging them and bringing them into our present. The core of worship is God acting to give His life to man and to bring man to partake of that life.
>
> Christian worship is God's revelation of himself in Jesus Christ and man's response, or a twofold action – that of God towards the human soul in Jesus Christ and in man's responsive action through Jesus Christ. Through his Word God discloses and communicates his very being to man.[14]

White perceives that the key words in Hoon's view of Christian worship seem to be 'revelation' and 'response.' At the centre of both is Jesus Christ who reveals God to us and through whom we make our response.[15]

But, a definition of Christian worship that did not refer to the Holy Spirit would also be incomplete. Cocksworth says: 'The Spirit is the one who enables us to worship because the Spirit brings us into fellowship with Christ and therefore with each other and with his Father. As we worship we enter into the movement of Christ's self-giving to the Father through the Spirit...Christian worship is participation in the eventful life of God through the presence and activity of the Holy Spirit in the life of the believer and in the midst of the fellowship of the Church.'[16] He also astutely adds: 'The confidence that God has given the Spirit to the Church should not lead us to complacent assurance that authentic worship will automatically happen simply by virtue of the fact we are the Church. It should compel us to enter more deeply into the gift God has given so that our worship can be truly inspired, by virtue of the fact that the Spirit is breaking us out of our preoccupation with ourselves and taking us into the love which Christ has for God.'[17]

In 'Worship At The Next Level' there is a focus on Trinitarian worship. James Torrance describes this as, 'our participation through the Spirit in the Son's Communion with the Father in his vicarious life of worship and intercession...Because Christian worship by definition is our participation in the life of the triune God, worship simultaneously expresses our theology and shapes it. Therefore, our worship must be *'intelligent'* using our minds (as well as our hearts, voices and bodies). Worship leaders are some of the church's primary theological educators and they need to work through the theological and cultural truths involved in worship.

> If our worship is to be intelligent, offered joyfully in the freedom of the Spirit, we must look at the realities which inspire us and demand from us an intelligent, meaningful response. As theological educators it is therefore essential that those leading worship be theologically, culturally and aesthetically educated.'[18]

Dennis Ngien in 'Gifted Response,' stresses that Christian worship is also God's gift to us in which we participate. It is first and foremost God's action in our hearts that we respond to. 'The chief motive of worship is grace – that the God who initiates his movement toward us in order to make worship through the Son in the Spirit possible, is the same one who draws us into the heavenly sanctuary through the Son in the Spirit...This is a reminder that there is a double movement in worship. God first descends to us in his Son, reveals himself by the Holy Spirit as the object of our worship – in which the Spirit elevates us to Christ's Ascension, to participate in the incarnate Son's communion with the Father that is understood as worship.'[19]

In 'Living In Praise' – Worshipping & Knowing God by D. F. Ford and D. W. Hardy, they focus on the significance of the praise of God as central to the whole of life. In chapter two they begin with the concept of praise being what we express when we find something of quality and declare our appreciation. They point out that this is true when we praise a person. 'To recognise worth and to respond to it with praise is to create a new relationship. This new mutual delight is itself something of worth, an enhancement of what was already valued.'[20] They believe that this can continue in an infinite spiral of free response and expression and like lovers the declaration of appreciation is not an optional extra in the relationship, but is intrinsic to its quality and vitality. The desire to delight in another person can bring an awakening of new responses that yearn to express in greater abundance their love and appreciation of the uniqueness of that person. In this context the logic of praise is that it results in an overflow of freedom and generosity.[21] What is striking about their train of thought is that it speaks to us about praise and worship being the overflow of a heart that has been won over by God and Christ. To deepen our corporate praise and worship, a good place to start is to ask the Holy Spirit to fill our hearts in a new way with their love, so that our souls may be filled with an outpouring of praise and worship.

Ford and Hardy point out that Dante's pilgrimage of praise and worship began in Florence as he met Beatrice and when they were children. Dante says: 'The young are subject to a 'stupor' or astonishment of the mind which falls on them at the awareness of great and wonderful things. Such a stupor produces two results, a sense of reverence and a desire to know more. A noble awe and a noble curiosity come to life. This is what happened to him at the sight of the Florentine girl, and all this work consists one way or another in the increase of that worship and that knowledge.'[22]

Dante was in love with Beatrice and as a young man wrote poetry about his love for her. When she died the vision he had seen through her inspired the Divine Comedy. His experience of falling in love was taken up into the vision of being transformed and led him to write the last canto of the Paradiso. To arrive at this he went through an experience of recognising his own sin and being humbled that radically changed the tone of his later poetry. His praise is the other side of a humility in which he sees himself realistically in relation to Beatrice and to God. What is striking is that Dante's progress through heaven continually astonishes in its ability to describe even greater expressions of praise, wonder and amazement to the growing revelation of God.

> Glory to the Father, and to the Son and to
> The Holy Ghost, all paradise began:
> And the sweet song intoxicated me.
> What I saw was like a universe in smiles:
> So that intoxication came to me
> Through my vision as well as my hearing.
> O joy! O happiness ineffable!
> O life entirely of love and peace.[23]

Dante's words strike a chord in our hearts about the desire to worship God that lifts Christian worship to a new and sublime level. 'To achieve this Dante travelled through hell where God was not praised and where the atmosphere is claustrophobic, smelly, noisy, colourless and restless – the very antithesis of the constant overflow of joy in heaven. Divine Comedy shows how right praise is not an optional extra in life but is the fundamental condition for happiness and for staying in harmony with reality. The claim is that the intrinsic logic of life and of Christianity are at one in this and that only in this activity are truth, beauty, goodness and love appropriately blended and fulfilled. Further, by telling the story as a journey from despair to the vision of God, Dante can say a great deal about education into the many stages and levels of praise.'[24] Dante speaks about the awe and unfathomable greatness of God that can profoundly move us to respond in worship to Him on a deeper level. Rudolph Otto in 'The Idea of the Holy,' alludes to this when he speaks about the sincerely felt religious emotion of faith, salvation trust and love.

> But over and above these, is an element which may also on occasion, quite apart from them, profoundly affect us and occupy the mind with a bewildering strength...we shall find we are dealing with something for which there is only one appropriate expression, *'mysterium tremendum.'* The feeling of it may at times come sweeping like a gentle tide, pervading the mind with a tranquil mood of deepest worship.[25]

Otto states that as a concept *'mysterium'* denotes that which is hidden and esoteric and that which is beyond conception and understanding. *'Tremendum'* implies a sense of awe and dread that we can feel in the overpowering presence of God...where the soul, held speechless, trembles inwardly to the farthest fibre of its being.[26] Otto brings to our attention attributes of God that constitute an element of authentic Christian worship. But, we should not forget the simple, yet profound truth, which undergirds our worship – keeping God's commandments.

Sotirios Christou   Autumn Cambridge 2009

CHAPTER ONE

WORSHIP IN THE OLD TESTAMENT

INTRODUCTION

When I was a student at theological college I discovered from my Biblical Studies that what our lecturers taught could be accessed from the books we used to write our essays. Now, as an ordained minister, I have found studying the Old Testament fascinating, because it means encountering the Lord through the ancient texts of our faith. Yet, as a Christian, I do not recall ever being gripped by any preaching on the Old Testament. David Peterson echoes a similar sentiment:

> For many Christians the Old Testament remains a mysterious and seemingly irrelevant book. At no point does it appear more distant from the needs and aspirations of people in secularised cultures than when it focuses on the temple, the sacrificial system and the priesthood. Yet these institutions were at the very heart of ancient thinking about worship and their significance must be grasped if the New Testament teaching is to be properly understood.[1]

As we explore how God instituted worship in the Old Testament this reveals a colourful drama of the theology of worship that enables us to discern principles of truth that can still inform and shape our worship in the 21st century. As Christian worship is often viewed subjectively an objective look at these principles can enable us to reflect on the content of our Services.

ANCIENT WORSHIP

The first instances of worship recorded in Scripture all involve individuals. In Gen. 12 the Lord calls Abram to leave his country and promises to make a great nation of him and to give his descendents the land. As a response he builds an altar to the Lord who had appeared to him – Gen.12: 7. Andrew Hill says: 'Abram's altar marked the site as holy because of the Lord's appearance and demonstrated Abram's reverence before God and his thanksgiving for the divine word of promise.'[2]

As we read about the patriarchs in Genesis we see that altars were a key element of their worship. Abraham built altars at Bethel,

Gen. 12: 8, Hebron, 13: 18 and on Mount Moriah, 22: 9. Isaac built
an altar at Beersheba, Gen. 26: 25 and Jacob at Luz, Gen. 37: 7.
Erecting an altar for worship involved offering sacrifices and was
also associated with prayer. 'Altar building and the offering of
sacrifice are linked on three occasions in the patriarchal narratives.
Twice Jacob worshipped God by presenting sacrificial offerings of
an unspecified nature Gen. 31: 54, 46: 1.'[3] Hill sees this aspect as
crucial to the development of Hebrew religion as it demonstrates
God's willingness to accommodate his revelation to cultural
conventions. He points out that human sacrifice was practiced in
ancient Mesopotamia and Abraham was no doubt familiar with the
ritual since he came from Ur of the Chaldees – Gen. 11: 31. As
Abraham was going to sacrifice Isaac, he also alludes to this
incident which Walter Brueggemann calls: 'the mystery of testing
and providing.'[4]

While we are aware that the call from God to sacrifice Isaac,
Abraham's only son, acts as a typology pointing to Christ being
offered for us as God's only son, this still raises difficult questions
that are not easy to answer. Although Hill points out that the Lord
accommodated the pagan practice of offering such sacrifices, this
is contradicted when the Lord rejects the golden calf as an act
of worship, even though this also reflected the culture of Egypt.
Hill's assertion seems too convenient an explanation and avoids
addressing the controversial command to Abraham to sacrifice
Isaac, which appears to be totally out of character with a loving
God. Westermann says: 'Its extraordinary, frightening dimension
one can only experience with empathy.'[5] Brueggemann similarly
says, 'It is notoriously difficult to interpret. Its difficulty begins in
the aversion immediately felt for a God who will command the
murder of a son.'[6] He also alludes to the fact that God wants to
know something. Something that God genuinely does not know.
Something that is resolved in Gen. 22: 12: 'Now I know.' Now the
Lord knows whether Abraham has faith to obey his command. 'We
do not know why God claims the son in the first place nor finally
why he will remove the demand at the end. Between the two
statements of divine inscrutability stands v. 8: 'Abraham said:
'God will provide himself the lamb for a burnt offering my son' –
offering the deepest mystery of human faith and pathos.'[7] While
God is omniscient he did not use his foreknowledge to anticipate
Abraham's decision. His test of his faith and obedience was
genuinely a test and not a foregone conclusion.

The reader knows Abraham is being tested by the Lord and Isaac will be reprieved whereas Abraham is ignorant about this. Hamilton says: 'The best known event in the life of Abraham is at the same time the most baffling.'[8] He points out that the divine command: 'take' is followed by the particle – *na* which is something like 'please' or 'I beg you.' This is rare and only occurs five times in the Old Testament when God speaks to a person. Each time God asks the individual to do something staggering that defies rational explanation or understanding. Here then is an inkling that God is fully aware of the magnitude of his test   for Abraham. The intensity of the test is magnified by the three distinct objects of the imperative: *your son, your precious son whom you love, Isaac*...and accentuates the solemnity of the divine imperative.'[9]

He also believes that the test for Abraham is not primarily about whether to sacrifice a beloved son, although that is no doubt involved. The real test is whether Abraham will sacrifice the one person who can perpetuate the promises of God and particularly those promises that his posterity should thrive. 'Abraham appears in superhuman, somewhat unrealistic dress. He never objects to the unreasonable, slightly insane commandment to sacrifice his son. To the contrary he seems to move about his grim task with silent resignation.'[10]

Hamilton comes nearest to perceiving Abraham's confidence that God would resolve the situation when he sacrificed his son and implies that he trusted the Lord to fulfill his promises to him. Deeply engrained in his consciousness is the fact God did the impossible by giving him and Sarah a son when they were in their old age. His faith had been deeply impregnated by the truth that God could do the impossible. Abraham in offering Isaac as a sacrifice only makes sense from this perspective of faith. Isaac who was born due to God's power and promise, could also be raised from the dead because of God's power and promise. How else was Abraham to make sense of such an outrageous command? Without this unquestioning trust in the Lord his action makes no sense and is the act of a deluded man.

One other aspect that biblical commentators fail to explore is Abraham's willingness to sacrifice Isaac as an offering of worship to the Lord. If his implicit trust in the Lord to raise Isaac from the dead if he killed him is correct, he may well have understood this as an act of worship. That is what offering a sacrifice on an altar to the Lord on special occasions signified, even if Abraham didn't comprehend why the Lord commanded him to do this. Matt Redman in 'Facedown' speaks about Abraham in Gen. ch. 22 as, 'worship with a price, but this is no ordinary worship time…As they reach the appointed place and build an altar there Isaac says to his father: 'The fire and the wood are here but where is the lamb for the burnt offering?' In other words, 'Everything seems as if it's in place but where's the sacrifice?' This is always a key question when it comes to real and meaningful worship. We would do well in our worship to ask the same question the boy Isaac asked, where is the sacrifice? Sometimes in our worship meetings the 'fire' and the 'wood' are there. In other words outwardly everything seems to be in place and we think we're set for 'great worship.' A skilled music team perhaps, or above average songs and an enthralling preacher. But something is missing. Where is the sacrifice?'[11]

Sacrifice can be shown in various ways in our lives. It may be seen as we give up things in order to follow Christ. Or it may be seen in our lifestyle as a Christian that Paul alludes to in Rom. 12: 1: 'I appeal to you brethren by the mercies of God, to present your bodies as a living sacrifice, holy and acceptable to God which is your spiritual worship.' Financial giving, prayer, praise and serving the Lord may all be seen as sacrifice. As Paul served the Lord and others he saw himself as, 'being poured out as a libation upon the sacrificial offering of your faith' – Phil. 2: 17.

In the Old Testament building an altar was also a sign that a person had encountered the Lord who had spoken to him and so the place was designated a holy site. Peterson informs us: 'The great concern of people in the ancient world was to know where the presence of a god could be found and to know the names of gods so that they could be approached and communion with them established. Certain localities came to be identified as the dwelling place of the gods and here altars were erected and patterns of worship established. Part of the tradition of the shrine or the temple would be the story of how the place had come to be recognised as the abode of the god.'[12]

ROOTS OF CHRISTIAN WORSHIP

The roots of Christian worship are traced to the spectacular saving activity of Yahweh on behalf of the Hebrews, when he rescued them from slavery in Egypt to bring them into a covenant relationship with himself, so that he could dwell amongst them through the gift of worship. In fulfillment of his covenant to Abraham Yahweh speaks to Moses and reveals his intention to liberate the Hebrews from their bondage to the Egyptians (which lasted 450 years – Ex. 12: 40). In Ex. 3: 7, 9, the Lord had seen the affliction of his people, heard their cry because of their suffering and had come to deliver them and bring them to a land flowing with milk and honey. He made a covenant with them and gave them the gift of worship. He came to establish them as a liberated nation and bring them into a land full of abundance – Ex. 3: 8, 17.

Yahweh dramatically demonstrated his power to the Hebrews through the ten plagues on Egypt, through the Passover, through the crossing of the Red Sea and through the pillar of cloud by day and fire by night, that symbolised his presence with them. Moreover, when the Lord led them to Mount Sinai his presence was accompanied by lightings and thunder – Ex. 19: 16. At Mount Sinai the Lord began to reveal his plans for his people to Moses culminating in the giving of the 10 commandments, the plans for building the ark, the tabernacle, and the ordination of Aaron and his sons as priests, along with the sacrificial system and the Day of Atonement. As we read about them we cannot fail to be struck by the comprehensive and elaborate details these things involved. Clearly, there was nothing careless or casual in the provision of worship designed and provided by the Lord.

THE TABERNACLE & WORSHIP

What clearly stands out is that all these detailed plans are divinely inspired and executed. Although God's people are invited to make freewill offerings to build the ark, the tabernacle and all the utensils in it and to make the garments for the priests, in this inauguration of Old Testament worship they are not invited to contribute to the Lord's design. Plans for worshipping the Lord are divinely conceived. They are divinely inspired. They are carried out according to divine instructions. The central truth that informs and shapes their worship is that the Lord is holy and had to devise a means by which his people were constituted holy to worship him.

Therefore, the priests and all the furniture in the tabernacle had to
be consecrated to be made holy in the Lord's sight.

It is instructive to note that nearly one-third of the book of Exodus
is devoted to details about the tabernacle. Here, Fretheim shows
acute perception when he points out that the extensiveness of the
repetition in Ex. ch. 35-40, stress the importance of obedience to
the divine command concerning worship.

> ...the worship of God is not a matter in which details
> can be neglected. Inattention to detail may well have been
> a major factor in the syncretism and idolatry that
> developed in temple worship. A change or compromise
> here or there and it does not take long for worship patterns
> to become diverted from their original purpose and for
> something quite inappropriate or foreign to emerge...The
> forms of divine worship are not to be fundamentally
> a matter of human innovation or effort. And so God is
> not only the architect, but the giver of the specifications
> for construction, and the bestower of the right spirit
> or inspiration for the artisans and builders. In every
> conceivable way the tabernacle and its associated worship
> must be built according to the will of God.[13]

Motyer also says: 'the tabernacle could make a strong bid to be the
greatest of all biblical visual aids...and it would be allowable to
say that there cannot be a single detail of the tabernacle devoid
of any meaning.'[14] He provides a detailed explanation of the
significance of the tabernacle, the ark and all the other ceremonial
objects, along with the robes which Aaron and his sons as priests
had to wear every day. He also explains the meaning of all the
different sacrifices the priests had to make which culminated in the
Day of Atonement. At first sight only a preacher or a theologian
would choose to study these things as they do not appear relevant
for worship today, especially as they have been made obsolete by
the atoning death of Christ. So it is not surprising if Christians find
more interesting topics about worship to focus on than the book of
Exodus. But we should not overlook the fact it contains truths that
can shape our worship today.

GOD'S PRESENCE

Studying the roots of Christian worship from the Book of Exodus
reminds us that God's desire is to dwell with his people. As a

sign confirming this he bound himself to them in a covenant relationship and gave them the gift of worship. God revealed himself through his saving activity and by speaking to his people on Mount Sinai through Moses and by giving them the gift of the law. For God's presence to remain with them and for the Lord to remain in relationship with his people, sacrifices had to offered up every morning and evening. This is a clear reminder of God's holiness and the separation that existed between him and his people. The Lord's appearance on Mount Sinai and the thunder and smoke that accompanied this were signs of his glory, his majesty and his transcendence. Here we are struck by the *'otherness'* of God, by his *'numinous character'* and that he is unapproachable. We are clearly dealing with the 'sacred' concerning God in Exodus. The otherness of God is something Matt Redman touches upon when he says: 'For worship to be worship, it must contain something of the otherness of God.'[15] Similarly, Tim Hughes quotes R. Webber: 'Worship needs to acknowledge the unknowable nature of God who is transcendent and other and dwells in eternal mystery.'[16]

HOLY – HOLY – HOLY

When we read how all the furniture and vessels in the Tabernacle and the priests involved in worship had to be consecrated, either with blood or anointing oil to be made holy, this highlights the truth that only by being constituted holy can God's people have access to worship him. We do not know how long the Lord took to conceive the gift of worship, but we do know that it involved elaborate details. It involved painstaking care in building the Tabernacle and the ark and ordaining the priests. It involved care in offering daily sacrifices of worship acceptable to the Lord. The focus on the holiness of the Lord and the necessity of consecrating everything and everyone involved in worship, so that they too were constituted holy, finds its fullest expression in the ark in the holy of holies, in the tabernacle. Motyer highlights this emphasis:

> The ark represented the Lord in his unapproachable holiness. It was the sole piece of furniture in the innermost shrine with not even a stand to support it. As a box it contained the stone tablets of the law which stated in ten precepts both what the Lord is like in his holiness and what he requires his people to be (holy)…It was a physical reminder of why God lives in isolation and why his people cannot enter his presence.[17]

At first glance the contemporary relevance of dedicating the furniture in the tabernacle that was used in worship so it was symbolically holy in the Lord's eyes may not be obvious and easily overlooked. This may be the case when the sanctuary-stage where worship is conducted has been taken over by modern technology, sound equipment, the band and the musicians. The tabernacle sets the precedent of dedicating everything used in worship so that it is constituted holy to the Lord. This would ensure that all those involved in leading worship and the musical instruments are dedicated to God so they are consecrated holy. The sanctuary can also be a reminder of drawing near to the holy of holies, into the very presence of God. To what extent should the sanctuary-stage where worship is led visually remind us that we are in the presence of the 'sacred?' Is it time for the Lord to be the central focus of this area by giving it back to him, and arranging the musicians and sound technology so they do not dominate this symbolically 'sacred space?'

THE GLORY OF THE LORD

In Exodus 40 the Lord told Moses to erect the Tabernacle and gave him the instructions for doing this. As all the parts were assembled and all the furniture put in place, the Lord instructed him to anoint the Tabernacle and everything in it with the anointing oil they had made. He also told him to wash Aaron and his sons with water and put on their holy garments as priests and to anoint them – Ex. 40: 1-15. After carrying out all the Lord's instructions we learn in v. 34 that the cloud then covered the tent of meeting and the glory of the Lord filled the Tabernacle. And Moses was not able to enter the tent of meeting because of the cloud upon it as the glory of the Lord filled the Tabernacle.

> When all is ready, God comes to dwell among the people in the completed Tabernacle. The sanctuary is not simply a symbol of the divine presence, *it is an actual vehicle for divine immanence,* in and through which the transcendent God dwells…The God who is present is present as the transcendent one. It is as the Holy One that God is present.[18]

Similarly, when Solomon consecrated the Temple and had the vessels placed in it, as they were praising the Lord the glory of the Lord filled the Temple and the priests could not stand in the presence of the Lord to minister – 2 Chron. 5: 14. Moreover, when

Solomon dedicated the Temple the glory of the Lord descended after he offered up sacrifices. Again the priests could not enter because of the cloud of the glory of the Lord – 2 Chron. 7: 2. Christopher Cocksworth, Bishop of Coventry, in a lecture on 'The Liturgy and the Spirit,' given at a conference in Norway early in 2007, refers to 2 Chronicles ch. 5 and 7. In this he raises questions about liturgy that can shape our encounter with God in worship.

> Did God by his Spirit, interrupt the carefully planned liturgy and elaborate ceremonial worship of the Temple consecration with his wild, untamable, unpredictable presence? Or did the Temple liturgy provide the structure within which, and the platform within which, God moved and worked? Did the sovereign God somehow manage to find his way around the *'liturgical police officers?'* Or had the sovereign God inspired drafters and leaders of the liturgy, to be architects of spiritual encounter to which God faithfully and graciously responded?

The liturgy of the Church and the liberty of the Spirit are not two opposites that have to be *chosen between*. They are gifts that are to be *woven together* in the rich ecology of God's grace. But this is a view which runs counter to many contemporary charismatic evangelical instincts.[19]

As we reflect on the Lord's plans for the tabernacle and the Temple we cannot fail to be struck by his attention to detail and the care that was required of the artisans to build them. Also, we cannot fail to be struck by God's holiness and his unapproachable presence that manifested itself in his glory in the sanctuary. So overwhelming was the holiness and presence of the Lord that the priests literally could not enter. As we reflect on these truths this is a reminder of the care required in coming to worship the Lord. In Exodus and 2 Chronicles the glory of the Lord militates against coming casually or thoughtlessly to worship him. These passages present us with the ultimate climax of Christian worship – the manifestation of the overwhelming glory and presence of the Lord.

As we have observed the detailed instructions God gave for the provision of worship so that the Lord could dwell amongst his people, this begs the questions: 'To what extent should this influence contemporary practice that often displays a casual approach to worship, and also a rather informal presentation? To what extent are we missing out on a much more powerful manifestation of God's overwhelming glory and intense presence amongst us, by being so casual in our approach to worship?' Robert Webber mentions that God's presence filled the Tabernacle (Ex. 40: 34-35), and that this 'acknowledges God's presence in a particular place...The act of consecration also emphasises the importance attached to a place...and sets apart a particular place for the community to publicly meet God.'[20] This implies our approach to worship should be one of reverence as we anticipate an encounter with God. It is also a reminder that as we worship we are dealing with the sacred and buildings can symbolise God's presence amongst us. The implication of the passages from Exodus and Chronicles is that we should take great care in our approach to worship God and the manner in which worship is conducted. These passages also imply we might not encounter God's *wild, untamable, unpredictable presence,'* if we ignore the principles about worship they contain.

J. M. Boice identifies the consequences when God's instructions for worship were ignored by his people. He points out that it may surprise many people that God gave specific instructions about how we worship him and he believes that not all currently passing for worship is acceptable. In the Old Testament worship took place at the Tabernacle (later in the Temple), and God was to be worshipped through the Levitical priestly system. And if people tried to approach him in any way other than by what he had determined, God's judgement was swift and terrible. We find examples in Naham and Abidu who offered unauthorised fire and were consumed – Lev. 10: 1-2: Korah who assumed priestly functions to himself and was swallowed up by the earth – Num. 16: 1-35: or Uzziah who offered incense that only the priests could offer and was judged by leprosy – Chron. 26: 16-21.[21]

While this may sound somewhat ancient in 1 Cor. 11: 17-33, Paul mentions that some Christians had died because of the way they had been taking part in the Lord's Supper. G. Fee identifies the behaviour of the well off Christians in Corinth who ate their rich food separately from the poor. Some were getting drunk and humiliating those who were poor and had comparatively little to eat. (*Their custom was to have an ordinary meal before they shared communion together*). Fee perceives that this was a serious action that abused the Lord's Supper and also those Christians of a lower sociological status, because it resulted in God's judgement on the rich.[22] A. Thiselton in his erudite exposition identifies the Corinthians as being accountable: 'for the sin against Christ of *claiming identification with him* using the celebration of the meal *as an occasion for social enjoyment, or status enhancement, without regard to what sharing in the Lord's Supper proclaims.*'[23] Paul identified this as 'not discerning the body'– 1 Cor. 11: 29. This unchristian behaviour towards other believers as they shared the Lord's Supper in their worship, violated the unity of the body of Christ. As a result Paul exhorted them to 'examine' themselves before taking part in worship.

THE FEAR OF THE LORD

Regardless of our style of worship how exactly is the fear of the Lord to be expressed in worship? In Exodus and Deuteronomy we come across the term, 'the fear of the Lord' in Israel's relationship with God. His people are to fear the Lord and this is found in the context of keeping his commandments. The knowledge of God's law and commandments is intended to affect their response to the Lord, so that their lives reflect a reverence towards him by living within the bounds he has set. This can be described in terms of personal piety and devotion to the Lord. Hill says: 'This fearful reverence for God Almighty motivated both worship and service on the part of the righteous according to the O. T. – Deut. 6:13, 10: 20.' It 'was religious devotion in the richest sense of the phrase and a reverence for God which expressed itself in positive responses to God and his word...The fear of the Lord is an attitude that includes the emotion of reverence and awe for a unique, holy, all powerful, all-knowing God. It is primarily a way of life based on a sober estimate of God's presence and care. This fear of the Lord fostered an awareness among the Hebrew faithful that God is clearly above all, providentially ensuring the outcome of a personal life in accordance with one's character and action.'[24]

Darlene Zscech's definition has another dimension to it. 'The fear of the Lord is a deep, reverential sense of our accountability to Him.'[25] Our fear of the Lord will also have an impact on the way we approach our worship and the manner in which we conduct it, regardless of whether our style is traditional or contemporary. And within the ethos of our worship we can express our reverence for, and our fear of the Lord, in all that we do and the way in which we do it. In such an atmosphere of worship I would go as far as to say that the fear of the Lord will have an evangelistic impact on any non-believers who are present.

RELIGIOUS FESTIVALS

Just as we have seasons in the liturgical calendar such as Advent, Christmas, Easter and Pentecost, Israel also had a rich tradition of festivals the Lord provided for them. These were incorporated into the festival liturgies of the Hebrew religious calendar. Seven major festivals were observed in New Testament times. Hills says, 'For the most part these festivals were connected to the important historical events of early Israelite history. The specific ritual re-enactments associated with each festival not only dramatised Hebrew history but also evoked memories of God and his covenant relationship with Israel. This liturgical symbolism was employed for the theological education of the religious community in the divine works of deliverance and redemption.'[26] Hill clearly identifies these major festivals.

'* The Feast of Booths/Tabernacles that is associated with the wilderness wanderings after the Exodus, is a reminder of Israel's temporary homes during her time in the wilderness - Lev.23:33-43.
* The Feast of Trumpets, later known as Rosh Hashanah or 'New Year,' when the blowing of the ceremonial trumpet marked the beginning of the new religious year – Lev. 23: 24-25.
* The Feast of Purim celebrates the deliverance of the Hebrews by Esther, Queen under Xerxes the King in Persia, Est. 3: 27, 9:20-32.
* The Feast of Dedication or Lights – John 10: 22-29 commemorates the cleansing and dedication of the second temple in 164BC. It is known as Hannukah and was marked by the lighting of candles for eight days. This symbolised the divine light of God's revealed word to his people – Psalm 27:1, 36: 9, 119: 105.
* The Feast of Unleavened Bread and Passover are the first of the major feasts in the religious calendar and historically and theologically the most important – Lev. 23: 4-5. The Passover was a family meal with the sacrifice of the lamb which re-enacted deliverance from Egypt, during which children were invited to ask questions about the meaning of this festival. The seven day feast of Unleavened Bread linked the Passover and was a reminder of the years of sorrow and bitterness in bondage in Egypt.
* The Feast of Weeks or Pentecost was also called the Feast of the Harvest or Day of first-fruits and celebrated the end of the barley

harvest – Ex. 23: 6. This festival was also called Pentecost (*pente* meaning fifty) because it came fifty days after the barley harvest, and was a time of great rejoicing before the Lord and a time for bringing freewill offerings to Him for the harvest.

* The Day of Atonement or Yom Kippur – Lev. 16 was the national day of repentance and sacrifice for sin in ancient Israel. Once a year on this day the high priest entered the Holy of Holies to make atonement for the sins of all the people. Of special significance was the symbolic transference of community sin to the head of the scapegoat led off into the wilderness. A typology of the substitutionary character of Hebrew worship that pointed to Christ. In contrast to other joyful religious festivals this was a day of mourning and sorrow. Important truths may be learnt from these Hebrew religious festivals.

First, God ordered Jewish worship in such a way that there were cycles of exciting worship celebrations at regular intervals during the year. Second, these festivals connected the worship of God with concrete historical events on the part of Yahweh for his people. Third, joyous celebration was balanced with sober reflection. And, fourth, the festivals offered a variety of participatory worship experiences…The festivals were elaborate. They were demanding. They were joyous for the most part and they were interesting.'[27]

MOUNT SINAI

In Exodus as we read about the plagues, the Hebrews' escape from Egypt, the miraculous crossing of the Red Sea, the Lord appearing on Mount Sinai, giving the 10 commandments, instructions for the building of the tabernacle and the elaborate ordination of Aaron and his sons as priests by Moses, we might well think we have entered the fictional world of the screen movie of Cecil B. De Milles' film 'The Ten Commandments.' He saw this as a spectacular movie with God as the central character and leading protagonist. It is a story set in an alien culture far removed from us. It is an ancient tale of God who has begun to reveal himself and come to dwell amongst his people. It is a record of elaborate rituals and blood stained sacrifices that result in the worship of Yahweh. Exodus may not appear scintillating reading but as we approach it with reverence, we find the origin of Christian worship that found its ultimate fulfillment in Christ.

Moses has been on Mount Sinai with the Lord forty days and
nights, meanwhile the Hebrews are getting restless. They are bored
waiting for him to return. Despite the Lord working mighty
miracles through Moses the people are not overly impressed with
him. In fact they are somewhat dismissive. 'When the people saw
that Moses had delayed to come down from the mountain, the
people gathered themselves together to Aaron and said to him: 'Up
make gods for us, who shall go before us: as for this Moses, this
man who brought us out of Egypt, we do not know what has
become of him' – Ex. 32: 1. B. Childs says: 'There is a certain note
of threat in the choice of the verb to describe the peoples' initial
approach to Aaron…The abusive reference to Moses with flippant
unconcern sets the tone for the coming activity.'[28]

The miracles the Lord performed, the covenant to be their God
and the words he spoke at Mount Sinai, introduced them to
revolutionary salvation theology. There is nothing to compare this
activity of God as he revealed himself with any religious belief
system they previously held. Meanwhile, all that Moses asked of
them was to wait for him to come down from Mount Sinai – Ex.
24: 14. What was asked and required of them was to trust the Lord
to show them the way ahead for the future. But they didn't trust.
And they didn't wait.

THE SPIRIT OF THE AGE
The Lord knew the provision for worship he was going to reveal to
them through Moses. Meanwhile, back on the mountain, the
Hebrews didn't know the Lord was giving Moses divine details
about worship concerning building the tabernacle and the Holy of
Holies, and instructions about the sacrificial system and the
ordination of Aaron and his sons as priests. The Lord was making
preparations to dwell amongst them through the gift of worship.
As the people took matters into their own hands Aaron capitulated
to their demand by forging a golden calf that reflected the
gods/idols in Egypt. This was tantamount to uninformed worship
which was impregnated with secular idolatry that reflected the
spirit of their age. Some biblical commentators think there may be
a certain ambiguity in interpreting this scene, although what they
do is explicit enough. Was the calf a substitute messenger for
Moses who had gone absent? Was it a symbol to represent the
Lord going with them? Was it a casual act to replicate an image of
a calf as a cultural symbol from Egypt? Here, Fretheim sees a

deeper, more calculated significance the Hebrews may have attached to this image. He perceives that the phrase 'go before' in connection with the calf is used only of God's messenger in Exodus, which suggests the people are requesting an image of the messenger of God. In this way they make the representation concrete and accessible, having a greater independence from Yahweh. The construction of an image of the divine messenger would give that figure a more permanent place at the lead of the community, no longer dependent on Moses' mediation.'[29]

The golden calf clearly shows how the Hebrews had been deeply influenced by the prevailing spirit of idolatry that pervaded their stay in Egypt. They assimilated this cultural icon that they had been exposed to. Aaron goes along with the people in making the idol presumably because he thought it was an acceptable way of celebrating their deliverance and worshipping the Lord. The people said: 'These are your gods O Israel, who brought you up out of the land of Egypt! When Aaron saw this he built an altar before it: and Aaron made proclamation and said: 'Tomorrow shall be a feast to the Lord.' And they rose up early on the morrow and offered burnt offerings and brought peace offerings: and the people sat down to eat and drink and rose up to play'– Ex. 32: 4-6. Childs appears to be somewhat generous in exonerating Aaron in this incident when he says: 'Obviously, Aaron had had a different intention from the people when he made the calf. The fact he could incorporate the calf in a Yahweh festival indicates that he did not understand it as blatant apostasy from Yahweh.'[30] But, he then contradicts himself when he says:

> The people have corrupted themselves. If in the instruct-
> ions of God to Moses one can see the true will of God for
> Israel's worship, in the golden calf one can also see the
> perversion of worship…the alternative worship to true
> worship is held up as a terrifying threat which undercuts
> the very ground of Israel's existence.[31]

Ratzinger perceives some important truths about liturgy in the connection with the golden calf. He believes that 'this incident is not intended to serve any of the false gods of the heathen. The apostasy is more subtle. There is no obvious turning away from God to the false gods. They want to glorify God who led Israel out of Egypt and yet it is a falling away from the worship of God to idolatry. The golden calf symbolises bringing God down to our level. He must be there when he is needed and he must be the kind of God that is needed. The worship of the calf is a self generated cult. When Moses stays away too long and God himself becomes inaccessible the people just fetch him back. Worship becomes a feast that the community gives itself, a festival of self-affirmation. It is a kind of banal self-gratification. The narrative of the golden calf is a warning about any kind of self-initiated and self-seeking worship. Ultimately, it is no longer concerned with God but with giving oneself a nice little alternative world, manufactured from one's own resources.'[32]

UNINFORMED WORSHIP

The Hebrews made a catastrophic error of judgement because the cultural assimilation of the golden calf in their worship was idolatrous and unacceptable to the Lord. The underlying issues involved not trusting the Lord, rejecting him and being unfaithful to the covenant he recently made with them. They also broke the first three commandments in Ex. 20. Fretheim draws a damning comparison between the worship the Hebrews initiated and the worship the Lord had planned.

> In every key point the peoples' building project contrasts with the tabernacle that God has just announced. The people seek to create what God had already provided. They rather than God take the initiative. Offerings are demanded rather than willingly presented. The elaborate preparations are missing altogether. The painstaking length of time needed for building becomes an overnight rush job. The careful provision for guarding the presence of the Holy One turns into an open-air object of immediate accessibility. The invisible, intangible God becomes a visible, tangible image. The personal, active God becomes an impersonal object that cannot see or speak or act. The ironic effect is that the people forfeit the very divine presence they had hoped to bind more closely to themselves.[33]

The Hebrews' worship is crude and tainted by the spirit of idolatry they had assimilated from Egypt. As yet they did not understand the implications of their sin and God's holiness: and that worship could only be offered to God on his terms, rather than by humanly instituted sacrifices that reflected the prevailing culture of their day. In our generation God's people would be prudent to take care as they seek to be culturally relevant in their worship.

PRIESTHOOD & THE DAY OF ATONEMENT

In the Old Testament to understand the theology about priesthood we have to start with God who took the initiative to instigate the sacrificial system, after he delivered the Hebrews from bondage in Egypt and drew them into a covenant relationship with himself. The tabernacle, the ark and the priesthood, along with the sacrificial system and the commandments, were all a gift and a sign of God's grace. The tabernacle acted as a perpetual reminder of God's presence with his people and the priestly sacrifices were also a reminder of God's holiness. Sacrifice as a gift enabled atonement for sin to take place as God had decreed. Therefore, God could dwell in the tabernacle in the Holy of Holies in the midst of his people. Concerning priesthood and sacrifice Gordon Wenham says: 'At the heart of this scheme was the establishment of a pure system of worship, in which God could be honoured and praised in a fitting manner and through which human sin could be atoned for.'[34] This highlights another important aspect of the sacrificial system – the offering to God of acceptable worship.

Just as great care and attention to detail were required by God of the people in building the tabernacle, the utensils in it, the ark and making the clothes of the priests, so too the rituals involved in the Day of Atonement instigated by God, equally required the same care and attention to detail. D. Tidball observes, 'everything about it indicates that it was a day of supreme importance. The high priest wore special clothes and had to go through very careful preparation, heightening its sense of importance and the rituals involved were unique. Right from the start we are made aware that this sacrifice required extra care. Every element of it demonstrates that God is awesome in holiness.'[35]

The Day of Atonement is associated with the high priest and had a marked emphasis on the ritual use of blood. To grasp the significance of this day it is important to remember that it prophetically pointed to Christ shedding his blood. Wenham says: 'Under the law almost everything is purified with blood and without the shedding of blood there is no forgiveness of sins (Heb. 9: 22).'[36] In Leviticus the shedding of blood is associated with cleansing and sanctification. 'All these sacrifices involved the shedding of blood and all these sacrifices reached their annual climax on the Day of Atonement. On this day each part of the tabernacle was smeared with blood.'[37] The purification of the sanctuary is central to this special day, along with the purification of the people from their sins.

Entry into the Most Holy Place, the Holy of Holies, where the ark of the covenant was, took place once a year on this special day and only after elaborate preparation by the high priest. The ark was the visible symbol of the presence and glory of God. Lev.16 outlines the preparation of the high priest and the people for this special day. Bellinger says: 'The priest functions as the mediator between the people and God and as we have seen before, he must be properly prepared for that role especially here where encounter with the divine presence is so intense.'[38]

Aaron is given specific instructions by the Lord about how to prepare himself for this day. This involved what he was to wear, how often he had to wash (five times), every time he changed his clothes, in addition to washing his hands and feet ten times and his need to offer a sin offering and a burnt offering. D. Tidball says, 'Complete physical cleanliness is required before entering the heart of God's sanctuary. His dress is unusual. On this day he is to lay aside the splendid and ornate garments of the high priest's office (see Ex. 28) and clothe himself in a *sacred linen tunic*. The simple white linen garment may be saying something about the degree of purity needed to officiate in the Most Holy Place, but most agree that it is more likely to stress the humility and penitential attitude Aaron requires to perform his duties. The garment is that of a slave – a significant reminder that when the high priest enters the very presence of God he is nothing more than a simple servant.'[39]

The Day of Atonement was a special day in the life of Israel, and before Aaron offered a sacrifice for the sin of the nation, he had to make a sin offering for himself and for his household, then the Holy of Holies had to be cleansed too. Aaron had to sacrifice a bull as a sin offering for himself and enter the Holy of Holies with a censer full of coals from the altar before the Lord, with two handfuls of incense beaten small and bring it within the veil and put the incense on the fire before the Lord: so the cloud of the incense covered the mercy seat which is upon the testimony, lest he die by being exposed to God's glory in the Holy of Holies. 'As the high priest goes behind the curtain...he is entering dangerous territory. He dare not enter it as if he had a right to be there, still less in a casual manner. He dare not enter without protection. So God thoughtfully commands him to bring fire and high-quality, finely ground incense with him and before he does anything else to create a smokescreen to serve as a wall of protection.'[40]

Aaron then had to take some of the bull's blood and sprinkle it with his finger on the front of the mercy seat and before the mercy seat, and sprinkle the blood with his finger seven times – Lev. 16: 11-14. This highlights the truth that in God's eyes the blood purifies the Most Holy Place from any defilement. He then had to kill the goat of the sin offering for the people, bring its blood within the veil and sprinkle its blood on the mercy seat on top of the ark and before the mercy seat. In this way he made atonement for the holy place because of the uncleannesses of the people of Israel and because of their transgressions. He also had to do the same for the tent of meeting. He then had to cleanse the altar before the Lord also with the blood of the bull and the blood of the goat by sprinkling it on the horns of the altar – Lev. 16: 15-19. Blood cleansed the altar as well as consecrating it. 'Usually blood is only sprinkled in front of the curtain or applied to the relevant altar in the Holy Place or the outer court. But on this occasion it is showered on everything...This is the most comprehensive act of blood cleansing that existed in Israel's sacrificial system.'[41]

Here, we are clearly dealing with ancient rituals concerning blood on this special day which God instigated to deal with the sin of the nation. Lev. 17: 11, spells out the significance of blood in God's eyes.

> For the life of the creature is in its blood, and I have given it to you to make atonement for yourselves on the altar: it is the blood that makes atonement for one's life.

From God's perspective the shedding of blood symbolises a life laid down for others and the sprinkling of blood acts as a sign of cleansing. In effect a life is given in exchange for a life. And the blood was the price to be paid if cleansing and forgiveness were to be given by God as he had decreed. D. Tidball points out that, 'Since the 14th century the word 'atonement' has its root in being 'at one' – that is of being in a state of friendship, reconciliation or harmony. The word used in Leviticus for 'atonement' comes from the Hebrew *kpr* and three different meanings lie behind it. It might mean 'to cover' as for example when a piece of wood is covered over with pitch, or a debt is covered by payment. Secondly, it might mean 'to ransom' having its origin in connection with bribery or the payment of a price to achieve a favourable result. Or thirdly, it might mean 'to wipe away' or 'purge.'

Traditionally, it was the second of these ideas that was thought to get at the heart of atonement: that is atonement was the paying of a ransom price. Many now prefer the third idea – 'to wipe away' – as a more accurate translation. The setting of the word in the context of the Day of Atonement's cleansing of the sanctuary favours this meaning, it is said, quite apart from any other considerations.'[42] With the purification of the holy place complete, we now have the third major element in the ritual on the Day of Atonement, the scapegoat. When Aaron had finished making atonement for these things he had to present a live goat in the Holy of Holies, and lay both his hands on the head of the goat and cover over him all the sin of the people of Israel. Then he presented the goat to the people and sent him away into the wilderness with a man ready to take him there – Lev. 16: 20-22. The goat was symbolically taking the sin of the nation away into the wilderness. This was a sign that God had put away the sin of his people. Bellinger says: 'The goat carries the sins to a solitary place far from the community and far from the divine dwelling place. The goat is then released in a place from which it is unlikely to return. The sins thus cannot threaten the holiness in the midst of the camp, and so can no longer bring damage to ancient Israel.'[43]

On the Day of Atonement the people (all the nation) also had their duty and responsibility as we see from Lev. 16: 29: 'And it shall be a statute *(a permanent rule)* that you must afflict yourselves and not to any work.' Preparation for this special day had connotations of penitence and probably involved prayer and self-examination. Ultimately, however impressive the ceremonies were that were carried out by the high priest, on their own they were insufficient. If they were to be effective the nation had to demonstrate true penitence.

The Day of Atonement had an emphasis on the shedding of blood – and it was not just a drop or two that was require to be neatly spilled. The rituals involving blood required by God demanded a 'drenching in blood.' From God's perspective this special day

effected a real atonement in his eyes. In his wisdom it was the way
he ordained which ultimately pointed to Christ who was to be the
perfect sacrifice for sins. This prophetically pointed to Christ the
lamb of God who was to shed his blood on the cross. The book of
Hebrews has a particular focus on Christ as our great high priest
who brought to an end the Old Testament sacrificial system, which
he fulfilled by being both priest and sin offering. The biblical
truths about Christ as our 'great high priest' in Hebrews is
astonishing in its scope, and as we shall see in chapter four this is
teaching that Christians should be aware of concerning Christian
worship. By understanding the extent of blood sacrifice required
by God on the Day of Atonement, we can more fully appreciate the
death of Christ on the cross, and the significance of his shed blood.

A MODEL OF WORSHIP

All the animal sacrifices which involved the shedding of blood that
culminated in the Day of Atonement with the high priest entering
the holy of holies in the tabernacle pointed to Christ shedding his
blood on the cross for our sins. While Christ's death ended the Old
Testament sacrificial system of worship the tabernacle can provide
us with a structure in our approach in worship. Also the tabernacle
can be seen as a model of worship.

S. Phifer believes the Tabernacle and Temple model of worship
teach us not only how to come into the Lord's 'manifest presence,'
but also how to come into the Lord's presence in our private
devotions.[44] In the Tabernacle and Temple there was the outer
court, the inner court (Holy Place) and the Holy of Holies. The
outer court is the place of praise where we offer ourselves to God
in repentance and humility. The inner court is where the table of
the shewbread represents the Word of God. Here the altar of
incense is a symbol of our prayers and the golden lampstand
represents the Holy Spirit. The Holy of Holies is where the ark of
the covenant is kept which houses God's glory and His manifest
presence and holiness...This model of worship is one of 'divine
genius.'[45] It involves both preparation and progression in worship.

Phifer says, 'We pass through the outer court of praise before we
enter the inner court of worship. Praise comes before worship.
Spirit precedes truth. Ministry *to* the Lord leads to ministry *from*
the Lord...Passing through the outer court of thanksgiving, praise
and humility prepares our hearts for the Word, for effectual

praying and for the illumination and regeneration of the Holy
Spirit. Time spent in the Word and prayer and in the light of the
Spirit prepares us to pass through the torn veil of the Holy of
Holies to wait in the stillness of God's awesome presence.'[46] The
Holy Of Holies is the ultimate destination of our worship, where
the Lord ministers to us through the power of the Holy Spirit, all
the riches of His glory in Jesus Christ. It is of interest to note in
ch. 6 that the charismatic worship of the neo-Pentecostals follows
the structure of this Temple model of worship.

The Tabernacle and Temple model of worship show us how to
approach God with care and attention to detail in our corporate
worship. Through Christ and his shed blood and with the help of
the Holy Spirit, our hearts are prepared to worship God and to
come right into his very presence. As Hebrews 10: 20 tells us, 'we
have confidence to enter the sanctuary by the blood of Jesus.'
Mark Stibbe in 'The Temple Model Of Prayer,' highlights the
importance of the help of the Holy Spirit in this model of prayer.
But, the same help is also required of the Spirit when we use this
as a model of worship. He says, 'Before we look at the first stage
of the Temple model of prayer, the gates of thanksgiving – it is
good to emphasise right at the outset the vital role of the Holy
Spirit in this model of praying (*and worship*). The Temple model
of prayer is a great structure but as with all structures there is
always a danger that the form may quench the fire...it will only
prove to be a great asset if the Holy Spirit is allowed to move
within this structure. We must always seek to invite the Holy Spirit
to lead us in our prayers (*and worship*) and to give us that divine
freedom within this orderly framework.'[47] *(Italics are mine).*

CHAPTER TWO

COUNTERFEIT WORSHIP

INTRODUCTION

As we read the prophetic books in the Old Testament it may be difficult to grasp how Israel succumbed to the temptation to worship idols of wood and stone instead of the Lord. It may seem incomprehensible to us how these pagan practices infiltrated the worship of the Temple. Jeremiah and his famous Temple sermon and the background to this, illustrates how this happened and what the Lord had to say about it.

From Jeremiah's priestly background he would have been familiar with the tradition of the law and the Sinai Covenant between Yahweh and Israel. He would have known that obedience and faithfulness to the Lord resulted in his blessing, but that failure resulted in judgement and the curse of the law – Deut. 30:1-20. He spoke about the covenant relationship between the Lord and Israel as a marriage commitment. And when he pointed to Israel's failure to keep the covenant he described this as adultery and harlotry in Jer. ch. 2-3. Now the historical background of the covenant occupies a central role in understanding the book of Jeremiah.

Jeremiah was a symbolic preacher and at times used visual aids to proclaim his message. One that contained repeated warnings to Israel to repent along with the warning of judgement if the nation failed to respond. His message of judgement was due to Israel's apostasy as she abandoned her allegiance to the Lord and her love for him. Jeremiah's ministry began in the reign of Josiah around 625 BC and spanned forty turbulent years. This continued throughout the reign of Jehoiakim, Josiah's son, and until the 11th year of Zedekiah, son of Josiah, until the captivity of Jerusalem in the fifth month – Jer. 1: 1-4. To appreciate the situation in Josiah's day when Jeremiah's ministry began it is helpful to know Josiah's background. His grandfather Manasseh did not walk in the ways of the Lord. He allowed all kinds of pagan religious practices that were idolatrous and broke Israel's covenant commitment with the Lord. He also tolerated prostitution in the Temple area – 2 Kings 2: 2, the worship of Baal, the erection of an Asherah, a statue of a pagan god to be worshipped, and the worship of astral gods and a host of other abominations. Clearly, authentic worship of the Lord as he had decreed was perverted beyond all recognition.

Josiah's father Amnon also continued in these evil ways during his reign – 2 kings 21. However, when Josiah became king, as a young man he began to seek the Lord and to walk in his ways – 2 Chron. 34: 1-3. He sought to bring about religious reforms and purge the land of pagan practices. During this time the Temple was repaired – 2 Kings 22 and the Book of the Law was found.

IDOLATROUS WORSHIP

Jeremiah ch. 2 is surely one of the most moving chapters in Scripture and the powerful impact it has is twofold. Firstly, the Lord reveals his deepest love for his people and like a spurned lover he pours out his heart at the loss of his loved one Israel. There is a beauty and a magnetic quality about God's unfettered love that he declares to his people. Secondly, the other piercing impact is the great sadness we glimpse at Judah's and Israel's apostasy, which resulted in idolatrous worship and ultimately led to God's judgement. In response to their apostasy the Lord declares his love for his people through Jeremiah and he calls them to repent and return to their first love for him. Tragically this was un-reciprocated. Consequently, we perceive a great sense of loss as the Lord is heartbroken by his peoples' failure to love him.

The structure of Jer. ch. 2 is like a court case in which the Lord brings charges against Israel and Judah by asking them questions. The main charge that the Lord brings against his people is that of apostasy. Apostasy means that Judah and Israel have changed gods. They have forsaken the Lord and no longer give him their allegiance or worship. Instead, they give it to the Canaanite gods, the Baals. As in a court case, the Lord asks his people certain questions: 'What wrong did your fathers find in me that they went far from me?'– 2: 5. 'For cross to the coasts of Cyprus and see or send to Kedar and examine with care, see if there has been such a thing. Has a nation changed its gods even though they are no gods? But my people have changed their glory for that which does not profit'– 2: 10-11. The people have rejected the Lord and their sin of idolatry is so serious it profoundly angers the Lord and is detestable to him. In 2: 12-13 there is strong emotive language to describe the impact this has on the Lord. 'Be appalled O heavens, be shocked be utterly desolate, for my people have committed two evils. They have forsaken me the fountain of living waters and hewn out cisterns for themselves that can hold no water.' Brueggemann says:

> But Israel in its recalcitrance exchanges the only true God for the gods of Canaan who cannot profit. Israel has distorted things at the foundation not being able to sort out what is real and unreal, what is true and false, what is life giving and death dealing.[1]

The deceptive nature of worshipping idols has led to their delusion. This is so insidious that what is real becomes false and what is false assumes reality. As a result God's people were not only deluded, but blinded to the true nature of their action. Adam Welch suggests that Israel trades gods because this one is too demanding. He is on to something here. Worshipping a domesticated idol makes no demands on the worshippers.

> There was no cause to forsake such gods because it involved so little to follow them. Israel forsook Yahweh because the relation to him was full of ethical content. Yahwism had this iron core in it. The iron core was that Israel could only have Yahweh on his terms. Yahwism was no colourless faith which was simply the expression of people's pride in itself and in its destiny. It laid a curb on men. It had a yoke and bonds. The bonds were those of love: but love's bonds are the most enduring and the most exacting.[2]

Jeremiah ch. 2: 4-37, divides into five sections and v. 4 sums up what happened to God's people: 'They went far from the Lord' – because they turned to idols and failed to worship him. There are four key words in these verses.

In v. 4 - 8   the key word is - FAITHLESS to the Lord.
In v. 9 -13   the key word is - FORSAKEN the Lord.
In v. 14 -28   the key word is - FEARLESS - no fear of the Lord.
In v. 29 -32   the key word is - FORGOTTEN the Lord.
Faithless, forsaken, fearless, forgotten – these are the four subidiary charges that the Lord brings against Israel as in a court case.

* In v. 5 we have the first charge. The people were faithless and went after worthless idols and became worthless themselves.
* In v. 6 they forgot the Lord's past faithfulness and to seek the Lord. They defiled and polluted the land through idol worship.

* In v. 7 Israel and Judah became an abomination to the Lord.
* In v. 8 four classes of rulers are charged with being faithless.
The priests are charged with not seeking the Lord. The Levites, the
teachers of the law are charged with not knowing God. The
political leaders are charged with sinning against the Lord, and the
prophets are charged with prophesying by Baal.
* In v. 9-13 the Lord continues with his charges and contends with
his people, challenging them about their idolatrous behaviour.
They have gone after Canaanite gods of wood and stone and
diverted their worship from the living God.
* In v. 10-11 the Lord confronts his people as they have changed
gods. Their behaviour is unparalleled and unprecedented. It is also
unheard of. Even pagan nations do not change their gods even
though they are non-existent.
* In v. 11 the Lord says: 'But my people have changed the glory of
knowing me, for that which does not profit.' In v. 12 the heavens
are called to act as witnesses to the court trial that God has
instigated against his people.

The Lord speaks passionately about his peoples' idolatry and the
serious nature of their sin. It no exaggeration to say when the Lord
sees his people giving their devotion, their love and worship to
other gods and idols, it is a horrendous sin in his sight. In v. 13 the
Lord points out the unthinkable. His people have forsaken him the
fountain of living water and hewn out cisterns for themselves that
can hold no water. In other words they made idols with their own
hands that had no spiritual life and worshipped them. In God's
eyes this was astonishing behaviour and resulted in his judgement.

We may well ask, 'What has their idolatry done to the people and
how has it affected them?' The first impression we get from Jer.
ch. 2 is the way the people see themselves.
V. 20 'I will not serve.' They rebelled against the Lord.
V. 23 'I am not defiled.' The people have been deceived.
V. 27 But in time of trouble they say, 'Arise save us.'
          Yet their faith had no foundation it was false.
          They had been deluded by their idolatry.
V. 31 'We are free we will come to you no more.'
          The people had become unfaithful.
V. 35 'I am innocent, surely his anger has turned from me?'
          The people who were deceived by their idolatry and
          had a false perception of their relationship with Lord.

The second revealing insight we glimpse from Jer. ch. 2 is the contrast in the way that the Lord sees his people.

V. 5   They went after worthless idols and became worthless.

V. 7   They have defiled the land through their idolatry.

V. 14 They have become a slave and prey to foreign nations.

V. 20 They bowed down as a harlot to idols in high places.

V. 22 The stain of your guilt is before me.

V. 27 They said to a tree: 'You are my father.'
          And to a stone: 'You gave me birth.'

V. 29 'Why do you complain against me?'
          They were blinded by their sin which is why the
          Lord didn't help them, despite their complaint.

V. 30 They ignored the Lord's discipline. Therefore as a result of these things the Lord says: 'Behold I will bring you to judgement for saying: 'I have not sinned.'

V. 39 The Lord is heartbroken by his peoples' idolatry. In contrast they have been totally blind and ignorant of what they have done. This is the result of their idolatrous behaviour which has utterly deceived them and led to false and polluted worship. Jer. ch. 2 is not only very moving and tragic. It is also very disturbing. Disturbing as God's people were unaware of how worshipping idols had affected them. In verse 32 the Lord says:

> Can a maiden forget her ornaments, or a bride her attire?
> Yet my people have forgotten me days without number.

God's people could not see how their idolatry had affected them and their relationship with the Lord. As a result under the terms of the covenant in Exodus they have brought judgement upon themselves. Jeremiah's preaching was an attempt to appeal to Judah's and Israel's imagination. He required courage to challenge and confront their idolatrous world-view they had constructed. Brueggemann says:

> The convergence of religious fickleness, political whoredom and covenantal disregard shows that Jeremiah is engaged in an acute critical analysis…He struggles here as frequently with the incredible obtuseness of this people. Not only is there an abandonment of God but covenantal sensitivities have so collapsed that Israel is unable to recognise the quality and shape of its actions. In the face of the data so clear to Jeremiah Judah continues to maintain innocence.[3]

Jer. ch. 2 presents us with three searching questions. Firstly, what idols have we inadvertently welcomed into our lives, or what idols have gained access into our lives by our deliberate sin? Let us ask the Holy Spirit to search our hearts and lives, to reveal any idols we have become blind to, that we may repent and evict them from our lives. Secondly, what idols may have insidiously gained entrance into our church life? Has our spirituality or worship become an idol? Let us ask the Lord by his Spirit to show us where any idols have infiltrated our worship that we may repent and evict them. Thirdly, how might Jer. ch. 2 apply to us as a nation? What comparison can we see between the idolatrous worship of Israel and Judah and our nation? Have we also become blind and deceived by the idols our nation has erected and worships? Over the past 30 years there has been much talk of spiritual renewal and revival, but the question Jeremiah leaves us with is a very disturbing one. He forces us to ask ourselves the most unpalatable question: 'Are we as a nation under God's judgement, because of the rampant idolatry in our nation and because of our failure to worship him?'

UNACCEPTABLE WORSHIP

Israel's religious practice is the target of Jeremiah'sTemple sermon that challenged their unacceptable worship. Jeremiah ch. 7 records this sermon and ch. 26 the response to it. It is helpful to have these passages before us as we consider the issue of unacceptable worship. Jeremiah 7: 1-15

> Stand in the gate of the Lord's house and proclaim there this word and say: Hear the word of the Lord all you men of Judah who enter these gates to worship the Lord. Thus says the Lord of hosts, the God of Israel, amend your ways and your doings and I will let you dwell in this place. Do not trust in these deceptive words: 'This is the temple of the Lord, the temple of the Lord, the temple of the Lord.'

> Behold you trust in deceptive words to no avail. Will you steal, murder, commit adultery, swear falsely, burn incense to Baal and go after other gods you have not known and then come and stand before me in this house which is called by my name and say: 'We are delivered!' only to go on doing all these abominations? Has this house which is called by my name become a den of robbers in your eyes? Behold I myself have seen it says the Lord. Go now to my

place that was in Shiloh where I made my name dwell at first and see what I did to it for the wickedness of my people Israel. And now because you have done all these things says the Lord, and when I spoke to you persistently you did not listen, and when I called you did not answer, therefore I will do to the house which is called by my name and in which you trust, and to the place which I gave you and to your fathers as I did to Shiloh. And I will cast you out of my sight as I cast out all your kinsmen, all the offspring of Ephraim.

We see the response to Jeremiah's sermon in 26: 7-16, 24. 'The priests, the prophets and all the people heard Jeremiah and these words in the house of the Lord. And when he had finished speaking all that the Lord had commanded him to speak to all the people, then the priests and the prophets and all the people laid hold of him saying: 'You shall die! Why have you prophesied in the name of the Lord saying: 'This house shall be like Shiloh and this city shall be desolate without inhabitants?' And all the people gathered about Jeremiah in the house of the Lord. When the princes of Judah heard these things they came up from the King's house to the house of the Lord and took their seat in the entry of the New Gate of the house of the Lord. Then the priests and the prophets said to the princes and to all the people: 'This man deserves the sentence of death because he has prophesied against this city as you have heard with your own ears.' Then Jeremiah spoke to all the princes and the people saying: 'The Lord sent me to prophecy against this house and this city all the words you have heard. Now therefore amend your ways and your doings and obey the voice of the Lord your God and the Lord will repent of the evil which he has pronounced against you. But as for me behold I am in your hands. Do with me as seems good and right to you. Only know for certain that if you put me to death you will bring innocent blood upon yourselves and this city and its inhabitants, for in truth the Lord sent me to you to speak all these words in your ears.' Then the princes and all the people said to the priests and the prophets: 'This man does not deserve the sentence of death for he has spoken to us in the name of the Lord our God.'...But the hand of Ahikam the son of Shapan was with Jeremiah so that he was not given over to the peoples to be put to death.'

FALSE CONFIDENCE IN WORSHIP

In Jeremiah's day the political and religious leaders believed that Israel was secure as a nation because they were God's covenant people. Their prevailing conviction was Jerusalem was inviolable (completely secure from her enemies). This was the religious philosophy that undergirded their national life and gave them a sense of security. They echoed this in the confident declaration: 'the temple of the Lord.' Their belief that the protection of the Lord was guaranteed was the foundation that underpinned the political and religious establishment. But the Lord called Jeremiah to challenge and refute this false temple ideology.

In his sermon Jeremiah challenged the Temple worship, along with the false confidence and trust that the people associated with it. They dogmatically clung to their religious belief that they had God's divine favour as his chosen people. Sadly, this public liturgical formula, 'the temple of the Lord' was not substantiated by observing the Lord's commands. In this religious context Jeremiah's message seemed blasphemous as it challenged the basis of their national and religious life. When he invited the people to 'amend their ways and their doings,' so that the Lord would allow them to dwell in Jerusalem – he sounded like a prophet who had lost the plot. Brueggemann says about 'the temple of the Lord:'

> This alludes to the words of the Jerusalem liturgy that were boldly, endlessly and uncritically repeated. Jeremiah dismisses those words of the liturgy as banal and ineffective and mocks the unthinking reliance on the status quo that they reflect and embody. The accent is on trust: do not trust in, do not count on, do not stake your life on. In one deft move the prophet has exposed the dysfunctional character of the Jerusalem Temple. The Temple and its royal liturgy are exposed as tools of social control which in a time of crisis will not keep their grand promises. The Temple is shown not to be an embodiment of transcendence, but simply an arena for social manipulation.[4]

Jeremiah declared that their worship was unacceptable to the Lord because they were neglecting to keep his commandments and laws. Ch. 7: 5-6 indicates they were worshipping other gods/idols and were unjust in their dealings with others. He exhorted them to amend their ways and not to trust in the deluded chant: 'the temple of the Lord,' as if this was a spiritual incantation that God would honour. So extreme was the situation in the Lord's eyes that he said to his people: 'Has this house which is called by my name become a den of robbers in your eyes?'– 7: 11. Brueggemann perceives that those who violated God's commandments tried to hide in the sanctity of the temple. 'Since the text addresses the power establishment, it is fair to conclude that the crimes targeted are not simply individual acts of exploitation but are acts of the entire system.'[5]

Their neglect of God's laws invalidated their worship so it became meaningless and unacceptable to the Lord. This was so serious that the severest judgement was on its way, hence the reference to the destruction of Shiloh. The peoples' failure to keep God's laws, along with their worship of other gods, violated the integrity of the Temple worship. As a result this brought calamity and destruction to the Temple. This was seen when God's people went into exile and were overwhelmed by a foe from the North that was predicted in Jeremiah chapter one.

WORSHIP THE LORD HATES

Closely aligned to worship that is unacceptable to God is that which the Lord hates and rejects. Amos ch. 5 describes such a scene when the Lord condemns his peoples' worship in the context of his judgement. The Lord pulls no punches. It is as if he is going for the jugular. Simundson says: 'The Lord is about to do something so terrifying that the land will wither and dry up. The terrifying roar coming from Jerusalem is a sign that this is about to happen. The roar will send chills of fear up the spine of anyone who hears it'– Amos 3: 4.[6] This is none other than the roar of impending judgement.

One of the issues that surfaces in Amos, as well as in Jeremiah, is that worship offered to the Lord cannot be separated from the way his people live. Jeremiah highlights that the idolatry of God's people deflected their worship to idols – a horrendous sin to him. Yet they chanted their mantra: 'the temple of the Lord,' oblivious to how abhorrent their worship was to the Lord. Similarly, in Amos ch. 5, the Lord states that his people have ignored the issues of justice and righteousness, therefore their worship is counterfeit. It is neither authentic nor acceptable to the Lord. There is in fact an earlier reference to the peoples' empty worship in Amos 4: 4-5:

Come to Bethel and transgress: come to Gilgal and mul-
tiply transgression: bring your sacrifices every morning,
your tithes every three days: offer a sacrifice of thanksgiving of that which is leavened and proclaim freewill
offerings, publish them: for so you love to do, O people of
Israel.

Amos sarcastically mocks their worship as he invites them to come
to Bethel and Gilgal and transgress. Has he like Jeremiah lost the
plot? Didn't he realise how controversial and offensive his words
were? 'Amos is not against religious practices in themselves. The
sacrifices mentioned here seem to be legitimate not the direct
object of his criticism…What Amos hates is the disconnection
between the outward practice of religion and injustice and
oppression so prevalent in the society…But know that each time
you come to the sanctuary and perform your ceremonies, your sin
multiplies because of your callousness, meanness and failure to
perceive God's true concern, that makes the gap between your
religiosity and your execution of justice all the greater.'[7]

Amos 5: 21-24 reveals how unpalatable the worship of God's
people had become to him. The Lord rejected their worship
because of their lack of justice and righteousness.

I hate I despise your feasts and take no delight in your
solemn assemblies. Even though you offer me your burnt
offerings and cereal offerings, I will not accept them and
the peace offerings of your fatted beasts I will not look
upon. Take away from me the noise of your songs: to the
melody of your harps I will not listen. But let justice roll
down like waters and righteousness like an ever-rolling
stream.

These are stunning words spoken by the Lord to his people who
imagined their worship was acceptable and pleasing to him. Words
intent on shocking them into seeing that their worship had become
counterfeit and lacking in integrity, because it was divorced from
any justice and righteousness. Consequently, their worship was
rejected because it had become repugnant to the Lord.

The hatred of Yahweh against the worship of his people,
that is the shock of this word…the first person verb in
which Yahweh discloses his reaction to their worship of
him, reiterate nauseated disgust and vehement rejection.[8]

Motyer adds: 'There cannot be a passage in the Bible more deliberate in expressing divine distaste than this: I hate: I despise: I take no delight: I will not accept: I will not look upon: take away from me the noise…I will not listen.'[9] Like a musical score each phrase builds to a climax that will stun the listeners.

This is a reminder the Lord expects us to embrace justice and righteousness as we cannot divorce the way we live from the way we worship the Lord. Similarly, we cannot give our devotion and love to idols and come to offer the Lord our diluted worship. This implies that we have a responsibility not only towards the Lord but to one another and towards those in our community and wider afield. This is a reminder that our worship should not reflect a preoccupation with ourselves to the neglect of these issues. One of the difficulties of a contemporary application of Amos' and Jeremiah's message about worship is that they were addressing the nation. The political, religious and social aspects of Israel were all inter-linked as they were not independent entities. However, in our nation we do not have a national consciousness of these things being closely aligned, or that the church has a prophetic role to address the nation in the way that Amos and Jeremiah did.

While we may well apply their message to any individual church one unspoken implication is, 'Should the Church be calling the nation to repent and worship the Lord and drawing peoples' attention to the issues of justice and righteousness?' The dilemma here is that we do not automatically think of the issues of idolatry, justice and righteousness, as being connected to the worship of the nation. It may also be that many see worship as the sole concern of the Church. While the issues of justice and righteousness Amos addressed can be seen as having national relevance or international significance, we may still not link them to our nation and its worship. Nevertheless, I would strongly suggest that it is time for the Church of England to recover its prophetic voice, and to declare to the nation the call to repent and worship the Lord and acknowledge him in our national life. I would even more strongly suggest that the Church should maintain a high profile in the coming years – in calling the nation to worship the Lord and living by the ten commandments – the foundation of Christian worship.

CHAPTER THREE

THE PSALMS AND WORSHIP

INTRODUCTION

In my former Church School in Marylebone Road not far from
Baker Street in London, for the second lesson at 10 am every
Tuesday the entire school attended church. St. Marylebone Parish
Church is very beautiful with an ornate sanctuary, a gallery and
attractive antique oak pews. Charles Wesley lived and worked in
Marylebone and is buried there with a memorial stone. Lord Byron
was baptised there. Admiral Lord Nelson worshipped there and his
daughter Horatia was baptised there. At the back of the church is
the Browning Chapel commemorating the marriage of Robert
Browning and Elizabeth Barrett. Sir John Stainer's oratorio 'The
Crucifixion,' was written for the choir of St. Marylebone in 1886,
and has been performed every Friday evening at 6. 30 pm ever
since. I would now value worshipping in such a beautiful historic
church but as a youngster these things passed me by.

During the church service a psalm was always included and as a
teenager they always struck me as boring. This is not surprising
seeing I was ignorant of their meaning and use in worship. Some
years later when the Lord spoke to me about learning to praise him
I began to use The Psalms as a means of praise. In later years I
also came to value them because they show us how to share our
feelings with the Lord. There are many psalms which I now find
very meaningful and I love Psalm 19, 'The heavens are telling the
glory of God,' which was read at my wedding. There are many
other psalms that I also love which can strengthen our faith with a
telling phrase that captures how we feel or which encourages us to
trust the Lord.

The Psalms express a kaleidoscope of feelings about everyday life
and faith in our relationship with the Lord. They contain feelings
of confidence, depression, doubt, faith, fear, grief, hope, joy,
penitence, praise, thanksgiving and worship. Our deepest emotions
and how we feel about our faith and our relationship with the Lord
can be expressed through the Psalms. Tom Wright, Bishop of
Durham says: 'The Psalms are inexhaustible and deserve to be

read, sung, chanted, whispered, learned by heart and even shouted from the rooftops. They express all the emotions we are ever likely to feel, including some we hope we may not, and they lay them, raw and open in the presence of God...One of the great tragedies in much contemporary worship is the great void at this point.'[1]

Those whose culture is more emotionally expressive may possibly relate more readily to The Psalms compared to those who are more conservative. The Psalms provide us with a model of writing down our feelings and thoughts and sharing them with the Lord. This can be very meaningful as it helps us to capture exactly how we feel as we look to the Lord to be involved in our lives. On occasions a church like those involved in alternative worship can creatively write their own psalms about issues that are important. Or they can write their own psalms of thanksgiving, praise, prayer and worship to the Lord to include in their corporate worship. The following is an example I wrote when I was much younger.

> Lord, who am I that I should praise you
> who am I to give you thanks?
> I want to reach out and embrace you:
> who can satisfy the desires of my heart
> more than you?
> Your love is ever constant.
> Lord, who am I that you love me so much -
> who am I yet you made me?
>
> I want to praise you
> I want to thank you -
> I want to glorify you in my life.
> Knowing you is to have life:
> what can compare or compete
> with your presence within me?
> I understand so little
> and long for so much.
> Lord, take me by the hand and lead me
> preserve my life.
> Give me humility and meekness
> but above all love.
> Lord, teach me to love you -
> I want to love you.

Teach me to love you
better and better-
day by day, hour by hour,
moment by moment -
until I see you face to face.

James Mays thinks the individual psalms of lament are not the
easiest ones for Christians to own. He suggests it is difficult to
relate to them as their content is about acute difficulty, suffering,
a preoccupation with enemies, or life threatening situations. The
other difficulty is that The Psalms allude to these grave issues
without naming them. Therefore, it is not easy to connect our more
ordinary concerns and culture with this ancient literature that is
often highly emotive. On the other hand, The Psalms give us a
model of how to share the emotional and psychological aspects of
our personalities with the Lord. In this way they can help us to
have an intimacy with the Lord. One that is based on God's
unchanging character, such as his steadfast love and mercy, his
faithfulness, his deliverance and his loving kindness. Often a
phrase from The Psalms can strengthen our faith or have a pastoral
impact that helps us to trust the Lord. Mark Ashton, Vicar of the
Round Church that meets at St. Andrew the Great in Cambridge
has this to say about The Psalms:

> If it is no longer appropriate to chant psalms, we must
> find other ways to incorporate them into our services.
> Psalms are the main biblical medium for the expression
> of human emotions. (Expressions of sorrow and joy,
> confidence and despair, anger and elation abound in The
> Psalter).[2]

BACKGROUND

The Psalms developed over about 1500 years and the earliest that
we have is the Psalm of Moses, Psalm 90. About 100 years before
Christ we have the Psalms as we know them today.[3] Psalms 1 and
2 act as an introduction to The Psalter and 150 as the conclusion.
The Psalms are divided into five sections by 41, 72, 89 and 106.
Kidd points out that as a major author of The Psalms David is a
biblical model of how we can relate to God through song. 'The
wildest extremes of human experience come together in him. He
triumphs and he suffers immeasurable tragedy and loss. He is also
the *'architect of praise'* who as king bequeaths a musical tradition
to Israel. His songs are the most abiding contribution he makes to

the construction of God's house. David had the combination of being larger than life and as frail as the frailest of us. He realised the atmosphere of God's presence should be made up of song. And he becomes, so to speak, the Temple's acoustics engineer. He designs its *'aural architecture,'* writes his songs and plays them for the Lord.'[4]

The Psalms have been divided into a number of categories, for example: hymns, individual laments, corporate laments, penitence, thanksgiving, wisdom and royal psalms. They were used in the annual national festivals especially in Temple worship. Broyles says: 'They can be simultaneously read as liturgies, literature and prophecies...The Psalms were composed not ad hoc but with careful craftsmanship and were written not for single occasions but for recurring occasions. They were not free verses but followed established patterns and conventions and were not merely read: they were performed publicly...many of The Psalms were sung with choirs at Temple festivals such as 135: 20, 'O House of Levi praise the Lord.' Psalms 15 and 24 have long been recognised as liturgies for worshippers entering the temple...entry into God's Temple was obviously a momentous rite of passage for worshippers.'[5]

P. Westermeyer points out, 'The Psalms along with Isaiah are the two Old Testament books most quoted in the New Testament. Many are relevant to Christology and contain titles that are applied to Christ. Behind the whole discussion of The Psalms has been an implicit sense that for Christians they are related to Christ. In the New Testament there are more than 93 quotations from more than 60 of The Psalms. Among the sayings of Jesus in the gospels there are more quotations from The Psalter than from any other book in the Old Testament. Not only are The Psalms referred to in the New Testament but they and especially the Royal Psalms have been 'applied to Christ' by Christians...Dietrich Bonhoeffer spoke for the Church when he viewed The Psalter as the prayer book of Christ, which means the one who prays The Psalms is Christ and it is in Christ that Christians then pray them.'[6]

PSALMS, HYMNS & SPIRITUAL SONGS

The Psalms have played an important part in the life of the Church throughout the centuries and biblical commentators affirm their central place in the Church's worship. They have been described as 'the womb of Church music' and Ambrose considers them 'the voice of the Church.'[7] Athanasisus said: 'It is my view that in the words of this book the whole of human life, its basic spiritual conduct and as well as its occasional movement and thoughts, is comprehended and contained.'[8] D. Bonhoeffer also wrote, 'The Psalter occupies a unique place in the Holy Scriptures. It is God's Word and with a few exceptions the prayer of men as well.'[9] Westermeyer points out that The Psalms are used in a variety of worship settings by different denominations. They can be used in the Eucharist to congregational forms of morning or evening worship, in the monastic offices and in 'free church' worship. They also have a place in Hebrew worship.[10] The Psalms were an integral part of the corporate worship of Israel and her common hymnbook. Weiser alludes to this when he says: 'The Psalter has been called 'the hymn book of the Jewish Church' and that with some justification, for it contains the various features which point to the cultic use of The Psalms in the worship of the Temple and especially in the synagogue service in late Judaism'[11]

In Eph. 5: 18-20 and Col. 3: 16-17, St. Paul exhorts us to sing to the Lord with our hearts and also to address one another in psalms, hymns and spiritual songs. David set the tone for doing this in the psalms he composed and there is no reason why we cannot include them regularly in our worship. We can incorporate The Psalms in different places in our services depending on their appropriate use. Equally, those gifted as songwriters in our churches can adapt The Psalms to music so that we sing them in a contemporary idiom. In The Psalms we can behold the Lord - 27: 4, delight in the Lord - 37: 4, desire the Lord - 27: 4, hope in the Lord - 31: 24, know the Lord - 100: 3, seek the Lord - 22: 26, taste of the Lord - 34: 8 and we can trust in the Lord - 118: 8-9.[12]

David was innovative as a songwriter and as a worshipper and also set the tone as a worship leader way ahead of his time. The Lord undoubtedly gave him the gift of music and a heart that loved to worship Him. He learned that God dwelt in the midst of his peoples' praise and that he is enthroned on their praises. When he was king David sought to bring the ark to Jerusalem as this symbolised the manifest presence of the Lord. He brought this to Mt. Zion and introduced musicians and appointed singers to lead. David sang to the Lord and danced before his presence which were for him an integral part of his worship to the Lord.

As I wondered how often The Psalms are used in sung worship I was pleasantly surprised to come up with the following list. Traditional hymns are Psalm 23, The king of love my shepherd is: Psalm 34, Through all the changing scenes of life: Psalm 46, God is our strength and refuge: Psalm 91, Safe in the shadow of his wings: Psalm 95, Come sing praises to the Lord above: Psalm 98, Sing to God new songs of worship: Psalm 148/150, O praise ye the Lord: Psalm 150, Praise him on the trumpet, the psaltery and harp. The following are either choruses or modern songs based on The Psalms, although almost all of them are somewhat dated. Psalm 8, O Lord our God how majestic is your name: Psalm 18, I will call upon the Lord: Psalm 19, The law of the Lord is perfect: Psalm 36, How precious O Lord: Psalm 46, Be still and know that I am God: Psalm 48, Great is the Lord: Psalm 68, Let God arise and let his enemies be scattered: Psalm 84, How lovely is your dwelling place: Psalm 92, It is good to give thanks to the Lord: Psalm 100, Jubilate everybody: Psalm 103, The Lord is gracious and merciful: Psalm 104, I will sing unto the Lord: Psalm 108, I will give thanks to you O Lord: Psalm 113, From the rising of the sun: Psalm 118, This is the day: Psalm 122, I was glad very glad when they said to me: Psalm 134, Come bless the Lord. One Taize song is based on Psalm 27, The Lord is my light, my light and my salvation.

A MODEL OF LAMENT

Herman Gunkel points out that the individual complaint songs, the Lament Psalms, form the basic material of The Psalter and these songs belong originally to certain worship activities. 'It is particularly clear that the complaint psalm belongs to the worship service in which it is sung, in those places where the sacrifice is named. For example, Psalm 5 presupposes that the psalmist stands beside his sacrifice. Alternatively, the complaint songs express a desire for YAHWH and Zion. The singer painfully misses the marvellous surroundings of the holy temple and buries himself in the majestic reminiscences of earlier pilgrimage journeys. These psalms indicate that they are not spoken in the sanctuary and so it would be impossible that they accompanied an act of worship. It is characteristic of all complaint songs that the psalmist has composed them in *apparently life-threatening situations,* such as 'distress' – 'danger' and 'fear' which they so often mention. These prayers do not treat everyday occurrences. Rather they treat the *terrible decision between life and death.*'[13]

Sigmund Mowinckel points out that another aspect of the Lament Psalms is the focus on acute illness. On occasions this is attributed to the psalmist's enemies afflicting him. At other times this is seen as a direct result of sin and is manifest in an emotional, physical or psychological malaise that the convicting hand of the Lord has allowed. The intensity of *'feeling ill'* is seen for example in Psalm 38 and even for non-believers the effect of sin may be similar. Mowinckel also mentions that to the Hebrew *'illness'* and similar words do not cover a medical notion as they do to us. A man may call himself *'ill'* even when he has been overtaken by misfortune and is low in spirits, disheartened and powerless. He also infers that *'illness'* is not infrequently a metaphor for a mental consequence of some kind of distress, such as direct defeat or political dishonour.[14] Psalm 38:1-8 is a good example of his thesis.

> O Lord rebuke me not in your anger nor chasten me in your wrath. For your arrows have sunk into me and your hand has come down on me. There is no soundness in my flesh because of your indignation: there is no health in my bones because of my sin. For my iniquities have gone over my head: they weigh like a burden too heavy for me. My wounds grow foul and fester because of my foolishness. I am utterly bowed down and prostrate: all the day long I go about mourning. For my loins are filled with burning and there is no soundness in my flesh. I am utterly spent and crushed: I groan because of the tumult of my heart.

The Psalms are also Israel's religious poetry in the context of her covenant relationship with God. Often they contain a dialogue with the Lord from the perspective of the individual, although there are also communal psalms. Brueggemann echoes this: 'The Psalms are helpful because they are a genuinely dialogical literature that expresses both sides of the conversation of faith. On the one hand as von Rad has seen, Israel's faithful speech addressed to God is the substance of The Psalms.'[15] One aspect of this dialogue is of particular relevance to the worship of God's people today. This is found in the psalms that have been identified as individual or communal lament. These are prayers that are a cry for help, for justice, or deliverance. Brueggemann thinks this dialogue has an enormous theological significance in the faith and liturgy of Israel and the Church. He suggests that this dialogue of faith permits those making petitions to be taken seriously, so that God who is addressed is engaged in the crisis in a way that puts him at risk. He believes the unmitigated supremacy of God is questioned, therefore the lament concerns a redistribution of power, otherwise docility and submissiveness are engenderd.[16] He astutely says:

> Where lament is absent, covenant comes into being only as a celebration of joy and well-being. Or in political categories the greater party is surrounded by subjects who are always 'yes-men and women' from whom 'never is heard a discouraging word.' Since such a celebrative, consenting silence does not square with reality, covenant minus lament is finally a practice of denial, cover-up and pretense, which sanctions social control...where the capacity to initiate lament is absent one is left only with praise and doxology. God is then omnipotent always to be praised. The believer is nothing and can praise or accept guilt uncritically where life with God does not function properly.[17]

In this dialogue of faith in the context of a covenant relationship with the Lord, Brueggemann, as I perceive it, implies that an audacious dimension emerges. God who evokes and responds to lament is neither omnipotent in any conventional sense nor surrounded by docile believers. Instead, He is like a mother who dreams with this infant, that the infant may some day grow into a responsible, mature covenant partner who can enter into serious communion and conversation. In this context there comes genuine obedience, which is not contrived to please, but a genuine, yielding commitment.

Here, Brueggemann takes us into the psychological dimension of the Lament Psalms, when he suggests that where there is no lament through which the believer takes the initiative in a dialogue with the Lord, God is experienced like an omnipotent mother. What is then left for the believer is a false narcissim that keeps hoping for a centred self but lacks the ego-strength for a real self to emerge. He believes what is at stake here is not only a true understanding of the real self, but also a radical discernment of this God, who is capable and willing to be respondent and not only initiator.[18] His thesis insinuates that where lament is absent our praise can lack reality and our faith remains powerless to influence the situation or find relevance in it, in relation to God. But, God is not looking for praise that circumnavigates the reality of our lives. He implies that we should show the Lord a mature faith that tenaciously appeals to him to be involved in our lives. We can interpret the dialogue of faith between the Lord and his people as one that appeals to God's faithfulness, his steadfast love and justice and his saving activity.

Brueggemann is sympathetic to those who suffer or are in pain in the context of worship that is celebratory. He sympathises because the message this style conveys is that everything in our lives and in the world is right. Such worship denies those who lament the opportunity to enter into dialogue with God. It prevents them from expressing their pain in the midst of the worshipping community. Pete Ward echoes a similar concern about charismatic worship when he says: 'Charismatic worship has no reflex which may accommodate those who are grieving or in the darker corners of spiritual experience. As a result some of the songs and the worship become a problem for some charismatics. Some speak of the tone and the language of the worship songs as a cause of spiritual harm in their lives…they feel their spiritual journey is more complex and ambiguous than what seems to be allowed in the regular worship of the church.'[19] Brueggemann voices a similar concern that identifies this as an important issue.

> A community of faith that negates lament soon concludes that the hard issues of justice are improper questions to pose at the throne, because the throne only seems to be a place of praise…The point of access for serious change has been forfeited when the propriety of this speech is denied.[20]

A community whose genre is primarily the *feel good factor of worship'* may inadvertently become self-indulgent. Such worship also runs the risk of preventing the Lord from engaging in a meaningful way with his peoples' deepest struggles. Equally, this worship borders on being superficial because it has been reduced to the level of comfort praise. Westermeyer says: 'In The Psalms we deal with the height and depth of human life articulated in a most compelling way. We see our struggles against the backdrop of God's goodness, our struggles with God and God's struggles with us in steadfast love and faithfulness.'[21] The Psalms do indeed allow the individual and the Christian community to express their struggles. Mike Pilavachi also believes we should not only focus on the joyful bits of praise as: 'The Psalms teach us we can express the hurts of life, cry out to God in intercession and still adore him. Worship was never meant to be an escape from reality, but praising his name in the midst of real pain in a real world is real worship...The Psalms incorporate honesty about where the psalmist is, as well as truth about who God is, and we must look to do the same in our worship.'[22]

The lament songs of Africans in Diaspora America show how the Lament Psalms were used and were part of African spirituality. In 1925, two brothers, Joshua and Rosamund Weldon published a collection of popular spirituals which included: 'Swing Low, Sweet Chariot,' 'Go Down Moses,' 'Roll Jordan Roll,' 'Little David,' 'Joshua Fit The Battle Of Jericho,' Play On Yo Harp' and 'Steal Away To Jesus.' All these songs except for 'Steal Away,' use themes and imagery from ancient Israel and most of the biblical images used in the spirituals are from the Old Testament.[23] Robb Redman also highlights the use of lament songs in African spirituality: 'Because it was dangerous for slaves worshipping God they gathered in clandestine meetings held in cabins or outdoors that often lasted all night. The call to worship went out long before the meeting began, as slaves passed word of the gathering to each other in the code found in such songs such as, 'Steal Away To Jesus' or 'Get You Ready There's A Meeting Here Tonight!'[24]

African American slaves found a common experience of bondage, suffering, loss of homeland and exile in common with the ancient Israelites. Of particular interest are those laments that evidence an absence of closure, ending not with resolution but a steady uncertainty. In 1925 James Weldon Johnson wrote:

> It is not possible to estimate the sustaining influence that the story of the trials and tribulations of the Jews as related in the Old Testament exerted upon the Negro...as God delivered Israel out of bondage in Egypt, so he would deliver them.[25]

We should take care to note that not all the Lament Psalms result in circumstantial struggles being resolved immediately which was also true for the African slaves. In this context what is important is the opportunity to express to the Lord through the dialogue of faith our emotional, existential, psychological and spiritual struggles and call on the Lord to be involved in them. We should also take care to note that the Lament Psalms of the individual and the community in Israel, were prayers for help and paradigms of hope. In the same way the African spiritual lament songs strengthened faith and gave hope of better things to come, albeit possibly in the next world.

WORLD-MAKING PRAISE

Sigmund Mowinckel's groundbreaking study identifies The Psalms as creative liturgical acts of praise. He sees praise as an act embracing an alternative future that ushers in, in a new way, God's creative action in the world. Brueggemann refers to Mowinckel's thesis as being constitutive – that is the notion that it is world-making. Similarly, Westermeyer also says: 'God's people impose order, shape, sequence, pattern and meaning, on already existing elements which are disordered and chaotic, until acted upon and in the sense that God has authorised this activity and is known to be present in it.'[26]

Mowinckel's thesis advocates that as God's people praise him in response the Lord renews their faith and his activity is released in a new way in their lives and into the world. This can be likened to the impact of prayer offered up to God, in response to which the Lord graciously acts in the lives of his people. Therefore, prayer, praise and worship can be seen to release God's creative activity into our lives and is *'world-making'* in the sense of ushering in something new. Brueggemann believes that 'praise is constitutive of theological reality. It not only addresses the God who is there before us, but is also an act of constructing the theological world in which we shall interact with God. Because praise is constitutive as well as responsive, practitioners of praise would do well to be critical, knowing and intentional about the enterprise of construction.'[27]

Brueggemann's and Mowinckel's view of the constitutive power of praise, draws our attention to the creative power of praise and worship that God's people offer up to him. This challenges us to move beyond these things being only a joyful activity that makes us feel good. Brueggemann's theology asserts:

> The human vocation of praise is to maintain and transform the world, obtain blessing that would not be obtained, maintained or transformed, except through this routine and most serious activity authorised by God and enacted by

human agents. 'World-making' is done by God...Praise is
not a response to a world already fixed and settled, but is a
responsive and obedient participation in a world yet to be
decreed through this liturgical act.[28]

This challenges us to have a renewed understanding of what God's
people are accomplishing as they offer up praise and worship
to him. It is thought provoking to consider the ways in which they
are contributing to God's *world-making* in their lives, in their
communities and in the world. It is creative to consider in what
ways their praise and worship is ushering in God's kingdom.

PSALM 22

It does seem surprising and even extraordinary that David the
successful warrior for whom defeat was a rare experience,
composed so many psalms that indicate a psychological weakness
about his enemies. We can discern that in Psalm 22 David's faith
and walk with the Lord is stretched and tested in a new way that
caused him considerable emotional and psychological distress.
But, this psalm is holy ground as it also speaks to us about the
emotional, physical, psychological and spiritual suffering of Christ
on the cross. Inspired by the Holy Spirit and without knowing it,
David prophetically points to the suffering of Christ. We can
approach this psalm in two ways. We can view it as a Lament
Psalm, a prayer for help Christians down the centuries have made
their own. Alternatively, it can be seen as a prayer from Christ's
lips. The first 21 verses are a prayer of lament voicing acute
suffering, asking the Lord for help, whereas verses 22-31 are a
testimony to the Lord's deliverance. Weiser says:

> The song first leads us down into the uttermost depths of
> suffering, a suffering which brought the worshipper to the
> brink of the grave and reduced him to utter despair. It then
> soars to the heights of a hymn of praise and thanksgiving,
> sung in response to the answering of the prayer...The poet
> who composed the psalm has the gift of describing his
> sufferings in words which deeply move our hearts and
> in figurative language which grips our imagination. His
> lamentation is one of the most touching in The Psalter.[29]

The Lament Psalms have a basic structure which enables the
individual or the community to express their prayer for help
and petition for deliverance to the Lord. Intense feelings that are

often overpowering are expressed in the context of a covenant relationship with the Lord. These strong emotions are voiced as a dialogue of faith by focusing on God and his character and his saving activity. The Lament Psalms alternate between expressing feelings and focusing on God. Towards the end of these psalms there is usually a resolution, an answer to prayer resulting in praise and thanksgiving. This comes in the form of the situation being resolved or how the psalmist feels being addressed. The psalmist then rises above the situation that emotionally and psychologically troubled him.

Claus Westermann also identifies the basic structure of the Lament Psalms and he sees five elements integral to them. '1. Address – introductory petition: 2. lament: 3. confession of trust: 4. petition: 5. vow of praise. The address is an introductory cry for help and turning to God. The lament shares the situation with the Lord and the petition is a prayer for help. The confession of trust becomes an assurance of being heard and the vow of praise is offered when the petition has been answered.'[30]

It is reassuring to know that in Scripture the Lord shares his feelings for his people and the world. He is not a God who is detached but emotionally involved. Through The Psalms the Lord invites us, and indeed gives us permission, to share our feelings with him. He doesn't expect us to hide or repress our emotions. Just as the Holy Spirit led David to share his emotional life with the Lord in Psalm 22, in this psalm the Lord also gives us a charismatic model of how to share our feelings with him. With the help of the Holy Spirit we can have an emotional intimacy with the Lord as we share the things on our heart with him. Psalm 22 also speaks about King David's fear of his enemies that play on his mind. One aspect of this relates to Saul and his soldiers who have been pursuing him on and off for a number of years to kill him. Understandably, every now and then, fear and panic grip his heart and greatly trouble his mind. Calvin saw how this psalm outruns any experience in David's life: 'From the tenor of the whole composition it appears that David does not here refer to one persecution, but comprehends all the persecutions he suffered under Saul.'[31]

The first two thirds of Psalm 22 is like a litany of personal disaster which shows that David could not comprehend why his prayer is being ignored by God. But, unknown to him, God had a greater purpose in not answering him immediately. Unknown to David his psalm was to have a significant prophetic meaning for Christ as he identified himself with it on the cross. At his crucifixion when Christ felt completely abandoned by his Father, he instinctively turned to this psalm to voice his sense of dereliction. Jesus' cry on the cross: 'Eloi, Eloi, lema sabachthani' (Matt. 27: 46, Mark 15: 34) is a direct quote of Psalm 22: 1. Mays points out, 'Citing the first words of a text was in the tradition of the time a way of identifying with an entire passage. The very experience of the psalmist becomes a commentary on Jesus' passion on the cross. In the intellectual world of Judaism one of the most important ways of understanding the meaning of present experience, was to make sense of the contemporary by perceiving and describing it in terms of an established tradition.'[32] Consequently, Christians down the centuries have seen the special significance of this psalm in relation to Christ.

> My God, my God, why have you forsaken me? Why are you so far from helping me, from the words of my groaning? O my God I cry by day, but you do not answer: and at night but find no rest.

The theme of David waiting for God to answer his prayer and save him from his enemies was not a new experience for him as this is also seen in other Psalms. In Psalm 13: 1-2 he says: 'How long O Lord? Will thou forget me for ever? How long will you hide your face from me? How long shall I bear pain in my soul and have sorrow in my heart all the day? How long shall my enemy be exalted over me?' In Psalm 62: 1, 3 he says: 'For God alone my soul waits in silence: from him comes my salvation.' In Psalm 69: 1, 3 he says: 'Save me O God for the waters have come up to my neck. I am weary with my crying; my throat is parched. My eyes grow dim with waiting for my God.' In Psalm 86: 1, 3 he says: 'Incline your ear O Lord and answer me, for I am poor and needy. You are my God be gracious to me O Lord, for to you do I cry all the day.' In God's providence David had to learn to call on him for help and deliverance from his enemies. He also had to learn to be patient and trust the Lord's perfect timing to answer his prayer. In Psalm 40: 1-2 David testifies to God saving him from his enemies when he says: 'I waited patiently for the Lord: he inclined to me and heard my cry. He drew me up from the desolate pit out of the miry bog.'

While David knows that on occasions the Lord may not answer his prayer immediately, his tone in Psalm 22: 1-2, clearly states the Lord is taking an unusually long time to answer him on this occasion. He is perplexed and does not understand why the Lord is doing this. In God's silence David feels he has abandoned and forgotten him. John Goldingay astutely perceives:

> The succeeding lines of the psalm will make clear that we should not infer the suppliant will be satisfied if this 'Why?' question were answered. The question is rhetorical and implies: 'You should not have abandoned me, and I appeal to you to come back now.' Abandonment lies in failing to act on the suppliant's behalf.[33]

In v. 1-2 God is silent and has not answered David's prayer. He is now becoming desperate as the Lord whom he knows intimately appears to have abandoned him. Emotionally and psychologically he is feeling threatened and needs assurance the Lord is going to help him. D. Tidball observes: 'In the moment when he needs God and seeks his comforting presence, fully expecting to receive it he is faced with the total absence of God…God neither steps in to deliver him from his affliction nor seems even to hear his prayer.

The God-forsakenness David feels is made worse by the massive tension between his belief and his experience. His theology tells him he ought not to be ignored by God at such a time as this. His experience tells him he is being deserted by God…The silence of God sometimes seems most unyielding precisely when we most urgently need him to speak to us.'[34] The absence of God has been supplanted by the presence of David's enemies. God now seems distant and his enemies feel near. Why is the Lord absent? Why is he ignoring his prayer for help? Why isn't he answering him? Perhaps there is sin in his life that has not been confessed? As he doesn't mention this anywhere in the psalm we can rule this out. We can perceive that the Lord is teaching David to trust him on a deeper level despite how he feels. He is taking him to a new level of trust even though the Lord is silent. The Lord is also teaching David to view how he feels in the light of his character, and to remember the Lord's faithfulness, his steadfast love and past deliverance. While his feelings are real they may be misleading and way off beam about the silence of God.

3-5   Yet you are holy, enthroned on the praises of Israel. In you
         our fathers trusted: they trusted and you delivered them.
         To you they cried and were saved: in you they trusted and
         were not disappointed.

Why does David focus on the Lord's character and how does this
help him? He recalls that God is reigning, enthroned on the praises
of Israel. This is a reminder the Lord is sovereign and in control of
his life. He remembers the Lord's past faithfulness in answering
his peoples' prayers when they trusted him and were not
disappointed. Focusing on the Lord in this way helps David to
express his feelings of abandonment and disappointment. And this
begins to renew his faith and hope in the Lord as he focuses on his
faithfulness.

6-8   But I am a worm and no man: scorned by men and
         despised by people. All who see me mock at me, they
         make mouths at me, they wag their heads. He committed
         his cause to the Lord: let him deliver him, let him rescue
         him, for he delights in him!

David began this psalm by sharing how he feels because the Lord
is not answering his prayer and appears to have abandoned him,
then he focused on God's character to strengthen his faith. Now
he shares with the Lord how he feels because of his enemies.
His self-esteem has been assaulted and he has no confidence in
himself. His imagination is running wild and getting things out of
perspective as he imagines what people are saying about him. He
feels scorned and despised. He feels humiliated and insignificant.
He feels his enemies are laughing at him and ridiculing him. They
taunt him and imply that God is not going to help and rescue him
and this only adds to his agony of mind.

9-11   Yet you are the one who took me from my mother's
         womb: you kept me safe upon my mother's breasts. Upon
         you I was cast from my birth and since my mother bore
         me you have been my God. Be not far from me for trouble
         is near and there is none to help.

After sharing for a second time how he feels with the Lord David
again focuses on God's character. He casts his mind back to when
he was young to describe a fond tenderness in his relationship with
him. He reminds the Lord of his past protection and how he relied
on him from a very young age. This is in sharp contrast to feeling
abandoned by him at the beginning of this psalm. David reminds

the Lord of their close relationship to prompt him into helping him. But the Lord's absence instead of his familiar presence, has now left David feeling acutely vulnerable.

12-21   Many bulls encompass me, strong bulls of Basham surround me: they open wide their mouths at me like a ravening and roaring lion. I am poured out like water and all my bones are out of joint, my heart is like wax it is melted within my breast: my strength is dried up like a potsherd, and my tongue cleaves to my jaws: thou dost lay me in the jaws of death. Dogs are round about me: a company of evildoers encircle me: they have pierced my hands and feet, I can count all my bones – they stare and gloat over me: they divide my garments among them and for my raiment they cast lots. But thou O Lord be not far off! O thou my help hasten to my aid! Deliver my soul from the sword, my life from the power of the dog! Save me from the mouth of the lion, my afflicted soul from the horns of the wild oxen!

David uses vivid animal images to describe the impact his enemies are having on him. Derek Tidball says: 'Using metaphors from the animal kingdom he feels surrounded by bloodthirsty, baying beasts that will not be satisfied with anything less than his total destruction inflicted in the most terrifying way. He feels surrounded by the bulls of Basham who were well known for their size and strength. He feels mauled by lions mercilessly tearing the flesh of their prey. He feels hemmed in by dogs snarling, growling and ready to pounce and destroy their prey. 'The words' writes Peter Craigie, 'evoke the abject terror of one who is powerless, but surrounded, with no avenue of escape.'[35]

In v. 12-21 there is an atmosphere of mounting tension. David is now panicking as he imagines what his enemies might do if they capture him. A frightening scenario that emotionally and psychologically overwhelms him. He is now feeling desperate and exhausted as he imagines being pinned to the ground and tortured by them. He visualises a terrifying scene as they gloat over him as a prisoner. His anxiety escalates as he fears for his life when he says: 'Thou dost lay me in the dust of death.' This suggests that the Lord allowed this to happen. An alarming prospect when he thought about the Lord's past protection.

As the Lord has been silent and deaf to David's request for help and as he feels abandoned by him, he vividly describes the situation so that the Lord will help him. The prospect of what might happen to David has reached the stage where he feels desperate. His prayer for help invites the Lord to, 'be not far off' – 'hasten to my aid' – 'deliver my soul' – 'save me from the mouth of the lion.' Tidball captures David's acute spiritual dilemma that his faith has been trying to make sense of. Although he views this situation in a somewhat positive way when he says:

> Battling with the dominant, haunting melody of trouble is the irrepressible music of trust. Terrified though he is at the mystery of God's desertion of him, he does not allow himself to lapse into unbelief. His 'restlessly searching mind'…brings the reality of his suffering into contact with another reality – the reality of his covenant God.[36]

In v. 22-31 there is a transition with David rejoicing in the Lord because He has answered his prayer. It is helpful to be aware that David's enemies were his Achilles' heel and also his psychological weakness. This is clearly seen as in around half of his psalms (around 37), his enemies are the subject of his prayer for help. A brief look at some of David's Psalms enables us to see the extent of his fear concerning his enemies. Psalm 31: 11-13: 'I am a reproach among all my enemies but especially among my neighbours, and am repulsive to my acquaintances: those who see me outside flee from me. I am forgotten like a dead man out of mind: I am like a broken vessel. For I hear the slander of many: fear is on every side: while they take counsel against me they scheme to take away my life.' Psalm 55: 2-6: 'I am overcome by trouble. I am distraught by the noise of the enemy because of the oppression of the wicked. For they bring trouble upon me and in anger they cherish enmity against me. My heart is in anguish within me, the terrors of death have fallen upon me. Fear and trembling come upon me and horror overwhelms me. And I say, 'O that I had wings like a dove! I would fly away and be at rest.' Psalm 69: 1-4, 'Save me O God! For the waters have come up to my neck. I sink in deep mire where there is no foothold. I have come into deep waters and the flood sweeps over me. I am weary with my crying: my throat is parched. My eyes grow dim with waiting for my God. More in number than the hairs of my head are those who hate me without cause: mighty are those who would destroy me, those who would attack me with lies.'

Verses 22-31 mark a turning point not only in Psalm 22 but also in how David feels. In hindsight he can see that the Lord is faithful and trustworthy even when he is silent. Even when he is not answering his prayer in the way he anticipated, expected or wanted. The danger he was in is now past and resolved although we are not told how. This is frustrating because his sense of desperation was palpable, and we do not know if he was getting paranoid and exaggerating. The Lord has answered his prayer but we do not know if he has rescued him from his enemies, or merely resolved how he was feeling because of them. Either way having been delivered David's heart is full of praise. Weiser says:

> The darkness which filled the worshipper's soul has vanished and rejoicing with great joy he begins to sing a song of thanksgiving. He has become assured that his prayer has been answered and that God has helped him…Having been delivered by God the psalmist is so fully conscious of his happiness which has been brought about by the re-establishment of his communion with God that even the fact that he is now able to give thanks to God is accepted by him as a gift from God's hands. As a visible sign of his gratitude he will pay a votive offering in the midst of the godly ones and invite the poor to a meal so that they may share his happiness.[37]

David wrote this psalm when he was feeling abandoned by the Lord and felt isolated as an individual. But, he ends it by placing himself firmly in the worshipping community of God's people. We have a sudden shift of scene as he wants to testify to the Lord's deliverance in the midst of the great congregation. Presumably, to fulfill a vow he made to the Lord as he called on him to answer his prayer. In the closing verses of Psalm 22 David is so grateful and relieved for being rescued from his enemies that he is now bursting with thanksgiving. He is elated and wants to testify to God's goodness. His audience is now not only the great assembly of God's people but nations and generations not yet born. 'With an elegant sense of style, David describes a community of worship in which Israelites are complemented by Gentiles, the poor by the rich and the dead by the yet unborn. Distinctive in this psalm is the way David sees in his own rescue a glimpse in the way God delivers others, beginning with Israel's faithful and poor but finally including everyone.'[38]

As we reflect on this extraordinary psalm, we are struck by the fact that after the Lord has answered his prayer, David does not question the reason why, or wonder why the Lord has deliberately delayed His answer. Seeing that he quite vocally expressed his dismay at the Lord's timing in answering his prayer, we may well express some surprise that there is no theological reflection on David's part, as to why the Lord did this. It almost seems as if he is in the Lord hands for him to do as he wishes, without the Lord explaining his action to him. Moreover, right at the beginning of Psalm 22 David does not understand why the Lord is ignoring his prayer, nor why he is not answering him. So too at the end of it, he is no nearer to understanding why this happened.

To a certain extent we can see a parallel in Christ's experience on the cross when he cried out 'My God, My God, why have you forsaken me?' Christ had not anticipated or expected to be abandoned by his Father and he too was dismayed and perplexed when it happened. At the time he may also not have understood God's purpose or reason for abandoning him and for removing his presence. But, just as God had a far greater purpose in mind for not answering David immediately and allowing him to compose this prophetic psalm, that in a remarkably accurate way describes Christ suffering on the cross, to which Christ alluded – so too God had a far greater purpose in abandoning Christ on the cross, that involved our salvation. And it may be that at certain times in our lives, we too might never comprehend why the Lord delayed answering our prayers, nor understand what this accomplished.

CHAPTER FOUR

CHRIST AND WORSHIP

CHRIST IS LORD

The centrality of Jesus as Lord in Paul's theology and worship is seen from his letters that have an introductory reference to 'our Lord Jesus Christ' or 'the Lord Jesus Christ.' 'The earliest Christian writings are Paul's letters and they provide evidence for the origin of a practice of referring to Christ as 'Lord' that antedates the apostle. From his earliest letters onwards he applies *"kurios"* – Lord to Jesus without explanation or justification, suggesting that his readers were familiar with the term and its connotation...The frequently occurring references to Jesus simply as the Lord – 1 Thess. 1: 6, shows how the term had acquired such a familiar usage for Christ that no further identification was necessary. Paul's letters presume a familiarity with the term as a Christological title from the earliest stages of his ministry.'[1]

In his relationship with Christ in Phil. 3: 8, Paul speaks about 'the surpassing worth of knowing Christ Jesus my Lord.' And at the heart of Paul's ministry, spirituality and worship is the truth that Jesus is Lord. F. W. Beare aptly remarks:

> Here and here alone in his writing, do we find the intensely personal 'Christ Jesus my Lord' – and it would be a dull reader indeed who did not mark the warm and deep devotion which breathes through every phrase...This same person Paul remarkably calls 'my Lord.' In using the singular pronoun rather than the plural 'our' – the apostle is in no way suggesting that his relationship to Christ is exclusive. Rather, the wonder of this knowledge of Christ Jesus as his Lord is so great, and the relationship so intensely personal that he focuses upon it in his testimony.[2]

In Paul's day, in Aramaic, in Hebrew and in Greek, the term for master or lord was used in two ways. This was used when addressing persons who were socially superior and also when addressing deities. Equally, there would have been political overtones associated with this title as Caesar was addressed as lord. The use of lord in these ways made its application to Christ

striking and to address Christ as Lord may well have been seen as
a challenge to Roman rule. M. Hooker says: 'In the Roman Empire
emperors came to claim divine honours and as a result there was a
growing emphasis on the imperial cult. Though Paul himself did
not challenge the claims made by the state of his day – Rom. 13:
1-7, he would certainly have refused to acknowledge Caesar as
kurios had that been demanded of him. By the end of the first
century AD the confessions that 'Jesus is Lord' and 'Caesar is
Lord' were recognised as expressing conflicting loyalties, and the
proclamation of Christ was seen as subversive.'[3]

Paul knew the use of 'Lord' had a religious association in the
worship of Israel. The Jews did not pronounce the name of God –
Yahweh, but instead used other forms to address him. In Hebrew
God was often referred to as *'adonay'*– 'the Lord.' In the first
century this could be used as a substitute for the name of God and
addressing Christ as Lord conferred on him the status of God and
worship as God. Anyone familiar with the O. T. would not fail to
recognise the allusion of 'Lord' to Isaiah 45: 22-23: 'And there is
no other god besides me, a righteous God and Saviour: there is no
one beside me. Turn to me and be saved all the ends of the earth!
For I am God and there is no other. By myself I have sworn, from
my mouth has gone forth in righteousness a word that shall not
return: To me every knee shall bow and every tongue swear
allegiance.' Dunn says:

> What is astonishing, however, is that these words in Isaiah
> are spoken by God and in one of the most unyielding
> monotheistic passages in the whole Bible. At the very least
> we have to recognise that the Philippian hymn in 2: 6-11,
> envisaged acclamation of and reverence before Christ,
> which, according to Isaiah, God claimed for himself alone.
> On any count that is an astonishing transfer for any Jew to
> make.

Even as Lord Jesus acknowledges his Father as God. Here it
becomes plain that "*kurios*" is not so much a way of identifying
Jesus with God, but if anything more a way of distinguishing Jesus
from God. We may note also from 1 Cor. 3: 23, 'you are Christ's
and Christ is God's' and in 11: 3 'the head of Christ is God.' And
again in 1 Cor. 15: 24-28, 'the Lord of all.' Christ has been given

his lordship by God and it is a lordship that will in the end be wholly subject to God.

The only obvious resolution of the tension set up by Paul's talk of Jesus as Lord, then, is to follow the logic suggested by his reference of Yahweh texts to Jesus as Lord. That is, that Jesus' lordship is a status granted by God, a sharing in his authority. It is not that God has stepped aside and Jesus has taken over. It is rather that God shared his Lordship with Christ without it ceasing to be God's alone.'[4] But, it is more than that. It also includes worship given to Christ as God.

In Phil. 2: 6-11, Christ is exalted as Lord by his Father and this is commonly known as the 'Philippian Hymn.'

> Christ Jesus who, though he was in the form of God, did not count equality with God a thing to be grasped, but emptied himself, taking the form of a servant, being born in the likeness of men. And being found in human form he humbled himself and became obedient unto death, even death on a cross. Therefore, God has highly exalted him and bestowed on him the name which is above every name, that at the name of Jesus every knee should bow, in heaven and on earth and under the earth, and every tongue confess that Jesus Christ is Lord, to the glory of God the Father.

O'Brien says, 'Jesus' self-humbling reached the absolute depths in his most shameful death, a death on a cross. But now, by way of vindication and approval…the Father has magnificently exalted his Son to the highest station and graciously bestowed upon him the name above all other names. This is his own name, Lord (Yahweh), along with all that gives meaning and substance to the name. In his exalted state Jesus now exercises universal lordship.'[5]

The exaltation of Jesus as Lord also has a liturgical nuance. In 1 Corinthians the references to Jesus as Lord indicate that this title was an integral aspect of their worship, as in 10: 21 and 11: 17-38. Also in 16: 22 we have 'Maranatha' – 'Come Lord Jesus.' For Christians in Paul's day the emphasis on 'every knee shall bow' expressed submission in worship to Jesus, worship that previously had been directed only to God. But now God has conferred on

Jesus divine status that qualifies him to be the recipient of worship too. In the early church there was a political cutting-edge to the acclamation 'Jesus is Lord' and bowing the knee to Jesus, as this was seen to be subversive to the homage Caesar demanded. Similarly Fee says: 'We should note finally that this declaration of Jesus as 'Lord,' would probably not be lost on believers in a city whose inhabitants are Roman citizens and who are devotees of 'lords many' including 'lord Caesar.' Paul well knows to whom he is writing these words, especially since he is one of the emperor's prisoners and the Philippians are suffering at the hands of Roman citizens as well.'[6]

As well as having contemporary relevance in Paul's day 'Jesus is Lord' has perennial significance, as Christians down the ages have offered their worship to Christ. Also, there is an eschatological dimension to the acclamation 'Jesus is Lord,' because at the "*parousia*"– the second coming, every knee shall bow at Jesus' feet. Because God has given Jesus the name that is above every name he exercises authority on a universal scale. Therefore, Jesus' lordship has a cosmic and an eternal dimension to it. 'There is in this language no hint that those who bow are acknowledging his salvation: on the contrary they will bow to his sovereignty at the end, even if they are not yielding to it now.'[7]

Concerning the universal lordship conferred on Jesus by God O'Brien says: 'This bestowal by God is the rarest of all honours, in view of his assertion in Isaiah 42: 8: 'I am the Lord, that is my name: my glory I give to no other.' God not only gave Jesus a designation which distinguished him from all other beings, a title which outranked all other titles. He also conferred on him all that coincided with that title, giving substance and meaning to it... All authority in heaven and on earth were his by nature as well as by gift.'[8] And as we have already noted, Jesus' lordship has also bestowed upon him the honour of receiving worship, that previously was only directed towards God.

CHRIST A HIGH PRIEST
Within Evangelical spirituality the relevance of Christ as a high priest in our faith and worship is neglected. While we speak about Christ as our friend, our Saviour and Lord, we do not expound the relevance and richness of Christ as our high priest. Yet the book

of Hebrews eloquently bears witness to Christ's priesthood. D. Peterson says about Hebrews: 'This is truly essential reading for those who would establish a theology of Christian worship. The writer takes up a number of Old Testament themes and shows how they remain an essential foundation for our thinking...A God ordained priesthood, authentic sacrifices, and effective cleansing and sanctification must be provided for those who would draw near to God and serve him.

The writer also shows us, however, how these foundational Old Testament themes must be re-interpreted in the light of their fulfillment in Christ...The perfect sacrifice of Jesus provides the basis of relating to God under the new covenant. His high-priestly work secures a once-for all atonement for sin, the cleansing of our consciences and continuing right access to God.'[9]

CHRIST A MERCIFUL PRIEST

In Heb. 2: 17-18 we read, 'Therefore, Christ had to be made like his brethren in every respect, so that he might become a merciful and faithful high priest in the service of God, to make atonement for the sins of the people. For because he himself has suffered and been tempted, he is able to help those who are tempted.' One aspect of being a priest is to represent the people to God and God to his people. As a result the priest identifies with the people he represents and has a solidarity with them. Heb. 2: 17-18 shows that the same is true of Christ. F. F. Bruce says: 'Any priest must be one with those whom he represents before God and this is equally so with Christ as his peoples' high priest. In order to serve them in this capacity he was obliged to become completely like his brothers and sisters apart from sin, of course...He is merciful because through his own sufferings and trials he can sympathise with theirs: he is faithful because he endured to the end without faltering,'[10]

The mercy of Christ reflects the merciful character of God. Christ is a merciful high priest not one who stands over us in judgement and condemns us. As Isaiah 1: 18 reminds us, 'Come now let us reason together,' says the Lord: 'Though your sins are like scarlet they shall be white as snow: though they are red like crimson they shall become like wool.' Christ is our merciful Lord who cleanses us from sin and takes away our guilt.

CHRIST A COMPLETE PRIEST

Hebrews is resplendent with priestly and sacrificial images about Christ and portrays him as a high priest who has passed into the heavens – Heb. 4: 14. He is a minister in the sanctuary and true tent which is set up not by man but by the Lord – Heb. 8: 1-2. As we recall God's initiative in giving Moses detailed instructions about building the tabernacle and the ark, setting up the sacrificial system and appointing priests – here we are also reminded that Christ being appointed a high priest in the heavenly sanctuary, is also God's initiative too.

Bruce says, 'Priesthood and sacrifice are inseparable entities,'[11] and in Hebrews the author compares priesthood and the sacrificial system in the Old Testament, with Christ our high priest and what he has achieved through his sacrificial death on the cross. The writer expounds some wonderful truths about Christ's complete priesthood, *(complete in the sense that it is perfect and lacks nothing)* that supersedes anything the priests in the Old Testament accomplished.

> The author was not a complete innovator in presenting Christ as his peoples' high priest, but he elaborates the priesthood of Christ in quite a distinctive manner, and he does so in order to establish that in Christ and the gospel, God has spoken his final and perfect word to mankind.[12]

R. Brown highlights aspects of Christ's complete priesthood. He see this as victorious because Christ's sacrifice for sin is complete and does not have to be repeated, whereas in the Old Testament sacrifices had to be constantly repeated. He also sees three strands of truths connected to Christ's priesthood. Firstly, Christ as a high priest surpasses the Old Testament priests because he made their sacrifices obsolete. Secondly, Christ is also portrayed as a human priest, who knows and who sympathises with our weaknesses, although he himself is perfect – Heb. 4: 15. Thirdly, Christ is a unique priest because he is the Son of God, as united with his divinity is his humanity.[13] There is also a fourth aspect of Christ's complete priesthood which Brown does not mention from this context in Heb. 4: 14-16. Namely, that Christ's sacrifice as a priest was possible because he was sinless 4: 15. A reminder of the sacrifice without blemish offered in the Old Testament.

CHRIST A COMPASSIONATE PRIEST

Heb. 4: 15 says: 'For we have not a high priest who is unable to sympathise with our weaknesses, but one who in every respect has been tempted as we are, yet without sinning.' In our struggle with temptation it is reassuring to know that Jesus also experienced his own particular temptations. Bishop A. T. H. Robinson says: 'His whole life was one of temptation and the very fact that he had powers and abilities which we do not have only added to the stress.'[14] Although we only have a record of Jesus being tempted by the devil in the wilderness, we can readily imagine that these insidious temptations came Jesus' way more often. P. Ellingworth perceives that Christ's earthly life gives him inner understanding of human experience and thus makes him ready and able to give active help.[15] Koester sees that sympathy is a heartfelt bond expressed in acts of mercy towards those who suffer and reflects the cultural context of Jesus' day.

> Jesus the high priest is identified by his ability to sympathise with the weak. Speakers in antiquity understood that listeners were moved not only by logic but also by appeals to emotion and character. Therefore, before engaging in exegetical argument, the author seeks to touch the feelings of the listeners inviting them to identify with the high priest who has identified with them. Christ manifests sympathy because he has been tested as the listeners have (Heb. 4: 15). They had previously been denounced, abused, dispossessed and imprisoned (10: 32-34) and they continued to experience friction with others in society (13: 13). Some remained in prison (13: 3). Those familiar with traditions concerning Jesus' passion would know that he too was denounced, abused and imprisoned.[16]

Heb. 4: 15 – 5: 4 also reminds us that priests in the O. T. had three qualifications. Firstly, they were called by God to act on behalf of men. Secondly, a priest had to be sympathetic so he could deal gently with the ignorant and wayward since he himself is beset with weakness. Thirdly, a priest being aware of his own sinfulness also had to offer sacrifices for his own sins. We know that Christ was called by God to be a priest and that he is sympathetic and compassionate, because he identifies with our temptations as he himself was tempted throughout his earthly life. Because of Jesus' total identification with us and his compassion towards us in our struggles – Heb. 4:16, we are reminded that: 'We may come with confidence to the throne of grace, that we may receive mercy and help in time of need.' We are assured of Jesus' sympathy in the midst of our struggles, temptations and weaknesses, if we face up to them with integrity.

CHRIST A SUBMISSIVE PRIEST

Heb. 5: 4-8 speaks about Christ's submissive priesthood. He did not presume to reach out for, grasp, or exalt himself to the status of a high priest. Christ was called and appointed by God because of his obedience, his godly reverence and his sinlessness. His priesthood was rooted in his submission as God's servant during his earthly life. We read in Heb. 5: 8: 'Although he was a Son, he learned obedience through what he suffered.' The submission of Christ to the Father is a sublime selfless quality. It reflects his love for God and his willingness to be his servant.

Heb. 5: 7 refers to Christ's suffering in Gethsemane when he offered up prayers with loud cries and tears. Brown reminds us of the 'spiritually daunting and humanly terrifying moment when Jesus did not resist the sovereign purposes of God. Gethsemane is the most moving example of that 'humble submission' that characterised his whole life. Even in his deepest agony he continued and maintained that same attitude of submission.'[17] Concerning Jesus' submission F. F. Bruce says: 'He set out from the start on the path of obedience to God, and learned by the Sufferings which came his way, in consequence just what obedience to God involved in practice in the conditions of human life on earth. Perhaps the obedient Servant of the Lord in Isaiah 50: 4-9 was in our author's mind. The Servant's eagerness to pay heed to the voice of God exposes him to ridicule and ill-treatment, but he accepts this as something inseparable from his obedience …these Sufferings which Jesus endured were the necessary price of his obedience, more than that they were part and parcel of his obedience, the very means by which he fulfilled the will of God.'[18]

Koester points out that people learned by suffering was common-place and Jesus' suffering even though he was a son, shapes the way the author's listeners see their own situation. 'They are among the sons and daughters that God is bringing to glory – Heb. 2: 10

and like Jesus the Son they are being tested. Although Jesus was never disobedient to God, he could not demonstrate obedience until he was placed in a situation where the will of God was challenged and obedience required. There was constancy in Jesus' unfailing obedience to God's will, yet as he encountered new situations, his faithfulness to God was challenged and his obedience shaped accordingly.'[19]

CHRIST A PERMANENT PRIEST

The readers of Hebrews were Jewish Christians who were in danger of reverting to Old Testament ceremonial rituals associated with Judaism. This explains the careful exposition of priesthood from the Old Testament in comparison to Christ's priesthood. The author has to be specific in referring to the priestly sacrificial system in order to show that Christ's sacrifice has put an end to this. He exhorts these Christians who are on the point of forsaking their commitment to Christ, to more fully hold onto their faith in him, by grasping how much more comprehensive, permanent and superlative Christ's priesthood is.

In Heb. ch. 7: 17 the author focuses on Christ's priesthood where he is compared to a priest after the order of Melchizedek. That Christ is a priest for ever is also alluded to in 6: 19-20: 'We have this as a sure and steadfast anchor of the soul, a hope that enters into the inner shrine behind the curtain, where Jesus has gone as a forerunner on our behalf, having become high priest for ever after the order of Melchizedek.' This obscure reference forms an integral part of the author's presentation about Christ. That he was a priest after the order of Melchizedek contrasts sharply with the Jewish priesthood that was after the order of Aaron. A reminder that the Scriptures spoke of not one but two types of priesthood. The Levitical priesthood established by the Law and that which was after the type of Melchizedek in Psalm 110: 4. Melchizedek's priesthood was understood to be eternal and effective whereas Aaron's was temporary, imperfect and was now set aside by Christ, because of its weakness and because it was obsolete. Consequently, Jesus is a priest after the order of Melchizedek and therefore his priesthood is permanent.

CHRIST A SUPERIOR PRIEST

Hebrews shows Christ to be a superior priest because he exercises a far more excellent ministry than any Jewish priest, as he mediates a far better covenant. This covenant is far superior to the old since it is established on far better promises. Jesus our high priest now reigning as Lord in the heavenly sanctuary guarantees to uphold this new covenant – Heb. 7: 22. This theme is taken up in Heb. 8: 6-13 and brings about a new covenant relationship with God, so Christ has fulfilled the prophetic utterance of Jeremiah 31: 34, that is alluded to in Heb. 8: 6-7. F. F. Bruce sees the superiority of this covenant as Jesus is the Mediator and the better promises on which it is established will appear in the quote from Jer. 31: 31-34.[20] But, R. Brown also sees the importance of the old covenant: 'Although the old covenant is a vanishing shadow, our writer does not dismiss it hastily, casually or unappreciatively. He recognises something of its former glory, even when he is explaining its partial worth.'[21]

Christ's priesthood is also far superior to that of the Jewish priests: 'For it was fitting that we should have such a high priest, holy, blameless, unstained, separated from sinners, exalted above the heavens' – Heb. 7: 26. This superiority is also emphasised in Heb. 7: 27-28: 'Christ has no need like those high priests, to offer sacrifices daily, first for his own sins and then for those of the people. He did this once for all when he offered up himself.'

The revolutionary theology about Christ as a high priest stands in sharp contrast to the sacrifices Jewish priests formerly made. These sacrifices culminated in the high priest entering the Holy of Holies once a year on the Day of Atonement. Heb. 9: 8 reminds us, 'By this the Holy Spirit indicates that the way into the sanctuary is not yet opened as long as the outer tent is still standing.' This was a perpetual reminder that access into the Holy of Holies, into the very presence of God was restricted. Christ's sacrifice is revolutionary because he entered the heavenly sanctuary not with the blood of goats and calves but with his own blood. And God accepted this as the final offering for sin. Therefore, access into the very presence of God is now freely available to his people. In the Old Testament only the high priest could come into the presence of God on behalf of the people once a year on the Day of Atonement. Now, those who trust in Christ have priestly access into the very presence of God. Unlimited access into the heavenly sanctuary, into the very presence of God to worship him, has been made possible by Jesus our great high priest. And drawing near to God and being in his presence, enjoying fellowship and communion with him is indeed a priestly privilege. It is much more superior to anything God's people had access to in the Old Testament.

CHRIST AN ETERNAL PRIEST

In Hebrews we glimpse the significance of Christ's priesthood: 'But when Christ had offered for all time a single sacrifice for sins, he sat down at the right hand of God' – Heb. 10: 12. Christ exercises an eternal priesthood because his ministry extends to the heavenly places as well as on earth. His ministry also transcends time and history. The eternal impact of Christ's priesthood is also echoed in Eph. 1: 9-10: 'For God has made known to us in all wisdom the mystery of his will, according to his purpose which he set forth in Christ as a plan for the fullness of time, to unite all things in heaven and things on earth.' Col. 1: 19-20 echoes a similar truth: 'For in Christ God was pleased to reconcile to himself all things, whether on earth or in heaven, making peace by the blood of Christ's cross.' So Christ's eternal priestly ministry embraces reconciliation and unity. But, Christ is also an eternal priest because of the value God places on his blood as our great high priest. W. Nee emphasises this profound truth when he points out the shed blood of Christ is effective because of the value God places on it, and because God accepted Christ's blood for the atonement of our sins.[22] R. C. Moberly says something similar about the culminating point of sacrifice in the Old Testament.

> This was not in the shedding of the blood. But in the presentation before God in the holy place, of the blood that had been shed.[23]

Christ's ministry as a high priest in the heavenly sanctuary, prepared by God, is also as Moberly points out:

> Christ's eternal presentation of a life, which eternally is the life that died. And in the life which Christ eternally presents to God, Calvary is eternally implied.[24]

CHRIST A JOYFUL PRIEST

In Heb. 12: 2 we read, 'Jesus the pioneer and perfecter of our faith who for the joy that was set before him endured the cross, despising the shame and is seated at the right hand of the throne of God.' We may glimpse aspects of Jesus' priesthood that were a source of joy to him in the gospels. Although there is scant reference to Jesus' reactions to the healings and miracles he performed and about the individuals he met, we can imagine how much joy these occasions brought to him. He would have been joyful at seeing the kingdom of God having an impact in peoples' lives. He would have been joyful when people responded to him and to his teaching about God as Father. We can readily imagine the crowds ecstatic with joy at the healings and miracles he performed: and individuals reacting in the same way when they were healed or set free by a personal encounter with Christ.

Jesus' joy is also seen in John 15: 11: 'These things I have spoken to you, that my joy may be in you and that your joy may be full.' F. F. Bruce says: 'It is not difficult to trace an affinity between the joy of which our author speaks here and the joy to which Jesus himself makes repeated reference in the upper room discourses of the Fourth Gospel. He tells his disciples there of his desire that his joy may be in them, so that their joy may be full (John 15: 11: cf. 16: 20-24): and in his high priestly prayer he asks the Father 'that they may have my joy fulfilled in themselves.' So here the 'joy set before him' is not something for himself alone, but something to be shared with those for whom he died as sacrifice and lives as high priest.'[25] As Jesus discerned he was the 'suffering servant' prophesied in Isaiah, Heb. 12: 2 allows us a glimpse into the joy he anticipated would result from his sacrificial death. We may perceive that his joy embraced many things, such as the joy of our salvation: the joy of seeing humanity reconciled to God: the joy of death being defeated: the joy of the coming of the Holy Spirit: the joy of anticipating his resurrection: the joy of returning to the bosom of the Father and the joy of the second coming.

WORSHIP AS A ROYAL PRIESTHOOD

To grasp the various nuances of meaning about Christ as a high priest reinforces the truth that it is through Christ we come to offer our worship to God as 'a royal priesthood.' Through the gift of priestly access into the presence of God in the heavenly sanctuary, the writer of Hebrews reminds God's people of their calling as a holy nation and a royal priesthood: 'Through Christ let us continually offer up a sacrifice of praise to God, that is the fruit of lips that acknowledge his name' – Heb. 13:15. Our priestly privilege in God's presence is not only to intercede, but to offer worship that overflows with thanksgiving and praise, for all that Christ our great high priest has accomplished for us.

Christopher Gray, a priest tragically murdered in Liverpool in 1996 refers to 1 Pet. 2: 5-9, where the people of God are described as a 'holy priesthood' and a 'royal priesthood.' He comments on these two texts: 'They suggest that the whole Christian body is called to be priestly, a royal priesthood dependent on Christ….any other sort of Christian priesthood if it is to be faithful to the New Testament, must fit in with the N. T. picture of Christ as the only true priest in the full sense of the term and the whole Christian body being priestly in a secondary sense, dependent on Christ. It must be a particular ministry that is derived from Christ and promotes the priesthood of the whole body.'[26]

C. Cocksworth, Bishop of Coventry, also alludes to the priestly people of God in 1 Pet. 2: 9. He believes that this makes some of the strongest statements about the priestly identity of the whole people of God to be found in the New Testament – 'you are a chosen race, a royal priesthood, a holy nation, God's own people, in order that you may proclaim the mighty acts of him who called you out of darkness into his marvellous light.' This is a quote from the O. T. as God's people have always been a 'royal priesthood' – Ex. 19: 6.[27] The concept of God's people as priests who offer up worship to him through Christ is also found in Rev. 5: 10: 'And thou has made them a kingdom and priests to our God.'

Michael Ramsey, former Archbishop of Canterbury points out that Christ's priesthood is unique and unrepeatable: 'but, if we shrink from saying that Christians are also to share in it, we seem compelled to say that Christians are called to reflect it. If indeed Christians are 'partakers of Christ' as this Epistle says, and if they are 'carrying about in the body the dying of Jesus' as St. Paul says, then his priesthood and sacrifice, unique as they are, are to be reflected in the Christians…and Hebrews tells of priesthood and sacrifice as describing the life of the church itself.'[28]

SPIRITUAL SACRIFICES IN WORSHIP

One aspect of the life of the church as a royal priesthood is to be expressed in our corporate worship as is reflected in 1 Peter 2: 4-5:

> Come to Christ to that living stone rejected by men but in God's sight precious, and like living stones be yourselves built into a spiritual house, to be a holy priesthood, to offer spiritual sacrifices acceptable to God through Jesus Christ.

Peter uses a metaphor that portrays God's people being likened to a spiritual house. Biblical commentators see this as a direct inference to being built into a spiritual temple. P. Davids says: 'The picture of the church as a temple is not only common in the N. T. but was also known in Judaism especially in the Dead Sea Community...The concept of the non-physical church replacing the material temple in Jerusalem is widespread in Christian writings.'[29] Schreiner indicates this house is spiritual, 'because it is animated and indwelt by the Holy Spirit. Despite the hesitation of some scholars here Peter clearly identified the church as God's new temple. The physical temple pointed toward and anticipated God's new temple, and now that the new temple has arrived the old is superfluous...The purpose of such a building is that they function as a holy priesthood.'[30]

Having been designated by God to be a holy and royal priesthood reinforces that God's people are righteous and sanctified by Christ. Holy has the connotation of being set apart and speaks to us about consecration to God as priestly worshippers. Schreiner says, 'The notion of the church as a priesthood anticipated v. 9. Peter was not thinking mainly of each individual functioning as a priest before God. The emphasis here is on the church corporately as God's set-apart priesthood, in which the emphasis is likely on the believers functioning as priests.'[31] At this point it instructive to note that as God designates his people a holy and royal priesthood, holy is an attribute that signifies we have been sanctified by the blood of Christ so that we can worship the Lord in his holiness. Royal indicates a title of dignity and priesthood is also honour of the highest rank bestowed upon God's people in order to minister to the Lord. This is one of God's most ambitious designs for his people. It also signifies great privilege in being able to come into God's presence to worship him through Christ our great high priest.

Our corporate worship is made in the context of offering spiritual sacrifices to God and we do so through the Lord Jesus Christ. So in our worship we offer sacrifices of praise and thanksgiving for our salvation: sacrifices of prayer and testimony to God's goodness: sacrifices involving our time and tithes and sacrifices of obedience, service and trust. At the same time we know from Rom. 12: 1, we are able to 'offer by the mercies of God our bodies as a living sacrifice, holy and acceptable to God which is our spiritual worship.' Hebrews 13: 13-15 also says: 'Through Christ then let us offer up a sacrifice of praise to God, that is, the fruit of lips that acknowledge his name. Do not neglect to do good and to share what you have, for such sacrifices are pleasing to God.' These verses bring together the importance of praising God with our lips and serving him with our lives by doing good. We see here that the worship of God involves our hearts as well as our hands.

CHAPTER FIVE

WORSHIP AT THE THRONE OF GOD

INTRODUCTION

One of the most remarkable things that Scripture provides us with is a glimpse into the worship that takes place in heaven. Isaiah, Ezekiel, and John on the Isle of Patmos all have visions of worship around the throne of God. And to closely look at these visions can shape our worship here on earth. It is particularly interesting to note that Matt Redman a leading contemporary figure in Christian worship, as recently as 2004 focused on the theme of worship at the heavenly throne.

> On several different occasions the Bible allows us a glimpse into an open heaven. Each time is a window of revelation through which we discover more of what worship looks like before the heavenly throne. So many clues as to what our congregational gatherings should look like are found in these accounts of the heavenly throne. When it comes to worship the throne always sets the tone. Each time we gather together we don't just journey to a church building, we journey before the very throne of God. To lose sight of this is to lose sight of the majestic in worship. Every kingdom has a king and every king a throne. And the kingdom of God is no exception. The Lord is the King above all kings and he has the throne above all thrones. There is no higher seat of authority, power and splendour in the whole of the universe. The elders bow low there, the angels encircle it and the whole host of heaven arrange themselves around it (1 Kings 22: 19). One day a countless multitude from every nation, tribe, people and tongue will gather there (Rev. 7: 9).[1]

ISAIAH'S VISION OF WORSHIP

The first five chapters of Isaiah speak about God's judgement on his people because of their sin. The death of Uzziah marked the end of an age of stability and the beginning of the threat by Assyria. But Isaiah ch. 6 takes us beyond human history and presents us with God's perspective on it. In ch. 6 the prophet unexpectedly has a vision of the Lord on his throne in the midst of heavenly worship.

ISAIAH 6: 1-9

In the year that king Uzziah died I saw the Lord sitting upon a throne, high and lifted up: and his train filled the Temple. Above him stood the seraphim: each had six wings: with two he covered his face, and with two he covered his feet and with two he flew.

And one called to another and said:
'Holy, holy, holy is the Lord of hosts:
the whole earth is full of his glory.'

And the foundations of the thresholds shook at the voice of him who called and the house was filled with smoke. And I said: 'Woe is me! For I am lost: for I am a man of unclean lips and I dwell in the midst of a people of unclean lips: for my eyes have seen the Lord of hosts!'

Then flew one of the seraphim to me, having in his hand a burning coal which he had taken with tongs from the altar. And he touched my mouth and said: 'Behold this has touched your lips: your guilt is taken away and your sin is forgiven.' And I heard the voice of the Lord saying: 'Whom shall I send and who will go for us?' Then I said 'here I am! Send me.' And he said: 'Go and say to this people: 'hear and hear, but do not understand: see and see but do not perceive.'

Although the holiness of God is a familiar concept I am not aware that sufficient attention is drawn to this in our worship. Yet it is clear that the holiness of God is central in Isaiah's vision of heavenly worship. The holiness of God revealed in this vision can inform and shape the ethos of our worship. Such was the powerful impact of God's holiness that Isaiah became acutely aware of his sin and the sin of the nation. 'He has been made aware of the awesome holiness of God with all that means of his transcendence and yet his immanence and now he is suddenly and brutally aware of himself.'[2] Brevard Childs also reminds us, 'Holiness in the Old Testament is not an ethical quality, but the essence of God's nature as separate and utterly removed from the profane. Holiness, 'the glory of His majesty' strikes terror in the unholy and proud, (Isa.2:19) but to his attendants awe and reverence.'[3]

Today, anyone with a vision of heavenly worship would probably be ecstatic, although if it followed the pattern of Isaiah's it would not only be for their benefit. As we shall see, glimpses of heavenly worship may not only have an unforgettable and life-changing impact, they can also come with a call to serve the Lord. In ch. 6: 10-13 Isaiah is called to announce a message of judgement on God's people that spells out certain disaster for them, although it also contains a seed of hope and renewal. The Lord may have given him this vision of heavenly worship to reassure him about the difficult nature of his message. Oswalt says: 'The vision was clearly fundamental to the entire course of Isaiah's ministry and to the shape of his book. The glory, the majesty, the holiness and the righteousness of God became the ruling concepts of his ministry.'[4]

Isaiah was probably taking part in the daily routine of worship when the Lord unexpectedly revealed himself in the vision of worship in the throne room of heaven. Whether or not he was actually in the Temple is irrelevant although this is the context of his vision. His perception of reality and who God is has been completely shattered. He had the privilege of seeing God in all his authority and glory and holiness and majesty. This is an awe-inspiring scene as he is overwhelmed by the vision of the holiness of God in this scene of heavenly worship. He has seen the Lord exalted and high and lifted up sitting on a throne in his kingly rule. 'Isaiah feels the raw edge of terror at being where humanity dare not go.'[5] And he is almost certain to have been lying prostrate before God at this scene of unprecedented holiness and majesty.

Isaiah saw the heavenly seraphim servants of God around the throne who were praising him, 'in rapt attentiveness, utterly devoted to Yahweh, fluttering around the Holy One...The primary activity that fills the throne room with glad surrender is the seemingly unending doxology of the divine choir. It sings of the holiness, the splendour, the glory and the unutterable majesty of the ruler of heaven whose awesome governance extends over all the earth (the same threefold 'holy' is echoed in Rev. 4:8).'[6] The overwhelming sense of God's holiness evokes in Isaiah a sense of his inadequacy and a fresh awareness of his sinfulness and he is reduced to nothing. Oswalt also says: 'The statement that the seraphim were calling to each other is probably an indication that the singing was antiphonal, but it also may be a way of saying that they were delighting with one another in the glory of God...It can hardly be doubted that this experience accounts for the common title for God in Isaiah 'the Holy One of Israel/Jacob.'[7]

As soon as Isaiah confesses his sin and identifies with the sin of the nation the Lord takes the initiative to cleanse him. He sends one of the seraphim with a burning coal from the altar who touches his mouth as a sign that his guilt was taken away. Although he records his vision, Isaiah is not the object of it. How he feels is also not the main focus, although we can easily see it that way. Brueggemann in his inimitable manner discerns that the Lord's forgiveness allows Isaiah a legitimate place in the very presence of God – but it is not for his enjoyment of the divine presence. 'The throne room of God is the policy room of world government. There are messages to be sent. The government of Yahweh needs a carrier.'[8] Oswalt echoes this: 'But for whatever reason, God makes it plain that while spiritual experience is never merely a means to an end, neither is it an end in itself. Unless that experience issues in some form of lived-out praise to God it will turn on itself and putrefy. That Isaiah is neither directly addressed nor coerced is suggestive. Perhaps it is so because Isaiah does not need coercion, but further needs an opportunity to respond.'[9] Similarly Childs perceives:

> Indeed the focus throughout is not on the spiritual experience of the prophet or on what this ecstatic event meant to him. To focus on such an individual, personal evaluation completely misses the point of the narrative. Isaiah has not time to revel in his private emotions. He is not concerned with re-imagining God! Rather, only when his sin, seen in all its massive and objective reality is removed, can Isaiah hear the voice of God. 'Whom shall I send and who will go for us?'[10]

As God reveals himself through Word and Sacrament in worship this is a reminder to firmly ensure the Lord is the central focus and object of our worship. Even though we may have ecstatic and memorable experiences as the Lord ministers to us, we are not to make ourselves and our feelings the hallmark or the quintessence of Christian worship.

EZEKIEL'S VISION OF WORSHIP

Those called by the Lord as a prophet in the Old Testament had one of two responses. Moses and Jeremiah classically protested they were unsuitable for the task, not that the Lord was going to be so easily rebuffed and take 'no' for an answer. Their resistance was countered by the persistent summons of the Lord. In contrast Isaiah and Ezekiel were constrained to respond to the supernatural nature of their call. Ezekiel the son of Buzi a priest was himself training as a priest. When he was younger he lived through the exciting days of the reforms of Josiah. The time when Jeremiah begun his preaching ministry. Eichrodt says, 'Ezekiel must have been profoundly impressed by the religious aspects of the reform as he saw the Temple being cleansed of the heathen filth that had settled in it, and the original forms and laws of Yahweh for worship being put into force. This must have aroused his enthusiasm at the thought of the greatness of the task that this would lay upon the shoulders of the Temple priesthood. The renewal of the covenant between Israel and her God, sworn to by king and people in a solemn act of state must have seemed to bring back the ideal period of David.'[11]

Unfortunately, Josiah the King was killed in 609 BC and his reign and reforms came to an abrupt end. As was predicted by Jeremiah, Jerusalem was defeated by a foe from the North, Nebuchadnezzar in 597 BC, when he deported around 10,000 of the population. Ezekiel was among the exiles taken to Babylon and the aspiration of being a priest in the Temple in Jerusalem was devastatingly snatched away from him. In exile the elders could order their own affairs and were able to continue worshipping the Lord but this was limited as there was no Temple. It is quite likely that many of the priests were also among the exiles.

D. Block points out that for Ezekiel, 'The exile of Jehoiachin the king, along with his own deportation probably meant the end of all his professional dreams. The use of the first person in 33: 21 and 40: 1, suggests that he was among the thousands of soldiers, craftspeople and nobility who had been sent into exile along with the king. They were the victims of a common ancient Near Eastern policy toward conquered peoples: the mass deportation of entire populations designed to break down national resistance at home by removing political and spiritual leadership, and to bolster the economy and military machine of the conqueror's homeland.'[12]

Five years after Ezekiel had been in exile the Lord revealed himself to him in his visions. These not only authenticated his call as a prophet, they also confirmed the strident nature of God's word that he was called to speak to his people in exile. As you read the early chapters of Ezekiel you almost recoil at the difficult nature of what the Lord summoned him to say and do as a prophet. Through his visions the Lord spoke powerfully into his life, and without them it is unlikely he would have had the assurance and courage to do what the Lord asked him. Blenkinsopp thinks Ezekiel may have been ordained priest in exile and that the 'mysterious divine glory which appeared to him was also thought to appear at the climax of the ordination service (Lev. 9: 6). So it is possible he was called to be a prophet in the same year in which he was ordained priest, perhaps during the act of worship accompanying the ordination. In what follows there is at any rate a clear connection with worship. The description of the divine throne is reminiscent of Isaiah's vision of a heavenly liturgy of which temple worship was the earthly counterpart.'[13]

In this context Ezekiel's vision of the glory of God is doubly striking, because it propelled him into a ministry that came completely out of the blue and one he had never entertained, nor consciously trained for. Having been born into a priestly family in Jerusalem his education from an early age evolved around his training to be a priest. We see from the book of Ezekiel that he was familiar with Israel's history and religious traditions. His theology embraced a worldview with God as the centre and his life as a priest also evolved around the things of God. C. Wright points out, 'few matched the sheer uncompromising singularity of Ezekiel's passion for Yahweh. Everything in his life and understanding was dominated by the attributes of Yahweh as God, especially the glory of God. We can trace his passion to the vision by the Chebar Canal when he was overwhelmed by the appearance of the likeness of the glory of the Lord. When God called Ezekiel through this extraordinary vision and transformed him, he had a powerful impact on a life and an intellect already thoroughly shaped by the centrality of Yahweh.'[14]

Although Ezekiel's training to be a priest had been woven into his entire life, at the age of thirty, he was an exile in a foreign land with no hope whatsoever of starting his ministry as a priest in Jerusalem. At times his disappointment and sense of loss must have been acute. He probably felt the Lord had let him down and on occasions he may have questioned why the Lord hadn't intervened so that he was not deported. Had He done so Ezekiel could have begun his ministry as a priest in the Temple. As his call and identity were inextricably bound up with being a priest perhaps being at ease and at peace with himself proved to be elusive, having been torn away from what his heart and soul was destined. W. Eichrodt captures how Ezekiel probably felt in exile:

> He was far from Yahweh's presence in the sanctuary, leading a shadowy existence in a lost world where there was not even the faintest glimmer of hope of liberation: all that must have weighed heavily upon the heart of the young priest...There in that unclean land there was nothing to hope for and no improvement could be effected. Jerusalem was the only place from which any light came... So the young priest had to pass though a waiting period of agonising tension in which hope and fear alternated.[15]

Wright also draws our attention to how traumatic it must have been for Ezekiel who trained as a priest to suddenly find himself called to be a prophet. 'The disjunction between the two was both theological and professional. While we can see the benefits that his training as a priest brought to bear on his prophetic ministry we should not overlook the immense personal, professional and theological shock it must have been to Ezekiel, when at the age of thirty when he was eligible to be ordained a priest in Jerusalem, God broke into his life and wrecked all such career prospects, and constrained him into a role that he had never previously entertained.

> No wonder the anger and bitter rage to which he honestly confesses disorientated and overwhelmed him for a full week – 3: 14-15. God would use all that he had built into Ezekiel's life during his years of preparation, but he would use it in radically different ways from anything he had ever imagined. Such is sometimes the way of God with those whom he calls to his service.'[16]

THE GLORY OF THE LORD EZEKIEL 1: 1, 22-28
In the thirtieth year, in the fourth month, on the fifth day of the week as I was among the exiles by the river Chebar, the heavens opened and I saw visions of God. Over the heads of the living creatures there was the likeness of a firmament, shining like a crystal spread out above their

heads. And under the firmament their wings were stretched
out straight one toward another: and each creature had two
wings covering its body. And when they went I heard the
sound of their wings like the sound of many waters, like
the thunder of the Almighty, a sound of tumult like the
sound of a host: when they stood still they let down their
wings. And there came a voice from above the firmament
over their heads: when they stood still they let down their
wings. And above the firmament over their heads was the
likeness of a throne, in appearance like sapphire and seated
above the likeness of a throne was a likeness as it were of
a human form. And upward from what had the appearance
of his loins I saw as it were gleaming bronze, like the
appearance of a closed fire and there was brightness round
about him. Like the appearance of a bow that is in the
cloud on the day of rain, so was the appearance of the
brightness round about. Such was the appearance of the
likeness of the glory of the Lord. And when I saw it I fell
on my face and I heard the voice of one speaking.

Although the word worship is not used, the scene around the
throne of God pulsates with divine worship. In the climax of
Ezekiel's vision a vast crystal expanse sparkled with awesome
brightness. Through and above this transparent crystal he saw a
throne in a brilliant rich blue, constructed from one of the most
precious stones of the ancient world – lapis lazuli. And on the
throne with all the added brilliance of contrasting fiery amber
was a figure like that of a man. 'His vision involves a fascinating
reversal of the concept of 'image of God.'...Here in anthro-
pomorphic reversal God appears in the likeness of a human being
albeit in glowing fiery splendour, that anticipates the trans-
figuration of the incarnate Son of God himself and certainly
provided the imagery for John's great vision of the heavenly throne
in Revelation 4...This is none other than Yahweh himself very
much alive and still on the throne...Nothing will ever be more
significant for Ezekiel than this encounter with the living God.'[17]

Lying prostrate captures Ezekiel's worship to the revelation of
God's glory. Wright perceives that God's glory reveals his
transcendence and the cosmic exaltation of the Lord pervades
the worship of Israel – and he warns worshippers against any
'chummy familiarity.' The glory of the Lord also reveals his

sovereignty and the image of a throne itself speaks of authority and power. It also manifests God's omnipresence because of the very location of the vision. God has arrived in Babylon in all his glory.[18] The vision of the Lord, a vision of divine heavenly reality, announces from God's perspective the reality of things as they are on earth and transforms Ezekiel. The Lord has taken the initiative to reveal that he is God and that he is in control of human history. Ezekiel has had the 'eyes of his heart enlightened' beyond belief and beyond imagination. What he has seen speaks into the very depths of his soul, even though no words are initially uttered.

This vision reminds us that Paul prayed for the Ephesians, to have 'the eyes of their hearts enlightened' and is a call to us to offer up the same prayer for the Church. He prayed that the Lord would give them a revelation to perceive spiritual truths. Such revelation from the Lord transcends intellectual comprehension and fills our hearts so they overflow with God's glory. It is a prayer for God to fill our hearts with himself, so that the Lord who dwells on the throne and is high and lifted up, will also reign in our hearts in all his glory. It can also be a prayer for God to inhabit our worship, so that the Lord who dwells on the throne and is high and lifted up, will also reign in the midst of our worship.

A SUPERNATURAL VISION

In Ezekiel's vision Block sees the significance of the supernatural creatures who had four faces, one of which was like a man's face. He points out that while to a modern reader the choice of animals in the vision may seem arbitrary they were a natural choice, as they frequently appear on ancient iconographic and glyptic art and for Israel they also had symbolic significance. 'The lion was renowned for its courage, ferocity and strength and also served as a symbol of royalty. The eagle was the swiftest and most stately of birds. The ox was a symbol of fertility and divinity. In the absence of abstract philosophical tools these images expressed the transcendent divine attributes of omnipotence and omniscience. Carrying the divine throne, the four-headed cherubim declare that Yahweh has the strength and majesty of the lion, the swiftness and mobility of the eagle, the procreative power of the bull, and the wisdom and reason of humankind.'[19]

The wheels in Ezekiel's vision symbolise some form of four-wheeled chariot able to move in any direction. Their wheels gleamed with the brilliance of beryl and their rims full of eyes represented the all-seeing, all-knowing character of God. The wheels moved with perfect synchronisation with those of the creatures, and the harmony between them is attributed to the 'spirit of life' (*ruach hahayya*) – denoting the life giving energising power of God. 'It was this energising spirit that also determined the direction and freedom of movement of the heavenly vehicle.'[20]

Ezekiel saw that above the heads of the creatures they appeared to be holding up a sparkling platform, above which was the likeness of a throne and seated above the throne was the likeness as it were of a human form. The wings of the creatures made a noise like the sound of many waters, like the thunder of the Almighty, a sound of tumult like the sound of a host. These loud sounds may be reminiscent of Yahweh's appearance to Israel on Mount Sinai that was accompanied by peals of thunder. Block concludes this section (v. 22-28) by indicating that Ezekiel has finally caught onto the significance of the vision:

> This is none other than the glory of Yahweh. The doors of heaven have been flung wide open and he beholds Yahweh in all his splendour, enthroned above the living creatures. The term '*kabod*' derives from a root meaning 'to be heavy' but when applied to royalty and divinity it denotes the sheer weight of that person's majesty, that quality which evokes a response of awe in the observer. The prophet has witnessed the incredible far away from the Temple, among the exiles in the pagan land of Babylon, Yahweh has appeared to him. Ezekiel responds by appropriately falling down on his face in worship.[21]

No vision in the Old Testament matches the supernatural impact of the theophany of Ezekiel's vision. It has profound theological significance for a number of reasons. Everything in his vision proclaims the transcendent glory of God, a supernatural glory beyond our imagination. His vision also emanates with God's holiness and sovereignty that are symbolised through his elevation on his throne. Ezekiel's vision embraces God's immanence as he revealed his presence in the likeness of human form in the midst of his people in exile. Block has this to say about it.

This vision serves notice that whoever would enter into divine service must have a clear vision of the One into whose service he is called. The ministry is a vocation like no other: it represents conscription into the service of the King of kings and Lord of lords, the One who sits on his glorious throne, unrivalled in majesty and power.[22]

THE FULLNESS OF GOD
EZEKIEL 47: 1-5, 8, 12

'Then he brought me back to the door of the Temple: and behold water was issuing from below the threshold of the Temple towards the east (the Temple faced east): and the water was flowing down from below the south end of the threshold of the Temple, south of the altar. Then he brought me out by the way of the north gate and led me round on the outside to the outer gate, that faces towards the east: and the water was coming out on the south side...Going on eastward with a line in his hand, the man measured a thousand cubits and then led me through the water: and it was ankle deep. Again he measured a thousand and led me through the water: and it was knee deep. Again he measured a thousand and led me through the water and it was up to the loins. Again he measured a thousand and led me through the water and it was a river that I could not pass through...And he said to me, 'This water flows towards the eastern region and goes down into the Araba: and when it enters the stagnant waters of the sea the water will become fresh...And on the banks on both sides of the river there will grow all kinds of trees for food. Their leaves will not wither nor their fruit fail, but they will bear fresh fruit every month, because the water for them flows from the sanctuary. Their fruit will be food and their leaves for healing.'

REVELATION 22: 1-3

'Then he showed me the river of the water of life, bright as crystal, flowing from the throne of God and of the Lamb through the middle of the street of the city: also on either side of the river, the tree of life with its twelve kinds of fruit, yielding its fruit each month: and the leaves of the tree were for the healing of the nations...the throne of God and of the Lamb shall be in it and his servants shall worship him.'

The fullness of God flows from the throne of God and of Christ the Lamb. The water and river alluded to in both Ezekiel and Revelation is also the fullness of the Holy Spirit. These passages of

Scripture represent important truths as water is consistently used to symbolize the flow of God's Spirit through his people. Psalm 36: 8 says, 'They feast on the abundance of your house: you give them to drink from your river of delights.' As we worship God we are refreshed by Christ and drink of the Holy Spirit. A reminder of Jesus' words in John 6: 37-38, 'If anyone thirst let him come to me and drink. He who believes in me as the scripture has said, 'Out of his heart shall flow rivers of living water' – which refers to the Holy Spirit.

The River of Life in Ezekiel which flows through theTemple flows from the throne of God in Revelation. The river is a symbol of the fullness of God's blessing for renewal and healing in our corporate worship and ultimately in the nations. In Ezekiel's vision of the Temple there were varying depths of water which progressively got deeper. At first the water in the Temple was a trickle, then a brook and then a river. This represents the inexhaustible abundance of water which has the power to transform the landscape. So too the 'River of Life' as we are immersed in it, in our worship, can bring spiritual life and transform our lives and bring wholeness and healing. Are we paddling at the water's edge in our worship and merely enjoying a trickle of God's blessing? The Lord longs for our worship to be immersed in the 'River of Life' that flows from the heavenly throne. A foretaste of heavenly worship in the new Jerusalem the City of God.

JOHN'S VISION OF WORSHIP

The author of Revelation modestly refers to himself as: 'I John your brother' – Rev.1: 9, rather than I John the beloved apostle, although he had every right to. He does not pull rank on these Christians or elevate himself above them as he feels no need to assert his authority. 'The early church generally accepted John the beloved disciple was the author of Revelation. This was confirmed as early as 150 AD by Justin Martyr and around 200 AD by Irenaeus and its apostolic authority was widely accepted by the ancient fathers. From the style of writing we can discern the author was a Hebrew who was very familiar with the Old Testament. While the language of the fourth Gospel is smooth and fluent and couched in accurate and simple Greek, that of Revelation is rough and harsh with many grammatical and syntactical irregularities. We can account for this difference as a disciple of John may have acted as a secretary to write the Gospel, while John himself wrote Revelation and his exile establishes the fact of persecution.'[23]

The book of Revelation is from Jesus Christ via his angel to John, written to be read out aloud as a pastoral letter to the churches in Asia who knew John. He may have intended it be read during a Communion Service as there is an allusion to the messianic banquet throughout his book. As we read it, it is important to bear in mind the original audience and how they would have understood it.[24] It also highlights that 'one of the most important things that worship accomplishes is to remind us that we worship not merely as a congregation or a church, but as part of the Church, the people of God. John reminds his readers that their worship is a participation in the unceasing celestial praise of God. So too, the worship of God's people today finds its place in the 'middle' of a throng representing every people and nation and tribe and tongue.'[25]

REVELATION 4: 2-11

At once I was in the Spirit and lo a throne stood in heaven with one seated on the throne. And he who sat there appeared like jasper and carnelian and round the throne was a rainbow that looked like an emerald. Round the throne there were twenty-four thrones and seated on the thrones were twenty-four elders, clad in white garments with golden crowns on their heads. From the throne issue flashes of lightning and voices of peals of thunder, and before the throne burn seven torches of fire which are the seven spirits of God: and before the throne there is as it were a sea of glass like crystal.

And round the throne on each side of the throne are four living creatures, full of eyes in front and behind: the first living creature like a lion, the second living creature like an ox, the third living creature with the face of a man and the fourth living creature like a flying eagle. And the four living creatures each of them with six wings, are full of eyes all round and within, and day and night they never cease to sing:

Holy, holy, holy, is the Lord God Almighty –
Who was and is and is to come!

And whenever the living creatures give glory and honour and thanks to him who is seated on the throne, who lives for ever and ever, the twenty-four elders fall down before him who is seated on the throne and worship him who lives for ever and ever: they cast their crowns before the throne singing.

> Worthy art thou, our Lord and God to
> receive glory and honour and power:
> for thou didst create all things
> and by thy will they were created.

The revelation of John draws aside the invisible curtain that blocks our view of the heavenly realm. A drawing back that reveals the world in a radically new light. His vision takes him into the throne room of the universe where God rules over the earth and from which emanates his ultimate authority and power. He now sees the worship in the heavenly places around the throne of God that is never ending. Aspects of Revelation are thought to reflect Ezekiel's vision of God's throne and Isaiah's earlier temple vision. Ezekiel describes what seemed like a human form seated above the throne, 'as the appearance of the likeness of the glory of God,' whereas John's figure on the throne has an appearance similar to jasper and carnelian. Ian Boxall says:

> The use of precious stones in John's description evokes the dazzling splendour of the divine adoration and worship. So too does the emerald which is used to describe the rainbow encircling the throne…Elsewhere in Revelation jasper will describe the radiance of God's holy city and its wall (21: 11, 18).
> While all three jewels will be found in the city's foundations (21:19), in Jewish tradition they are among the jewels on the high priest's breastplate (Ex. 28: 17-20).[26]

The reference toan emerald like a rainbow shows the magnificence of the heavenly scene. As we view the throne of God and the heavenly court around it, we have a glimpse of the transcendent beauty and awe-inspiring worship that takes place there.

In John's vision there are twenty-four thrones with twenty-four elders on them who are identified as exalted human beings, dressed in shining white garments with crowns upon their heads which may indicate priestly and royal functions, although their garments are also reminiscent of those worn by angels. Boxall says: 'In short the twenty-four elders are almost certainly the angelic heavenly personification of the people of God. Their presence here close to the divine throne serves as an assurance to the vulnerable, but faithful among the seven churches (Rev. 1-3), that the promises made to them by the son of man figure will indeed come to fruition. As in heaven so ultimately on earth.'[27] At the heart of this vision is the phenomena emanating from the throne of God, flashes of lightning, voices and peals of thunder. These awesome sounds are reminiscent of the theophany that accompanied God's glory and presence at Mt. Sinai (Ex. 19: 16-18) following the deliverance of the Hebrews from Egypt. 'At strategic points throughout Revelation similar phenomena will recur with increasing intensity, as God acts again with judgement to overcome injustice and save his people (8: 5, 11: 19, 16: 18).'[28]

The four living creatures in John's vision resemble those in Ezekiel's and Isaiah's visions and here they are immersed in divine worship day and night, every day, without ceasing. Ladd says: 'It is quite clear that these four living creatures are analogous to the Seraphim of Isaiah 6: 1-3 and the cherubim of Ezek. 10: 14…Either the cherubim represent the praise and adoration extended to the Creator by the totality of his creation: or else they represent angelic beings who are used by the Creator in exercising his rule and his divine will in all the orders of his creation.'[29] The first part of their canticle is the same as Isaiah's as they declare that God is holy. Their worship is complemented by that of the elders around the throne of the Holy One. 'But theirs is no merely cerebral activity of speaking or singing. They fall down in front of the one seated on the throne in a gesture of divine worship, casting their golden wreaths before the throne. It may be that such a ritual parodies practice in the imperial court, where senators and representatives of the provincial cities presented the emperor with golden crowns on specific occasions. It is not the emperor but the Holy One seated on the authentic throne who deserves such honours. This vision is a salutary reminder that the rather cerebral activity which often passes for religious worship, would have been unrecognisable as such in the ancient world and certainly finds no support in Revelation. Here the worship of heaven is an activity which involves the whole person and all the human senses: speech: sight: hearing: touch and even smell.'[30]

WORSHIPPING THE LAMB REVELATION 5: 6-14

And between the throne and the four living creatures and among the elders, I saw a Lamb standing as though it had been slain, with seven horns and with seven eyes which are the seven spirits of God sent out into all the earth: and he went and took the scroll from the right hand of him who was seated on the throne. And when he had taken the scroll the four living creatures and the twenty-four elders fell down before the Lamb, each holding a harp and with golden bowls of incense which are the prayers of the saints: and they sang a new song saying: Worthy art thou to take the scroll and to open it seals for thou wast slain and by thy blood didst ransom men for God, from every tribe and tongue and people and nation, and hast made them a kingdom and priests to our God, and they shall reign on earth.

Then I looked and I heard around the throne and the living creatures and the elders the voice of many angels, numbering myriads of myriads and thousands of thousands, saying with a loud voice: 'Worthy is the Lamb who was slain, to receive power and wealth and wisdom and might and honour and glory and blessing!' And I heard every creature in heaven and on earth and under the earth and in the sea and all therein saying: 'To him who sits upon the throne and to the Lamb be blessing and honour and glory and might for ever and ever!' And the four living creatures said: 'Amen!' and the elders fell down and worshipped.

In John's vision the Lamb now replaces the allusion to Jesus as 'someone like a son of man' and is the central Christological title (this occurs 28 times in Rev.). Ch. 5 opens with a moving scene culminating in Jesus the Lamb being worthy to open the scroll, (this significance is revealed in the following chapters) because his death on the cross and his blood ransomed people for God from every tribe and nation. This is the enthronement and worship of Jesus the Lamb that reflects the worship that took place in ch. 4. The heavenly creatures who have a harp and golden bowls of incense, is reminiscent of the worship in the Temple at Jerusalem. A reminder that the 'earthly liturgy of both the Tabernacle and the Temple, was patterned upon the true heavenly sanctuary.'[31]

John's vision bursts into a panoramic scene of worship of unrivalled splendour. 'The angelic liturgy is impressive indeed in its scale and intensity. These lesser angels also sing a canticle which proclaims that the Lamb is worthy...As this vision reaches its climax with ear-splitting intensity the whole of creation is caught up in the praise of God and the Lamb...We catch a glimpse here of what creation was intended for and what can in God's great plan be on earth, as it is in heaven. God and the Lamb hitherto addressed separately are now acclaimed together in one great concluding doxology, the objects of praise and honour, glory and strength, for ever and ever...Then the elders fall down before the throne and the Lamb, in a posture of silent and profound worship.'[32] The worship of God and Jesus the Lamb that takes place in heaven is in an atmosphere that is profoundly moving as the elders fall down. The posture of lying prostrate on the floor is evocative of total submission in worship to God and Christ. Christians in the Orthodox Churches do this and it may be timely for God's people in the West to also prostrate themselves in worship before the Lord. M. Redman calls this *'face down worship.'* Such worship can powerfully symbolise lives yielded to the Lordship of Christ.

WORSHIP, CONFLICT & VICTORY REV. 9: 1-19

After this I heard what seemed to be the voice of a great multitude in heaven crying: 'Hallelujah! Salvation and glory and power belong to our God, for his judgements are true and just: he has judged the great harlot who corrupted the earth with her fornication, and he has avenged on her the blood of his servants.' Once more they cried: 'Hallelujah! The smoke from her goes up for ever and ever.' And the twenty-four elders and the four living creatures fell down and worshipped God who is seated on the throne saying: 'Amen. Hallelujah!' And from the throne came a voice saying crying: 'Praise God all you his servants, you who fear him, small and great.' Then I heard what seemed like the voice of a great multitude, like the sound of many waters and like the sound of mighty thunder-peals crying: 'Hallelujah for the Lord our God the Almighty reigns. Let us rejoice and exult and give him the glory, for the marriage of the Lamb has come and his bride has made herself ready: it was granted to her to be clothed with fine linen, bright and pure, for the fine linen is the righteous deeds of the saints.

Rev. ch. 18 announces the fall of Babylon and opens our eyes to the invisible spiritual powers opposed to God's kingdom. When John wrote to the seven churches Rome would have been seen as Babylon. Now in the 21st century it may represent a power that seeks to establish control over peoples' and nations' lives. In Rev. ch. 12 and 13 we also read of a dragon and a beast being worshipped by men. These disturbing chapters introduce us to an underlying theme in Revelation that involves worship and conflict. Noel Due echoes this theme, 'Behind the scenes of history lie spiritual powers, unveiled in the book of Revelation for what they really are. The principle of their operation is imitative in that they seek to set up a counterfeit to the reality of God and his purposes. The red dragon who is Satan has the incarnation of his 'son' in the beast who is the counterpart of Christ, i.e. who is the antichrist. He has a 'death' and 'resurrection' (Rev. 13: 3) and the power of his death and resurrection is to make all men worship the beast. The second beast who is the false prophet, the evil counterpart of the Holy Spirit causes humanity to worship the image of the beast: and the beast is in collusion with the unholy woman, Babylon, who is the foul counterpart of the pure Bride the church of Christ.'[33]

In Rev. ch 19 in the throne room of heaven true worship pervades the atmosphere, where the victory of Christ over evil results in resounding liturgical praise in a canticle involving heavenly worshippers. The shout of 'Hallelujah' resounds four times in six verses and occurs only in the New Testament in Revelation. Once again the twenty-four elders and the four creatures fall down and worship God. This heavenly liturgy is resplendent with the choral singing of a vast multitude of worshippers. They rejoice in God's salvation and final victory over evil and also rejoice in His justice and in His Kingly rule. The ecstatic worship of the angelic hallelujah chorus, the elders and the creatures ushers in the second coming of the marriage of the Lamb with his Bride, the Church. This is a scene of great celebration. E. Boring says:

> Even with all the language of judgement the scene never ceases to be a worship scene. The smoke of Babylon that ascends forever is only a grisly contrast to the incense of heavenly worship. Worship celebrates 'the mighty acts of God' not our pious feelings…Worship is the dominating note of the concluding scene of this vision.[34]

CHAPTER SIX

CONTEMPORARY & CHARISMATIC WORSHIP

INTRODUCTION

This chapter is not a definitive text for any church, but, it is an example of an exploration of these styles of worship. My first experience of charismatic worship can be traced back to the time I was the Manager of a leading, fashionable unisex salon in Baker Street, London, when two Greek friends invited me to go with them on a Christian holiday at Ashburnham in Sussex. This was run by the Fountain Trust where Tom Smail was the speaker. If they had told me that this was a charismatic holiday this would have meant absolutely nothing to me. This was my first experience of charismatic worship and one particular evening stood out because the presence of the Lord was so real. On Wednesday at 10pm Tom Smail apologised that we had to stop the meeting as the coffee was ready. But who wants to stop worshipping when the presence of the Lord is so real? At Ashburnham there was the opportunity to be prayed for to receive the baptism of the Holy Spirit. Around 30 of us sat in one of the meeting rooms and a member of the team came and laid hands on us and prayed for us. At around this time I listened to songs by The Fisherfolk that were especially worshipful and intimate with the Lord.

Over the years I have come into contact with other charismatic churches, denominations and conferences/holidays. I went to the Dales at the beginning of the 80s where Bryn Jones was the leader and speaker. The first evening we were part of 4-5,000 thousand people enthusiastically worshipping the Lord. The celebratory worship felt overwhelming but we adjusted to it the next day! During the middle of the 80s as a theology student at St. John's in Nottingham, I was part of a student church, St. Nicks that embraced the teaching of John Wimber. Between 1986-87, I was on placement as a student at St. Margarets, Aspley in Nottingham. A few years earlier the church had experienced charismatic renewal. But sadly the vicar was not able to lead them deeper into renewal so that it matured.

On a few occasions I also worshipped with my wife Sarah at the Pentecostal Assemblies of God in Talbot Street, Nottingham where her cousin was a member. Here the Service consisted of 45 minutes of sung worship, the notices and then a 45 minute sermon. Every Friday night between 8-12 pm they had a half night of prayer for their church and the city. Attendance on Sunday morning was around 300, later when they moved to a warehouse it was around 500 and it is now 2000. In their worship that lasted 45 minutes there was a tangible sense of the presence of the Lord. Yet this passed quickly and there was a sense of being in a dimension where time stood still. On one occasion after the sung worship there was an altar call and around 20 people responded.

Over the years I went to Spring Harvest and visited St. Andrews Chorleywood when Bishop David Pytches was the Vicar. At the end of the nineties I also visited two churches where the Toronto Blessing had arrived. This was the latest wave of charismatic renewal to come to Britain and originated at the Toronto Airport Vineyard Fellowship. My first curacy in 1988, an Anglican, Evangelical charismatic church, was a spiritually gifted fellowship. Although not everyone identified themselves as charismatic, many believed in baptism in the Holy Spirit and the use of spiritual gifts. St. Barnabas, in Cambridge where I worship, is a large eclectic Evangelical church with charismatic leanings. This is a young congregation predominantly under 40 and it is a privilege to see so many young people and adults there.

In 1992 for just over two years I was a full-time Non Stipendiary Curate in two parishes just outside Cambridge. Having been part of two rural congregations whose main worship was Eucharistic (Holy Communion) was completely outside my experience as I was primarily used to a morning Service of the Word with a strong slant on preaching. But, I believed the Lord guided me there. In the parish of St. Edmunds, Hauxton, the congregation numbered around 35-40 and used the Rite A Communion Service. A mile down the road at the parish of All Saints, Harston, they used the Rite B Communion Service which closely followed the 1662 Prayer Book Communion. Both Communion Services lasted an hour and we had around fifteen minutes to talk to the congregation at Harston before we went to Hauxton. I had not been involved in Eucharistic worship in any meaningful way prior to this. I was subsequently struck by the profound and lasting impact this worship was to have on me. On my first Sunday at Harston the congregation of six was boosted to nine by Fraser Watts, the priest in charge, Jean the Lay Reader and myself. I was involved in parish visiting after Easter and by the end of June 36 people attended. Although I had never before been part of such a small congregation as the one at Harston, I was particularly struck by how prayerful and worshipful their Communion Service was. Also, in the weeks that followed I was equally struck by the depth of content that this hour long service included. There were three Scripture readings and a Psalm was also included. There were five hymns although the sermon was only ten minutes long. What also made a profound impression on me was that the Rite B Communion Service was steeped in Scripture. Having been used to a Service of the Word with one Scripture reading and a long sermon at the eclectic church in Cambridge prior to arriving in the rural parishes, it was readily apparent that the scriptural content of this hour long service was clearly greater.

PRAISE & WORSHIP

The second half of the 20th Century gave rise to new models of praise and worship based on the emergence of the choruses that sprang from the Jesus movement in the early 70s and The Fisherfolk. It soon spread to the charismatics and then to the Pentecostals, and towards the end of the last century it became prevalent in many Evangelical churches as well as spawning new church movements like the Vineyard. As a result there has been an increase in worship songbooks published. From the heady days of Youth Praise in the 60s there came new songbooks such as Mission Praise, Songs of Fellowship, Spring Harvest, Graham Kendrick, Hosanna – The Vineyard, Hillsong and Soul Survivor. They have all contributed new praise and worship songs in their respective eras.

Worship that includes contemporary songs also has its roots in the House Church Movement and in Christian holidays like Spring Harvest and latterly New Wine and Soul Survivor. When Spring Harvest began in 1979, 3,000 people attended in Prestatyn, North Wales. By 1987 this had increased to 50,000 and by 1990 the number attending was 80,000. Pete Ward says: 'Central to the impact of Spring Harvest was the way that the event spread charismatic styles of worship around the country...With these changes also came a shift in fortunes within the Charismatic

Movement. Walker argues that their success is one of the main
reasons for what he sees as the decline in the 'Restoration' group
of churches...Through Spring Harvest individual Christians were
able to experience a similar excitement and style of worship to
that which was on offer at the Restorationist Dales and Downs
Bible weeks. At Spring Harvest however, they were able to do so,
without taking on board the restrictive authority structure.'[1]

THE RESTORATION MOVEMENT

James Steven points out that the Restoration Movement was part
of the Charismatic Movement in the 60s. However, in the 70s
it began to take on its own distinctive characteristics, as the
Charismatic Movement diverged into the two main streams of
Renewal and Restorationism. The former focused in the Fountain
Trust, sought to live out the implications of charismatic life within
the Anglican, Catholic & Methodist churches. The latter had roots
in the Brethren, Independent Baptist, Evangelical Free Church, and
the Assemblies of God and were used to the concept of local
autonomy. But, they went further in radically altering church
structures according to their perception of biblical principles.
In the early 70s many of the small house church fellowships in
the Restoration Movement began to order themselves in larger
network fellowships, such as New Frontiers led by Terry Virgo,
the Pioneer Trust led by Gerald Coates and Ichthus led by Roger
Forster. The songwriters, Graham Kendrick (Ichthus Fellowship,
London) and Dave Fellingham (Clarendon Church, Hove) are also
associated with this movement. The services consist in worship
lasting up to 45 minutes, followed by the notices and then a
sermon also lasting up to 45 minutes.

Steven also mentions that The Restoration Movement exclusively
adheres to the Bible and is Conservative Evangelicalism at its most
fundamental. One of the other distinct aspects of its theology is
'Baptism in the Holy Spirit.' This enables Christians to have power
to witness, be effective in prayer, and minister using spiritual gifts.
Many of their songs emphasise the sovereignty and majesty of
God and the ascended Christ seated at the Father's right hand.
They also have a sense of being 'kingdom people' with a
commitment to God's purposes of restoring the Kingdom of God.
Another major emphasis of the Kingdom is a renewal of worship.
Here, Scripture controls the songs and there is an expectation that
'God will be in their midst.'[2]

CHARISMATIC WORSHIP

Robb Redman describes charismatic worship by comparing the John Wimber, Vineyard Model with neo-Pentecostal practice. 'In the Wimber model there are five distinct phases in free-flowing praise. 1. invitation: 2. engagement: 3. exaltation: 4. adoration and 5. intimacy. In this model the first 3-5 songs are often upbeat and focus on gathering to worship God and then focus on the nature and attributes of God in exaltation. The music often shifts at this point to a softer, mellower sound to permit the worship to acknowledge God's presence in adoration. Thematically, the adoration and intimacy sections feature songs that address God personally. The final intimacy phase is the quietest. In many Vineyard churches songs rich in biblical and non-biblical language predominate: many songs describe a relationship with God in physical terms, seeing, hearing, touching holding, kissing. As biblical justification for this, Vineyard worship leaders emphasise a meaning of the New Testament Greek word for worship (*proskuneo*) 'to turn towards to kiss,' which they take to mean intimacy or closeness to God.'[3]

The neo-Pentecostal approach to worship also has a five-stage process, but this draws on an understanding of worship in the ancient Jewish Tabernacle and Temple. 1. Outside the camp. 2. Through the gates with thanksgiving. 3. Into his courts with praise. 4. Onto the holy place and 5. into the holy of holies. The service begins with the gathering of the people outside the dwelling place of God, rejoicing in the encounter with God about to take place with upbeat and energetic songs. Psalm 100 is the cue for the next two stages: 'Enter his gates with thanksgiving and his courts with praise.' The songs celebrate the greatness of God and offer thanks for God's goodness. The mood changes as worshippers move into these two phases, 'all attention is now directed solely to God, Jesus or the Holy Spirit.'[4] These two models of sung worship with their five stages are of particular interest as they have to be more creative in their content. They are also more comprehensive and are likely to have a greater variety of songs, and have a progression into God's presence worshippers can be aware of.

Integral to the theology of the Charismatic Movement is that God comes to meet his people and the worshippers have the expectation they will meet with God. Chris Bowater says, 'The desire to know God, to meet with him. This is the key to Spirit-filled worship of

God. Without this desire to stand in his presence, worship becomes a fruitless experience…The most important fruit of worship is God's presence. This is the very heart of worship.'[5] Also at the heart of charismatic worship is the desire to experience the 'glory of God.' The glory of the Lord is seen in the manifestation of his overpowering presence in the Old Testament when Solomon consecrated the temple. Bowater points out that, 'charismatic worship has readily adopted the idea that to speak of God's glory is to speak of his immanent presence.' And it is this concept which leads to songs of awe and glory having such a prominent feature in charismatic worship.[6]

Mark Bonnington in 'Patterns Of Charismatic Spirituality'– 2008, elegantly describes the issues of incandescent glory and intimate love in this genre of worship. He points out that it is God who is being encountered in the Spirit, Almighty God, the God who created the world, who is the source and end of all, the God of glory, the God of majesty and power. A fully biblical God eventfully encountered is not a God reduced to that eventfulness, a God domesticated and controlled.

> *It is precisely the interplay between God experienced as incandescent glory and unapproachable holiness and God immanent, real and present experienced in intimate love, the interplay between God worshipped in awe and God known as loving Father, that drives the dialectic at the heart of charismatic spirituality.*

This restless interaction never lets worship settle for a distant, powerful but ultimately uninvolved God or for an intimate, loveable but rather domesticated undemanding friend…This interplay between immanence and transcendence is economically expressed in the use of the word 'glory'– *doxa* and comes to expression in some of the most popular charismatic songs of the last 20 years. Two examples show this: 'Be still for the presence of the Lord, the Holy One is here' and 'My Jesus, my Saviour.'[7]

Jeremy Begbie writing as far back as 1991 in an article in 'The Spirituality of Renewal Music,' identified the main themes of charismatic worship songs in six groups. 1. Songs of exuberant praise. 2. Songs of jubilant testimony and exhortation. 3. Songs of intimacy with God. 4. Songs of majesty. 5. Songs of hushed reverence. 6. Songs of battle. Victoria Cooke in 2001 commented,

'Whilst not comprehensive Begbie's summary provides us with a helpful starting point. Since 1991, however, there have been significant developments in the predominant trends of worship – so much so that I believe it is now necessary to re-categorise the main worship themes in charismatic hymnody.'[8]

Cooke identifies five categories which are not too dissimilar to Begbie's. '1. Songs of Praise. 2. Songs of Love and Commitment – while Begbie wrote of simple intimate love songs to the Father/Jesus/God, these songs have proliferated and speak of total surrender and commitment to God. 3. Songs of Intercession – this refers to songs that were previously identified as warfare and declared God's victory over all other powers. These are not so prevalent now and it is more usual to have songs of intercession looking to God to answer his peoples' prayers. 4. Songs of Ministry – some of this genre are sung to a congregation and their main focus is on encouraging listeners to be open to God and be honest about their feelings and problems. Others focus on God's attributes and the believer's relationship with him which seek to bring healing. 5. Songs of Awe and Glory – include a petition for an intense encounter with God.'[9]

Peter Hocken 'In Streams Of Renewal,' that charts the origins and early development of the Charismatic Movement in Britain, highlights some of its distinguishing features that are also relevant to charismatic worship. He points out that while it is not unusual for charismatics to become preoccupied with spiritual gifts and the manifestation of spiritual power that is associated with them, such an assumption could easily lead to the conclusion that the possession of these gifts is the central focus of the movement.

> It is then worthy of note that the participants constantly testify that the primary aspect of accession to the sphere of spiritual gifts, is a new quality in their knowledge and experience of God…Some spoke of a conscious inflowing of God. Some had a clear sense of the presence of God and his glory, some an inner peace and knowledge of God's love. There is a particular place in the witness for the person of Jesus Christ, with frequent mention being made of a new knowledge and love of the Saviour.[10]

A feature then of charismatic worship is a new or renewed desire to praise God. 'This new capacity to worship was often experienced in terms of a welling up within one's heart as the work of the indwelling Holy Spirit. This is especially associated with receiving the gift of tongues itself experienced as spontaneous praise. Also, there is a new capacity for hearing God speak in a number of ways: by receiving pictures or impressions, or words of knowledge or wisdom.'[11]

Hocken believes that the Charismatic Movement has a distinctive shape with baptism in the Spirit being a core, central experience. Evidence of this is seen when a person exercises any of the spiritual gifts listed in 1 Corinthians. Another aspect is having the Lord's authority when preaching or using spiritual gifts. There are two other key features to understanding it. The first is the transforming power of the Holy Spirit in peoples' lives to bring salvation, deliverance and healing where there is addiction or brokenness. The second involves:

> A new closeness to and love for Jesus Christ: a new joy and peace: a new capacity to praise God: a new desire to read the Scriptures: a new power for ministry and witness, a new confidence in God.'[12]

A defining aspect of being filled with, immersed in or baptised in the Spirit, is a new or renewed relationship with God, Christ and the Holy Spirit. It is a relationship with the Trinity on an intimate, intuitive level that touches people in a profound way in their heart, mind and innermost being. As a result God, Christ and the Spirit become very alive and real to them and is fellowship with the Trinity in a new way.

The following are two moving testimonies of baptism in the Holy Spirit which show its profound impact. The first is from Michael Harper who was the first Director of the Charismatic Movement – The Fountain Trust. Although this dates to the beginning of the 60s his testimony captures something of its life changing impact. 'I was *"filled with all the fullness of God"* and had to ask God to stop giving me more – I could not take it...so filled was I at one moment with *"joy unspeakable and full of glory"* and then deep conviction of sin, as the Holy Spirit revealed areas of my life that had not been under his sovereign control...I experienced as I had never before the love of God literally poured into my heart...Prayer was a new experience of intimate communion with my Master and the element of worship which had been totally absent before, became an important part of my devotional life.'[13]

Raniero Cantalamessa also describes a thrilling experience of baptism in the Holy Spirit, by someone who took part in a retreat in 1967 which was the start of the charismatic renewal in the Catholic Church.

> Our faith has come alive, our believing has a kind of knowing. Suddenly the world of the supernatural has become more real and natural. In brief, Jesus Christ is a real person to us, a real person who is our Lord and who is active in our lives. We read the New Testament as though it were literally true now, every word, every line. Prayer and the sacraments have become truly our daily bread, instead of practices which we recognize as 'good for us.' A love of Scripture, a love of the church I never thought possible, a transformation of our relationships with others, a need and a power to witness beyond all expectation, have all become part of our lives. The initial experience of baptism in the Spirit was not at all emotional, but life has become suffused with calm, confidence, joy and peace...We sang the Veni Creator Spiritus before each conference and meant it. We were not disappointed. We have also been showered with charismata. This also puts us in an ecumenical atmosphere at its best.[14]

JOHN WIMBER

Contemporary worship owes an incalculable debt to the late John Wimber and the Vineyard Movement he founded, so it is appropriate to chart his contribution to worship. One major factor that influenced John was his background as a musician. As an only child he spent long hours alone and learned to play over twenty different musical instruments, his favourite being the saxophone. And by the age of fifteen he was an accomplished musician. After graduating he pursued a professional music career and in 1953 he won first prize at the Lighthouse International Jazz Festival. In 1962 he bought an up-and-coming group called the Righteous Brothers and played sax for them, and in 1964 they released their hit single, 'You've Lost That Loving Feeling.'[15] Not long after he came to the Lord John sold all his musical instruments. He loaded up an entire station wagon with boxes of music, records and arrangements that represented his whole life's work that he loved, and took them to the dump and disposed of them. His wife Carol described this as, 'the corn of wheat that has to die to bring forth much fruit.'

John's background as a musician was an influential factor in Christian worship and he passionately called his worship leaders to make 'Jesus famous' and to be servants, instead of promoting their own ministries. He discouraged musical exhibitions that would steal the church's affection for Jesus, by drawing attention to the worship leader or band. Simple, pure devotion to Jesus was the outstanding trait of early Vineyard worship.[16] Before he was the leader of the Vineyard Movement John was one of the Pastors of a Quaker Church. Many years before his Vineyard ministry evolved both he and his wife were led to the Lord by a friend called Gunner who was a Quaker. The model of evangelism they had in the fellowship was to befriend people, teach them about the Christian faith and share the Lord, their lives and their homes with them, something that John and Carol became involved in. They were also influenced by the Quakers' emphasis on waiting for the Lord and openness to the Holy Spirit.

> The silent meeting for worship is the most visible element of classical Quaker worship. The worshippers assemble without leader or program, stilling their minds and focusing their attention waiting to sense the presence of God and then to respond as they are moved in their own spirits.[17]

Andy Park informs us that John Wimber had a genuine desire to have deep communion with God in worship and he resisted any manipulative techniques that would cheapen the worship experience. God met John and Carol in their Quaker worship in a small group in 1977 which later became the Anaheim Vineyard. This is how Carol describes those early days.

> We began worship with nothing but a sense of the calling from the Lord to a deeper relationship with Him. Before we started meeting in a small home church setting in 1977, the Holy Spirit had been working in my heart creating a tremendous hunger for God. One day as I was praying the word 'worship' appeared in my mind like a newspaper headline. I had never thought much about that word before.

After we started to meet in our home gathering we noticed times during the meeting, usually when we sang, in which we experienced God deeply. We sang many songs but mostly songs about worship or testimonies from one Christian to another. But, occasionally we sang a song personally and intimately to Jesus, with lyrics like 'Jesus I love you.' Those types of songs both stirred and fed the hunger of God within me.[18]

In the early days Carol recalls learning to sing *to* Jesus *not* about him. 'We realised that often we would sing about worship yet we never actually worshipped, except when we accidentally stumbled onto intimate songs like, 'I love you Lord.' Ever since, the Vineyard has placed an emphasis on singing to the Lord and their worship is marked by simple songs of love and devotion. From this an intimate kind of worship evolved that has had an influence around the world. John felt the Lord had entrusted the Vineyard with a gift of worship to share with God's church.[19]

An integral feature of Vineyard worship is God's love for his children. The 'Father Heart of God' is a phrase which is found in their worship albums and indicates this is an important doctrine in their theology. In the UK Vineyard this is seen in the emphasis in their love songs on the fatherly nature of God and the intimate relationship between the Father and his children which reflects the intimacy of their worship. This also reflects God's compassion as he responds to the needs of those who seek him. This includes an emphasis in their worship on physical healing and also emotional/psychological healing. Equally, their worship seeks to communicate to the worshipper the confidence that they are a child of God.[20] 'The 'Father Heart of God' was one of John Wimber's main theological concerns in his teaching. It was of prime concern to him that worshippers both understood and experienced the love of God as father rather than as a dictator, bully or tyrant. This aspect was therefore central to his teaching and subsequently of prime importance to the themes of Vineyard worship and forms a vital part of the their contribution to songs.[21] In response to God's fatherly love, praise and surrender are also central themes in Vineyard worship. An integral aspect of self-surrender is the pursuit of holiness, as God is a holy God and those who seek him must also seek his holiness – to bring an offering of a consecrated life in their sung worship. This is expressed in the song: 'Over every thought, over every word, may my life reflect the beauty of my Lord.'[22]

While Vineyard worship has had a wide influence, John Leach, a former Director of Anglican Renewal Ministries writing towards the end of the 90s, felt their songs did not have the range of feel, colour and tempo as a selection of the type of songs Spring Harvest used at their Easter Celebrations. He felt the Vineyard lyrics that were simple and intimate to one worshipper could be slushy and theologically bereft to another, especially if you have been singing them for 45 minutes. He felt that while their music was good on adoration and love, with at least two songs of celebration and joy, that is about it. 'Particularly noticeable by its absence is any hint of the victorious mood of many of our spiritual warfare songs such as, 'Let God arise' or 'For this purpose.' I feel this is a serious lack.'[23]

John Wimber had a call to the style of worship that evolved as the Vineyard model. Equally, Matt Redman's and Tim Hughes' style of worship evolved when they were young teenage Christians seeking to express their love for the Lord. To replicate these styles of worship requires more than enthusiastic musicians playing loudly, or having long sessions of sung worship. We have to take into account their spiritual formation that evolves over a period of years, while their call and vision for worship matures. Of equal significance is the development of their relationship with the Lord as he moulds them and their ministry. Paul Oakley echoes this when he says: 'There was a time when God called me to lay down music indefinitely to pursue him and know him more. I just kept an acoustic guitar in my room just so I could worship with it. It was almost a full two years before I felt God say, 'Now is the time to pick it up again' – but those two years were critical and foundational.'[24] There are no short cuts to replicating styles of worship well known leaders have cultivated over many years. Learning to lead others in worship, acquiring the skills this calls for and the sensitivity to the Holy Spirit this requires, involves being dedicated to continue learning about worship, and how to lead it and release others as worshippers too.

SOUL SURVIVOR

Mike Pilavachi points out that worship has always been a core value of Soul Survivor and in his own words shares what this means. 'At our church, Soul Survivor Watford, we put a large emphasis on singing songs of worship in our meetings, not because we're more musically talented than others, but because when we fell in love with Jesus that was the first way we wanted to express it. We wanted to tell him how much he meant to us, to adore him publicly and privately by singing words of love and praise, to give something back to him for all he had given to us. One thing we quickly discovered was that you can't out-give the Giver. As we sang to him, he met with us in ways we'd never expected. As we told him we loved him, he was pouring more love into our hearts.'[25] While worship is an integral feature of Soul Survivor the defining purpose of this charity is to envision young people of all denominations to first capture a vision of Jesus, and then to equip, train, empower and release them into his ministry in their lives.

Therefore, to trace the roots of Soul Survivor sets the scene for their style of worship. In the 90s Mike Pilavachi was the youth worker at St. Andrews, Chorleywood, when Bishop David Pytches was the Vicar. In his youth group there was a 15 year old boy, Matt Redman, who 'worshipped his heart out' at the back of the meetings. As Mike encouraged Matt he started to lead the worship at church. As they both longed to grow in their understanding of worshipping Jesus, they decided the best way to do this was to spend one night a week outside the church structure. They chose Saturday and over the next few months with Matt playing the guitar the two of them sang their hearts out to Jesus, praying, reading their Bibles and singing in the Spirit. Over a period of time a number of other young people started to join them and that's how Soul Survivor started. In Mike's words, 'It was all pretty much an accident!'

When Mike Pilavachi began leading the youth work at New Wine, founded by David Pytches, he had the recurring dream of having a similar event just for young people. He wanted it to be evangelistic and a lot of fun, but at the heart of it would be worship, teaching and ministry, three things he saw as being core to developing genuine and lasting relationship with Jesus. He went to David and shared his vision with him thinking he would say, 'No way – it's ridiculous.' Instead he listened and said: 'Mike it sounds ridiculous to me.' He then paused and said, 'But, it sounds like it may be from God. Let's have a go.'

In 1993 the first Soul Survivor took place at Shepton Mallett and just under 1900 young people turned up. This figure is accurate because Mike counted them all in himself! The next year there were 4,000 and this gradually increased to 23,000 young people in the summer of 2006. Lots of young people bring their friends, many of whom make a commitment to the Lord. Soul Survivor's work with young people is impressive, but equally impressive is their emphasis on evangelism and social action/justice. This evolved as they realised that many worship leaders were being raised up but few evangelists. As a result, in 2000, instead of having their annual festival in Somerset they arranged for 11,000 young people to go and serve the City of Manchester in a mission. Afternoons were spent cleaning up estates, working on peoples' gardens, creating community gardens and play areas and re-furbishing community centres. Residents stopped to talk to the delegates amazed that young people would do something for nothing, and were invited to evangelistic events held every evening in the Manchester Evening News Arena. The impact was widespread. Communities were changed and crime rates went down and 1,700 people gave their lives to Jesus.

Similarly, in 2004 Soul Survivor was involved in Soul in the City in London. During the morning around 12,000 delegates and young people worshipped in song at three main venues. They then spent the afternoon worshipping God through acts of service for local communities in the form of 432 projects. 9,500 Christians from 772 partnering churches were also involved and provided a place for new Christians to be discipled. It is estimated that 1,200 people made first time commitments to Jesus and through other aspects of the mission another 4,800 people responded to God. The work of Soul in the City has continued through the local churches, who seek to maintain and develop the relationships built, as they love and serve the people of London.

Another place to serve that Mike Pilavachi has initiated is the mission to Durban 2009. South Africa being one of his favourite countries he has often visited Durban. Here his encounter with a number of homeless, parentless children, who were begging made a deep impression on him and his friends. As the Lord has shared his heart for the lost, a sister charity has been set up called Soul Action. The aim is to encourage sustainable initiatives that will continue after the volunteers have returned home.[26]

Anyone who has been to Soul Survivor knows 'the heart of worship' represents their ethos. It is a key metaphor in their songbook. There is a heart to worship that seeks to express the intimacy between the believer and the Lord. Pete Ward says:

> This heart is located in acknowledging that worship is all about Jesus. Heart here relates to the essence of the deepest truth of worship. It is possible to drift from this 'heart' to be distracted even by worship itself. We can make worship something that it should not be but this is a mistake because the pure, essential nature of worship relates to Jesus. This is its heart.[27]

In worship we can also seek the heart of God the Father. 'To approach God's heart is to experience the grace of God who gives and gives. This is the heart of the Father, the merciful graciousness of the Lord...Searching for God's heart is the response of one lover to another. God holds our heart in his hands and we are committed to seeking after him.'[28] When speaking about the believer's heart Ward also says: 'Pouring out the heart in worship comes through the closeness of the Lord. At the same time the worship of the believer is a demonstration of love for Jesus. Such worship itself may be said to bless the heart of Jesus. Worship in the secret place where Jesus and the believer share their intimate connection. In the song 'I'm giving you my heart' the believer surrenders themselves to God.'[29]

One of Matt Redman's best known songs, 'When The Music Fades,' challenges us to think about what we are doing in sung worship. The birth of this song in 1997 is particularly interesting. The Soul Survivor congregation in Watford began to experience problems and Mike Pilavachi the leader shares what happened. 'Instead of focusing on God the whole thing had become so cluttered, so concerned with details that everyone in the church leaders and congregation alike became distracted by the worship. Was it Redman's fault? I listened...he wasn't singing any more duff notes than usual. Then it clicked. We had become connoisseurs of worship instead of participants in it...Then the truth came to us: worship is not a spectator sport, it is not a product moulded by the taste of the consumer. It's all about God.

We needed to take drastic action. So we banned the band. For a couple of months the church services were totally different:

nobody led worship, if someone wanted to sing they started a song. If not we would have silence. We agreed that if no one brought a sacrifice of praise we would spend the meeting in silence. At the beginning we virtually did! It was a very painful process. We were learning again not to rely on the music. After a while we began to have some very sweet times of worship. We all began to bring our prayers, our readings, our prophecies, our thanksgiving, our praise and our songs…The excitement came back. We were once again meeting with God. With all the comforts stripped away people worshipped from the heart. When we had learned the lesson we brought the band back. It was at this point that Matt began to sing the song he had written out of this experience, 'The Heart of Worship – When The Music Fades.' The words express exactly what was going on.

> I'm coming back to the heart of worship
> And it's all about You Jesus.
> I'm sorry Lord for the thing I've made it
> When it's all about you, all about you Jesus.'[30]

M. Redman and T. Hughes are outstanding contemporary song-writers and worship leaders. When Redman was a young teenager the Lord touched his heart and he was bursting to express his love for him, but didn't know how. He says: 'I was desperate to somehow let this worship out.'[31] This reflects one of the aims of Soul Survivor which is to enable young Christians to express their love for the Lord and arguably this is one of their most distinctive contributions. Soul Survivor's contribution to the spiritual growth of many young people is also incalculable. The DVD 'In Spirit & Truth'– 2006, shares the enormous debt of gratitude young people owe to Soul Survivor.

It is interesting to note how Matt Redman's songs have evolved over the years as there has been a distinct shift of emphasis from praise to commitment. Many of his early songs focused upon praise, thanksgiving, the wonder of the cross and the gift of salvation. While these themes have continued during the last few years there has also been a focus on personal sacrifice.[32] Cooke points out, 'The cross is a recurrent theme, not only in Redman's more reflective songs, but also in his songs of praise. 'The Cross Has Said It All' is representative of his early approach to the cross, where the main focus was on rejoicing in the gift of salvation. This is a lively song and the tempo is meant to reflect the joy and confidence that comes from knowing the effects of the cross. The lyrics are almost a compendium of biblical quotations and imagery demonstrating God's love, the effect of the death of Christ and the human condition…While the cross remains a source of joy and praise it was also to form the basis of Redman's approach to a response of love. 'Jesus Christ' (Once Again) was one of his songs which was to find a lasting place in many charismatic worship services, especially in association with Communion Services. Here, the worshipper is invited to consider the cross and make a humble response to the gift of love it reveals.'[33]

At the heart of this song 'Jesus Christ' (written in the same year as 'The Cross Has Said It All'), is the way in which he draws the worshipper from focusing on the sacrifice of Christ, to making a response to this sacrifice. The response of praise and wonder is complemented by a hint of something more – 'once again I pour out my life.' This emphasis on offering a response of more than 'thank you' is to be found again and again in Redman's songs.[34] Similarly, another response in Redman's songs to the sacrifice of Christ is one of awe, commitment and love. These reflect an intimate relationship between Christ and the believer, and praise and worship takes on a very personal note. Intimacy can be seen to be one of his main desires in worship as in such songs as 'One Thing My Heart Is Set Upon.'[35]

Matt Redman's songs reflect his personal experience of Christ and the Father, coupled with his desire to respond to their love. There is clearly an authenticity and integrity about them. I wonder though if at times churches sing his and other songs of intimacy far too readily? I find that on occasions during sung worship I prefer to listen to these songs rather than thoughtlessly sing them, when I find it hard to genuinely identify with the emotions they express. A song like 'Blessed Be Your Name' is tremendous and I can really enjoy listening to it at home without necessarily connecting with the lyrics. Christians in corporate worship may also find they enjoy similar songs without connecting with the lyrics. It requires integrity to sing these songs of abandonment, commitment and love. One way of drawing this out from the worshippers is to sing these songs in an attitude of prayer. Equally, those involved in sung worship and the ministers who lead the services, can spend time during the week praying that these songs will not just indulge the worshippers so they feel good. But, that there will be genuine worship in their hearts for the Lord. This can help to avoid creating a romantic element in sung worship. We do well to remember that sung worship which expresses the believer's feelings, is authentic and pleasing in God's eyes, when it is undergirded by holiness and obedience, abandonment and love.

The song 'It's Rising Up,' reflects another theme that has become central to Matt Redman's songs, the notion that commitment to evangelism is a central response to be offered in worship. Cooke concluded in 2001 and it is probably just as true now: 'Matt Redman is possibly the most popular and widely used worship song-writer in the UK at the current time…He also takes seriously both Christian discipleship and mission, though on each of these themes his work could be criticised for lacking a breadth and depth of theological vision. Redman's focus is necessarily on facilitating engagement with God in worship and motivating for Christian service.'[36]

M. Redman says: 'I try increasingly to write worship songs with one eye on the un-churched person. In 'Beautiful News' the bridge sections says, *"There's a God who came down to save/and he calls your name"* – which is the first time I've written a lyric in the context of a worship song that speaks directly to people who don't know Jesus. It's important at the time of writing to run everything through that 'unchurched-person filter.' We have to ask, "Are we conveying Jesus in a grand, gracious and relevant way?"

ALTERNATIVE WORSHIP

Alternative Worship can be traced back to the mid 80s and the Nine O'Clock Service in Sheffield which began at St. Thomas Crooks. What I remember about St. Thomas' from the 80s is the tangible presence of God in the church. Neil Hopkins a former member gives a summary of how this service started and about its demise. In the early 80s Chris and Winnie Brain moved to Sheffield and formed a band (Tense) and became involved with St. Thomas Crooks, a large Evangelical church. Chris was appointed a house group leader by the vicar Norman Warren. Chris and about ten others formed the Nairn Street Community based on Acts about holding all things in common. In November 1985 John Wimber led a signs and wonders conference in Sheffield City Hall and Warren persuaded a number of Nairn Street to attend. They did so reluctantly at first, but quickly became enthusiastic. A team from

John Wimber held a follow up meeting at St. Thomas Crooks, the place was packed and a large number of Nairn Street were 'zapped.' Warren had a vision of 'several hundred young people being added to the church in a fairly short space of time.' He soon gave the go ahead for Nairn Street to set up an experimental service for their own culture.

At the beginning of March 1986 Neil went to the first Nine O' Clock Service. This was introduced by Steve Williams a former youth group leader at the church and now a Nairn Street member. The lights were dimmed and a series of slide projections were displayed around the walls of St. Thomas's whitewashed interior. The worship began and the music was choppy mid 80s Gothic rock, unremarkable in places like the Leadmill and the Limit, but spine tingling in a church environment. The lyrics were projected at the front, white on a black background. In retrospect this doesn't seem all that radical, but it managed to simultaneously attract and repulse a large number of people. Theologically NOS was initially quite conservative with a strong emphasis on spiritual discipline, prayer, charismatic gifts and ministry. People were interviewed and counselled before being admitted into membership and then assigned into an area of ministry. This structure had benefits and disadvantages, people felt valued and part of a team that was achieving things and were also stretched in unfamiliar areas. The downside was that there was a lot of work to do and a lot of pressure to get it done by deadlines, and key ministries could be granted or withdrawn by the fiat of the leadership team. You didn't volunteer for jobs, rather it was seen as a privilege to be allowed to do them. It was very difficult to turn things down.

Through the late mid 80s NOS evolved in parallel with the culture of the time. Acid house music and style was adopted around the summer of 1988 and a greater emphasis was placed on dance, performance and multi-media in the services. The charismatic theology peaked with the influence of Mike Bickle and the Kansas City prophets. Two important landmarks around this time were the biggest ever Confirmation Service in the diocese and possibly the UK, with about 100 people being confirmed by the Bishop of Sheffield. The other step was the development of the Communion Service, complete with incense, Gregorian chants sung in Latin and a meditative, ambient slant to the music. Three things then happened which were to radically change the nature of NOS. First, it outgrew St. Thomas' and relocated to Ponds Forge. This had the effect of leaving NOS in a limbo state in the Church of England, not truly independent, but certainly not under the direct pastoral leadership of the Bishop of Sheffield. Chris Brain trained for ordination on a fast track approved by the bishop. Lastly, the theological base switched towards creation spirituality and a global mission and away from local social action.

The Planetary Mass – Communion Service was certainly the most spiritually moving and joyous worship that Neal and a lot of other people had ever experienced. But the message seemed to slowly become colder, more intellectual and less personal. Chris Brain resigned from the direct leadership, with the amorphus goal of setting up a service in America, although he retained control of the finances and indirect control of the service. There are lots of ins and outs to the story at this point – but suffice it to say that Chris Brain was involved in abusive relationships with a lot of very vulnerable people. He exercised his power and the hard work of a lot of people towards satisfying his own particular goals. The story of this abuse came to light in the public media in August 1995 and left everyone feeling dazed, confused and hurt. As a result of this scandal the NOS then closed down. Had the last ten years been for nothing? I don't think so. Thousands of people had the kind of spiritual experience normally denied to our culture. People were healed. Lives were changed. The gospel was preached.

Phil Catalfo shares about a Planetary Mass that took place in San Francisco's Grace Cathedral in 1995, led by some 35 members of the Nine O' Clock Service at the invitation of William Swing, Episcopal Bishop of California. The ritual also known as the 'rave mass' was inspired by the creation spirituality of maverick priest Matthew Fox. Phil was amongst some 300 curious people arriving at Grace Cathedral, a familiar place to him. This was a fitting site for the country's first Planetary Mass as it had been the setting of more than a few ephiphanies and welcome experiments in spirituality. The services were not actually held in the Cathedral's great Gothic nave, but in one of its basement rooms, better suited to creating a plugged-in, interactive, post-modern crypt. The first thing he noticed in the basement were the video screens. There were about a dozen in various sizes and the most striking was a large white globe hanging from the ceiling in the middle of the room which acted as a spherical projection surface. Off to one side was an impressive bank of audio and video consoles and a production crew to run them. As people came in, many of them recruited by canvassing the 20 something club scene and local environmental groups, the sound system played soothing music and the video monitors showed footage of cloudlike patterns. Occasional laser lights flickered. The music gradually phased into a light hip-hop then escalated into a more arresting dance beat. The worship made quite an impact on Phil and after Matthew Fox preached, the Sanctus chant took place and Communion followed. He felt this was the part of the service that convinced him that what he was experiencing was truly innovative. Half a dozen people carried stuff to the altar – one had wafers, another wine, another earth, air, fire and water. These were representative sacramental substances which he interpreted as a Communion of the Elements. As each person offered their substance at the altar a brief blessing was pronounced upon it. This was the first time in 20 years that he had received Communion and in his own words *'he was quite blown away by the experience.'*

Alternative Worship takes place when people participate in an act of worship that reflects who they are and the culture of their everyday lives. This stands in contrast to church worship in general that is deemed to be disconnected from the real world. Alternative Worship uses contemporary technologies, media and the arts and much of its content is creative and earthed in the reality of the world around us – because it perceives the presence of God in these things. However, it is not doing church in a contemporary idiom to appeal to outsiders. It is a work of the people – liturgy, to make worship for themselves that is real and enables them to bring the whole of their lives and themselves before God. Yet, this can be accessible to outsiders and have an appeal to them because the worship connects with their lives. Alternative Worship is also deeply concerned for community that is attractive to believers as well as to reaching out to others. Its ethos embraces the concept of people having an authentic encounter with God without being overly prescriptive about this. 'In alternative worship the act of worship is not mediated by any single medium, but takes place as a multi-media-ritual. As such, no single element of the rite takes any precedence over another, be it words, music, singing or visuals. This is reinforced by the fact that any number of things can be happening at the same time. One radical expression of this is

when worship occurs through means of 'installations,' 'labyrinths'
or 'stations.'[37]

Paul Roberts in effect points out that projected images, physical
objects, words, music and movement may all be taking place
simultaneously. At times the plethora of points of focus is
deliberately designed to obscure a single focus point – so there is
the freedom to locate one's attention on a point of choice. At other
times, they are designed to co-ordinate, so that a single point is
elaborated using different media. Each activity or media represents
the fruit of considerable amounts of local creativity, whether it is
the words of the prayers or other aspects of the worship. While
Alternative Worship also embraces contemporary music, nightclub
lighting and multi-media, equally it embraces theology, the nature
of church life and how the gospel is applied in proclamation and
personal life. It arises from the need for the church to engage
with a culture shift, from the patterns of Christian life which took
shape in modernity, to a faith which brings the authentic message
of Christ to bear on life in post-modernity.[38]

At the same time it is helpful to be aware of one or two possible
weaknesses in alternative worship. Congregations can be treated
like a passive audience when services are too prescriptive and
where a theme is not explored using sufficient media resources –
and when there is insufficient opportunity or instructions given for
participation. Also services can be seen to be chaotic where the
congregation have little option other than to watch and try to make
sense of it all. As a result the congregation does not connect with
what is happening and is not engaged properly, leading to the event
failing to function fully as an act of worship.[39]

'Alternative Worship' – 2003, with Jonny Baker being one of the
authors, points out in the introduction, that Alternative Worship
was seen to attract young adults alienated from mainstream
churches and was deemed 'post-charismatic,' in that most groups
rejected the culture of chorus singing and the worship group/
leader. Baker at Greenbelt in 1999 demonstrated the liturgical
aspect of Alternative Worship when a Communion Service was led
with music and liturgy specially composed for the occasion when
all the liturgical texts were sung. The music is available on
the album – 'The Eucharist' originally created for Greenbelt.
In Alternative Worship people also reacted against the model

of the Holy Spirit that stressed immediacy, spontaneity and extemporising as the true signs of the 'Spirit moving.' The charismatic movement embraced quite an explicit critique of the liturgical tradition seeing it as 'formal therefore un-free.' Most Alternative Worship groups have rejected this opposition and turned back to embrace form, set prayers and liturgical patterns as they felt the ethos of charismatic worship produced a culture of banality. Paul Roberts highlights another important distinction between charismatic and Alternative Worship. 'Whereas for the former the experience of God is located 'outside' the physical domain (the ecstatic) for the latter worship relocates God within the physical domain. Therefore, to experience God means to encounter him in and through the created order – symbolically, iconically and sacramentally. Theologically, this return to sacramentalism is accompanied by a renewed emphasis on the incarnation.'[40]

Pete Ward comments on the distinction Roberts makes between charismatic worship and Alternative Worship, (he sees the former as *'ecstatic'* and the latter as *'incarnational')*. Those involved in Alternative Worship work together in groups and plan the worship. Through this activity and through what they create they encounter God. Roberts calls this *'incarnational'* because the experience of God is mediated through cultural events and artefacts – the things of the world. By contrast in charismatic worship there is some kind of ecstatic, interior experience of God which may be seen as – out of this world. Ward believes that such a distinction must be challenged because in effect you cannot precisely prescribe the ritual of worship. He sees no reason why so called incarnational worship constructed by a group, at its best, cannot result in an encounter with God and be ecstatic. Alternatively, he believes it is a false notion to assume charismatic worship is only an internal experience. Because the experience of God is mediated not only by songs but also by other people involved, which means Christ will be communicated through the worship of those who gather together. 'In this sense charismatic worship is every bit as incarnational as any other kind of worship. There is nothing to say that 'incarnational' worship will not occasionally be escapist or that 'ecstatic' worship can never lead towards an increasing concern for mission and social justice.'[41]

J. Baker points out that charismatic worship has embraced free expression in singing intimate songs along with ministry, but this can lack depth and be predictable. Sooner or later worshippers want something more as the range of themes and language in the songs and prayers simply doesn't address the issues of life. This is where Alternative Worship turned back to the liturgical traditions of the church, but reframed them often in simple but imaginative ways, making connections with everyday life. The experience of many alternative worshippers was like that of people suddenly discovering a birthright, a heritage which had been hidden from them. The riches of Catholic liturgical tradition were suddenly spread out before them, overflowing out of the old treasure chest: texts, chants, rituals, use of colour and gesture. The impact of these new discoveries was to generate new respect for Catholic tradition. The distinctive thing about Alternative Worship was that it arrived with a new appetite for imagery in worship and with new media for displaying it. But, few clergy were skilled or trained in the visual arts and few artists had developed theological and liturgical instincts. Alternative Worship groups have also been concerned with the prophetic 'reading' of the visual culture around them in Western mass media.

J. Baker in 'Alternative Worship and the Significance of Popular Culture,' identifies the extent in which popular cultural resources are used in Alternative Worship. The use of multi-media rituals or resources, are indicators of the underlying themes of authenticity and meaning that they seek to establish in their worship, and are also very significant in establishing their identity. In this genre a struggle for meaning takes place on two fronts – resistance to the dominant capitalism in the Western world, and also resistance to the dominant forms of church. In effect Alternative Worship groups are resistant communities. But, this requires underpinning by theology as well as its intuitive grasp of the language, signs and symbols of the culture. While every group is different, for most the incarnation is a theological foundation. It undergirds their seemingly intuitive approach to using popular culture. With this incarnational approach the use of popular culture in worship powerfully brings the 'real world' into the presence of God and enables God's presence to be discerned in the 'real world.' Any notion of a split between sacred and secular is rejected. Implicit in this incarnational approach is a very positive theology of creation and redemption.

On his blog J. Baker shares a bit about his involvement in the Worship Symposium held at the London School of Theology in September 2008. 'When I was standing on the Millenium Bridge it struck me as a picture of the challenge we face in worship. When I look one way I see St. Paul's Cathedral. It reminds me of the gift of the tradition that has meant that the dangerous memory of Jesus has been passed on to me. But culturally I don't fit there. If I look the other way I see the Tate Modern on the South Bank in London which is always buzzing. Culturally I love it, am at home there with its postmodern creativity. But, I want to mess things up and bring the riches of the Christian tradition across the bridge and the cultural world of postmodern London into the church.'

One of the most creative aspects of Alternative Worship is their own liturgies. A fabulous Eucharistic prayer was composed for the Communion Service at Greenbelt in 1999 that Jonny Baker was involved in.

> The Lord is here
> *God's Spirit is with us*
> Lift up your hearts
> *We lift them up to God*
> Let us give thanks to the Lord our God
> *It is right to give thanks and praise*
>
> O Lord our God, sustainer of the universe
> at your command all things came to be:
> the vast expanse of interstellar space
> galaxies, suns, the planets in their courses
> and this fragile earth, our island home
> by your will they were created and have their being.
> Redeemer God, word became flesh
> we remember you in bread and wine
> your body, your blood
> broken so we with all creation may be made perfect.
> Through your sacrifice death is nullified.
> Through your resurrection we have a future - thank you.
>
> Therefore with angels, microbes and mountains
> and all that lives for you
> we proclaim how wonderful you are
> we pour out our thanks to you
> in song that never sleeps:

Holy Holy Holy Lord
Holy Holy Holy Lord
God of power and might
God of power and might
Heaven and earth are full of your glory
Heaven and earth are full of your glory
Hosanna in the highest
Hosanna in the highest

And now we ask that by the power of your Holy Spirit
this bread and wine may be to us Christ's body
and his blood: who on the same night that he
was handed over to suffering and death,
took bread, thanked you and broke it.
He gave it to his friends saying
'Eat this, it is my body given for you.
Do this in memory of me.'
Later after supper he took the cup
thanked you, and gave it to them saying
'Drink this all of you,
this is my blood of the new covenant
which is shed for you and for many
for the forgiveness of sins.
Do this whenever you drink it in memory of me.'

Christ has died, Christ is risen
Christ has died, Christ is risen
Christ will come again
Christ will come again

In this place where heaven and earth meet
under the rainbow of God's promise
in this sharing of bread and wine
future hope becomes reality now.
So bring your scorched earth
bring your harvest
bring your open sky
bring your restless guilty waters
bring your swift unbending road
bring your urgent inner city
to the table where your hosts says:
'I make all things new.'

Lamb of God you take away the sin of the world
Lamb of God you take away the sin of the world
Have mercy on us
Have mercy on us

Bread and wine were shared. Then the following hymn was sung.

Come and be here
Steal past my fears
O wounded healer
O humble leader
Show me your hands
Show me your side
O holy victim
O crucified

Chorus
I will receive you now
I will receive your love
I will believe in you
I will go on with you

Speak to my heart
Bring me your peace
O broken Saviour
O gentle fighter
Breathe on my face
The breath of life
O my Christ let me
Share in your life
Bring to my lips now
Your body and blood
O bread of heaven
O hope of glory
Send me in love
Into the world
O faithful teacher
Wisdom of God

Alternative Worship is creative, innovative, interesting and ground breaking. It is also holistic and those involved take responsibility for the entire component parts of their worship, whether it is the multi-media content, blessings, prayers, the prayer of thanksgiving in Communion or communicating the Word.

ALL-AGE WORSHIP

All-Age Worship may well be seen to be the successor to Family Services or the equivalent dressed up in another name. But, they are not the same although both aim to include all ages. The term Family Service may sound as if it ignores singles and older people when in fact they are usually present. As Sunday Schools declined in the 1960s and 70s informal Family Services were introduced designed to attract children and parents who otherwise might not have attended church. A Family Service can be combined with baptisms and include the relatives and friends who normally do not come to church. Some regular church members might feel it is very positive to welcome new families while others feel their morning worship is hijacked by them once a month by baptisms and stay away. Finding the balance of being worshipful and appealing to newcomers is a juggling act and some may feel it borders on entertainment not worship. For churches mission minded All-Age Worship and Family Services can be seen as a positive thing to attract non-regular members or those on the fringe.

At the beginning of the 90s in All Saints Harston, in Ely Diocese, we began a monthly Family Service. This proved to be successful and we attracted around 40+ children and adults. Some of these adults also went to the regular 9am Eucharist but it was thrilling for them to see the children and their parents at this new service. What worked particularly well in this village was that one of the ministers went into the school during the week and spent time with the children, who did some paintings, poems or prayers on the theme of the Family Service for the following Sunday, and many of the children then shared these during this Service.

At this stage it is helpful to define what is meant by 'All-Age Worship' – AAW. Chris and John Leach point out: 'Very simply it is worship designed to engage people of all ages. Again, and obviously, it happens whenever people of all ages are present.'[42] They believe there are two reasons for AAW. The first is because of a theology which says that we ought to worship together, instead of children being shunted off to do their own thing on Sunday soon after the start of a service. However, they don't go into a detailed outline of what this theology is – although they imply it involves children and adults being pilgrims together, walking in the way of Christ, who need to learn the give and take involved in worshipping together.[43]

Being pilgrims refers to the model that is found in a General Synod report 'Children In The Way' – 1988. This report describes the development of both adults and children through worship and teaching using the term 'Pilgrim Church.' Anne Barton in 'All-Age Worship' – 1993, points out that it is this model that is generally described as AAW. The Pilgrim Church model likens the church to a group of people of all ages going for a long walk together. During this there will be opportunities to talk, to share and to observe different things and discoveries. At times the children will lag behind, some of the smallest may have to be carried and at other times they will dash ahead and make new discoveries.[44]

I obtained a copy of the 'Children In The Way'– CITW report from the archives of General Synod. As I read this, it struck me that the Pilgrim Church as a model for AAW using the analogy of going for a walk together, was not the most convincing aspect of it. Pilgrim sounds old fashioned and I wonder if children/teenagers would relate more to the call of Christ to follow him? The call to follow Christ is linked with his command to go and make disciples of all nations – Matt. 28: 19. I am inclined to think that following Christ sounds a far more attractive concept to have as a model for children/teenagers than being a pilgrim. But, I may be wrong.

There are many other points that CITW raises apart from being a Pilgrim church that seem far more important, which Baker and Leach do not even mention. I may be missing something here, but the idea of children and adults going for a walk doesn't address the complex issue of having an act of worship and nurturing faith, that includes the very youngest to the very oldest members. It doesn't address the different cognitive learning stages that children and young people go through, or how the learning process for adults might differ. We have to take into account for each respective age group, exactly what this means in the formation of their faith and in their expression of worship. Ronni Lamont suggests AAW should be more 'slanted' towards the children as they do not usually have the cognitive processes required for adult liturgies. This needs to be borne in mind when 'all-age' liturgies are planned. If it is to really be 'all-age' then something different for several age groups will be needed at the teaching slot, if all those present are to be stretched and their worshipping needs met.[45]

C. & J. Leach's second reason for AAW is connected to mission, as they believe churches which try this generally find it is more accessible for visitors, newcomers and particularly young families – those most notably missing from our churches.[46] But, then they disingenuously say about AAW: '...you will nevertheless hear a bias towards the younger and towards those feeling their way into the church and faith. Let us face it: in churches the elderly and the 'churched' already have plenty which is accessible for them!'[47] Of course one of the challenges, and probably the most difficult one, is to put together an act of worship for 45 minutes or so that not only is inclusive to all ages present, but which is also relevant to their faith and worshipful to them. These are key elements in AAW which demand to be explored in some depth.

To ensure that AAW can achieve its potential and relate to all ages, it may be helpful to have some teaching about this for each respective age group, including the adults, For example, a couple of Sundays could be devoted to sharing about AAW which would involve some research and teaching by the ministry team and those who work with the children/teenagers. To complement this we can also explore what worship involves and means for all the children/teenagers and adults, which we can then seek to include in an AAW structure. The leaders and helpers working with the children/teenagers can think about worship with them and find out what they understand by it and what it means to them. Involving the whole church in AAW allows the congregation to own it.

Over the years as a minister I have had to preach or lead worship and I have always made it a point to prepare thoroughly. So for example, if I had to preach a 20-30 minute sermon my planning and preparation would begin two weeks in advance, as I have found this method suits me best. In the first week on a couple of mornings I would look at my Scripture text and make a note of the main points. I would then pray that the Lord would impress on my heart the truths to highlight in my sermon. Then during the week that I was due to preach this would form the basis of the content of my sermon. I would also think how I would introduce my text and capture the congregation's attention. I would ask myself how familiar the congregation might be with my text and would assume people are already familiar with it especially if it is well known. If this is the case I would point this out, and say 'the challenge for us is to think about our text in a new way, or see it from a different perspective.' I would also think how I might include a story or illustrations to highlight the main points. But, I would ensure they did not take over and was the only thing the congregation remembered. Also, I would be praying that the Lord would speak to his people through me, through his Word. And I would aim to establish a rapport with the congregation at the start of my sermon, to ensure I spoke to them rather than preached at them.

It is generally acknowledged that to prepare a 20 minute sermon demands around eight hours of study and a 30 minute sermon requires even longer. The point I am highlighting is that putting together an AAW Service requires a considerable amount of thought, planning and preparation well in advance, so that there is time for ideas to be refined and become a coherent act of worship. You have to take into account very young children who will wander around and be noisy. You also have to take into account the children whose attention may usually be taken up by play stations and sophisticated computer games: and you have to take into account teenagers, young adults and older members. Whether it is the drama, an interview, a presentation, the prayers, the songs, the talk, telling a story, the visual aids, or everyone walking up the front to stick something onto a board – it has to engage all ages at some level and also nurture their faith, have a spiritual impact and help them to worship the Lord. One of the things I value most in AAW is when the adults and children/teenagers share what the Lord has been doing in their lives.

There are three main weaknesses in AAW that I have come across. The first concerns the content. Here, the component parts of the content can fail to nurture people's faith or have a spiritual impact. When this happens the different parts of AAW come across as items which fail to convey the theme or illustrate the scriptural truth. For example, I recall a dramatic presentation involving two people that was too adult in content and which went on far too long. But, I do not remember the truth it was meant to illustrate. I also recall a visual aid story by one person which also went on far too long and didn't illustrate the point intended. On both occasions the presentation remains the memorable point. The content in both instances failed to point people to the truth and nurture their faith or have a spiritual impact. Secondly, AAW does not always succeed as an act of worship. This happens because people focus on what they are doing in the service, perhaps the drama, a visual aid, etc – without first ensuring this will help everyone to worship. Alternatively, AAW can consist of items that are not worshipful. For example, the two presentations mentioned earlier did not come across as an act of worship or help others to worship, because they remained at the level of a performance. Thirdly, the content of AAW can fail to relate to all ages. I have found this often happens when the sermon is much too adult and doesn't relate to all the children/teenagers. This is surprising as I would have expected the speakers to be aware of this. To ensure we avoid these three weaknesses, it is important to ask questions during the planning about all aspects of AAW. For example: 'What is the main point/theme of our service? 'Will the content illustrate the theme?' 'How will the content help everyone to worship the Lord?' 'How will the content nurture the faith of the children/teenagers and adults?' 'What sort of response will this elicit from the different age groups?' Of course it is also important to pray about all aspects of the service and for those taking part to be filled with the Holy Spirit. And to remind everyone who takes part up front in AAW, that they too are involved in an act of worship.

Planning AAW may well involve a number of people who will represent the different age groups in the congregation. It is helpful to plan at least a month in advance, with a second meeting two weeks later and a third meeting a week before the service takes place. C. & J. Leach also advocate planning well in advance and collecting good ideas for the Bible passage/theme, activities, music, liturgy, responses and so on. At a second meeting you can see which ideas are still glowing. What is the one thing you hope the service will achieve? What response do you hope and expect people to make? They also advocate you ensure the flow of AAW goes smoothly and that the different parts feel like an act of worship and not a variety show.[48] The beginning of an AAW Service is important and should specifically welcome the children, young people and adults, along with any visitors. Apart from giving any notices the theme can be announced at the start. Anne Barton thinks the atmosphere is set before the actual service begins and that the beginning of the worship requires thoughtful preparation. As people are chatting beforehand, the person leading at the start of AAW looks to focus their attention onto the Lord and create a sense of anticipation as we begin our worship.[49] This is echoed by J. Berryman and S. Stewart who say concerning children and worship, 'As we gather we need a way to get ready to be with God, to move our attention from ourselves and our world to God. So our approach to God, our gathering in God's name, is a time for preparing ourselves to listen to God. While getting ready comes from within, the liturgy helps us to refocus and centre in God as it shifts our everyday language to religious or biblical language, images, symbols and signs of God...Two things are essential in the first part of the order for worship: our awareness of the presence of God and our ability to get ready to be with God.'[50]

About 30 years ago Jerome Berryman became involved with the Montessori method of religious education with children which he calls 'godly play.' His interest is on the function of religious language, parable, sacred story and liturgical action, in the moral and spiritual development of children. This method describes an exciting way that children experience God while learning about God. The key to this approach is a worship context for telling and working with biblical stories instead of a school environment – as the intent of worship is to experience and praise God which is one of awe, mystery and wonder.

N. Harding author of 'Children Can Worship' has worked with children and youth for many years and acknowledges AAW is demanding. In effect he points out it requires time, prayer, thought and a real commitment to prepare to be successful. AAW Services require the need to focus on one message which is interpreted and made appropriate to all the age groups represented. While action songs are likely to be included it is important to have songs with good content too. AAW Services are really difficult to get right. They need to be prepared and led by people who have appropriate gifts, the aim being not to do a 'children's service' but to give children a positive image of God's church meeting together. Do the gimmicks, tricks and visual aids get in the way of the message? Are children used with integrity rather than being used to perform? If we are using liturgy how appropriate is the use of language? Do the prayers relate to the theme and teaching? Can the Bible story involve volunteers and visual aids? Does the talk have a clear point? If possible have something for everyone to take home. It could be a fun sheet, a relevant item as a reminder of the message or a piece of paper with a key text.[51]

'We should regularly ask whether the children are being stretched in their faith by the worship? There is such a lot to God that we miss if we don't look deeply enough. If we fail to reveal a little more of God to the children we work with through worship, we could be failing in our ministry. I have seen from experience that children and young people who are not stretched and challenged tend to become stale and bored, especially if they have grown up in the church and know all the Bible stories.'[52]

Catching the attention and interest of children/teenagers during AAW and in their respective age group meetings is something to carefully monitor. This can be done by asking them to fill out a simple evaluation sheet at the end of each term. Equally, they can suggest how they can both be improved and be more relevant to them. This is important as leaders can assume that the content of AAW and the material they are presenting to their respective age groups is interesting, when in reality the children/teenagers may find it boring or irrelevant. Finding out from the children/teenagers what they are doing in Religious Education at school might be a good indicator at what level to pitch our presentation.

In the formation of their faith we should aim to teach our young people to think Christianly and critically. We should encourage them to ask searching questions about the Christian faith and its relevance to issues in their lives and in society. Jason Gardner in 'Mend The Gap,' which focuses on bridging the gap between young people and adults in the church similarly says: 'What we need to help our young people develop is a faith that can meet the challenges of a constantly changing world…Too much of church today cushions believers from the abrasive critiques of a society frequently at odds with religious conviction.' He also questions whether the way the church disciples young people is rigorous enough or engaging enough.[53] For example, one Sunday I was with my 10 year old sons. The theme was listening to God and obeying him and also their parents. But those leading the session didn't get the children to think about these issues. They didn't get them to identify the different ways that God might be speaking to them, or what he might say to them. The leaders didn't get them to discuss why they should be obedient to God and their parents!

Roots Magazine also has some guidelines about AAW. Here are some of their helpful points. Is there a balance between action and praise, word and prayer? Does the service have an overall coherence, or is it just one item after another? What space is there

The child explores, tests, imagines and creates, observes and copies, experiences and reacts.
So faith first comes, not through theological words, but through experiences like those of trust, love and acceptance related to those words.[58]

The next stage is an *'affiliative faith.'*
We need to belong to and participate in, an identity-conscious community of faith.
This involves opportunities to deepen religious feelings through creative activities, to share in the community's stories, and to experience awe, wonder and mystery. Beliefs and attitudes are more consciously assimilated from others.[59] 'As a child's world expands he carries with him the powerful influence of his parents. Because he wants to please them and adopts their beliefs and values, their faith becomes his.'[60]

The next stage is a *'searching faith'* that strives:
To work out a consistent personal faith with reference to an authority within, rather than that of other people.
There will need to be elements of doubt and critical judgment: a need for experimentation, as alternative understandings and traditions are explored.[61] 'When capable of abstracting cognitively, a child will search for himself and discover his own faith.'[62]

The last stage is *'owned faith.'* This holds the tension of truth viewed from different perspectives and finds new meaning in myth, symbol and ritual.[63] 'The child/young person commits to a set of beliefs and a way of life which may be very different from that of his parent.'[64]

Now most people want to put their faith into personal and social action and they are willing and able to stand up for what they believe, even against the community of nurture. [65]
Marion Carter in 'All God's Children' takes into account Westerhoff's four stages of faith and believes that children make their own sense of faith and are active thinkers in their own right, although the influence of home and faith community is significant. Through her research she is led to believe:

Young children are spiritual. They have a sense of awe and wonder and an innate spirituality of everyday life that challenges the religion and spiritual atrophy of many adults. In each child is the spark of divine nature. Every child knows something about God, even if they struggle to find words to explore their experience. This innate spirituality is irrespective of learning ability or articulateness.[66]

Being aware of the cognitive learning processes children have in these stages of faith and their instinctive awareness of God, can inform and shape the way the church nurtures their Christian faith. Although we should not be too dogmatic about the transition from one stage of faith to another and the age at which they occur. At the same time it is important to be aware of the support any children/teenagers with special needs will require in their faith formation in their age group. Special needs might involve some sort of disability or children from a difficult background/situation.

CITW highlights the importance of the quality of leadership for those working with children/teenagers and points out that dioceses offer training courses for leaders working with children. It also mentions that many of those involved in leading felt a sense of dissatisfaction because they were aware of the need for additional skills, support and resources. CITW recommends the provision and expectation of adequate training for them.[67] Similarly, the Mission-Shaped Children report recommends:

> It is strongly advised that such a leader will have considerable experience and have received appropriate training. This includes having a mature faith and an awareness of how children learn and develop spiritually.[68]

Core Skills For Children's Work – CSFCW, suggests that those working with children need to understand a little about what it means to be a child in today's world. There are many important and powerful influences on children and the values strongly communicated through the media are significant and formative.[69] CSFCW suggests three theological models for working with children and one is pertinent to AAW.

> If children are seen as being as much of today's church as the rest of the congregation, and equally valuable members, then it will be vital that children's provision in

the church is of a high quality, aimed at equipping their ministry. Children will be enabled to take part in all aspects of church life.[70]

As we think about AAW and children/teenagers, many churches probably rely on volunteers to work with them, even if there is a Youth Worker/Coordinator. Yet, it is clear that an understanding of children's cognitive development and how their faith is formed is required. Moreover, it is also clear that they should have some formal training to assist them in this task. We have to ask whether we are failing our children/teenagers if the church is not more selective in its approach to those who work with them. M. Carter puts her finger on an important point in this area when she says: 'The nurture of children is too important to leave to conscripts or those who express an interest…Work with children within the church is a significant vocation and is entered into with care.'[71] While this may seem an obvious point it may well be a timely reminder those called and gifted to work with children/teenagers (although they may require training) will be the ones who are most effective with them. These are the people we should be looking to identify and release in this ministry.

The inclusion of children/teenagers in AAW can have a greater focus by involving them as much as possible in these Services. It is also sensible to ensure that the content clearly appeals to and relates to as many of their age groups as possible. Their inclusion in worship can also be reinforced on other Sundays apart from AAW. For example when there is a Communion Service children at secondary school age can stay in for the entire service. During this they can be involved in reading the lessons, the prayers, be in the music group, and act as stewards when the congregation receives Communion. Equally, the younger children can come and join the congregation at the peace, and go forward to the front to receive a blessing. Or, if the church has explored the possibility of children receiving Communion and the PCC and the Diocese have approved this, it would demonstrate to the children/teenagers they are an integral part of the church. On other Sundays during the first part of the service, the different children/teenager groups can in turn share what they are learning. On occasions, the adults can also be invited to go and see what these groups have been doing or view any displays they have made, or be invited to share on occasions with them. The children/teenagers on special occasions such as Pentecost can be involved with adults in making colourful banners as part of the worship for these services. Also the whole church can have a project that they are all involved in as part of their worship, for example, in raising money for an overseas project or one nearer home.

Just as there is a news sheet telling the adults what the service themes are for each Sunday in the term, it would help to have a news sheet informing the congregation of the children/teenagers programs. This would enable the adults to pray in an informed way for these groups. Seeking to involve children/teenagers in a much more significant way in our worship and in other ways in the life of the church, gives out the message that they really belong as much as the adults. All these things show that the church values children/teenagers, takes an active interest in them and ensures they have a real sense of belonging in it. What we should bear in mind is that our young children/teenagers are leaders of the church in the future and everything should be done to help them grow in this way. Perhaps, there should be a rite of passage at a certain age (16), when teenagers are welcomed as adult members into the church. From that age onwards they would worship with the adult congregation and be included as much as possible in the Sunday Services. And of course they can be consulted about issues for sermon topics they are concerned about or interested in.

Margaret Withers in 'Mission-Shaped Children'- moving towards a child-centred church, reminds us the CITW Report recommended research into the spiritual development of children, and new liturgies to serve AAW including a form of the Eucharist when the children were present. With the publication of the Anglican Prayer Book, Common Worship in 2000, an opportunity was missed to examine the need for new liturgies to serve AAW, and in particular a form of the Eucharist when children/teenagers are present.[72] It is of interest to note that probably the most suitable Eucharistic prayer for use at Communion with children/teenagers present is the last one of eight – prayer H.

Once a PCC and their Diocese have agreed to their proposal for children to be admitted to take Communion, there will be a need for some teaching to prepare the children/teenagers and also adults for this. All-Age Communion – AAC, in the context of AAW and the faith formation of the children/teenagers is important. We can become very set in our pattern of worship when thinking about the alternatives that are available to us. But, the inclusion of children/teenagers at Holy Communion is an exciting possibility. If we want to involve them in our corporate worship then we must be more innovative.

As children will be present in AAC the presentation of this service is important. A good place to begin is the sanctuary-stage where the altar-table is. The aim is to make this attractive to catch the children's interest, not as a gimmick but to help focus their attention as we worship. Communion is a special service and this is a sacred space, where we encounter Jesus. The altar can have colourful vestments for the liturgical season and there can also be lighted candles on it. The sanctuary-stage where the altar is reminds us that this is a sacred space, so musicians/singers and sound technology can be arranged so that they do not dominate it. The minister who is leading can wear a minimum of clerical robes, perhaps an alb and stole, or a clerical collar and smart jacket, rather than come casual and risk looking scruffy. Being up front and leading worship in this special service, in this sacred place, invites us to come with reverence. Not because this makes us more spiritual, but because the Lord is worthy of our best. And we want the children to sense the special atmosphere, in this special service of Holy Communion.

There are many ways in which children/teenagers can be involved in the worship at AAC. They can make banners as an act of worship to decorate the church and make this a colourful occasion. They can compose a Eucharistic prayer of thanksgiving for special occasions. They can be part of the music group or choir to help lead the sung worship. They can bring the bread and wine forward and families can take it in turn to specially bake the bread for this service. They can help take the offering and they can lead the prayers and read the Scripture lessons. They can also pray for other children or adults – one lady in our church recently testified that she had a back problem for years and her young daughter prayed for her and she was healed. If there is drama they can be involved in this and also narrate it. During some of the songs they can wave their flags or lead the congregation in the actions. On occasions they can also give testimonies about their experience of Christ and what God has been doing in their lives, and share what they have been doing in their respective age groups. If there is a story connected to the theme of the service this can be read out to the young children as they gather around the front of the altar. During the Eucharistic prayer the children and the teenagers can be invited to come and gather round the altar. The teenagers can be stewards when people go forward to receive Communion and they can also be involved in giving the bread and juice to the children (wine to the teenagers). When they receive bread and juice/wine their Christian names can used, as they can indeed be for the adults. All these things can be signs of their full inclusion in this colourful, moving, simple and yet profound act of corporate worship.

A CRITIQUE OF CONTEMPORARY WORSHIP

The term contemporary implies being up-to-date with the latest trends. It also implies creativity and innovation in worship rather than being old-fashioned. Contemporary worship can stand in contrast to traditional worship where the latter can refer to formal, liturgical services. The former is usually informal and primarily includes the latest Christian songs and quite likely no liturgy. It may aim to attract and look to be relevant to those who are non-church goers. It can also be interpreted in a number of ways. Contemporary worship may include a wide range of styles ranging from alternative worship, café worship, emerging and liquid church worship. Equally, the culture and churchmanship of a congregation is likely to determine what the term 'contemporary worship' means for them. For example, an inner city church in a working class, multicultural community may consider their worship contemporary, because their format and language aims to share the gospel in a way relevant to their context. Alternatively, a city centre church with a well educated congregation, may consider their worship contemporary because of their informal presentation, and because their music in sung worship is not restricted to the loud rock, pop model. Equally, a liturgical service of Holy Communion can be considered to be contemporary because it includes clusters of modern songs.

Contemporary worship can take place in a modern building, or a school hall, or a warehouse, or a café, or pub, or in a church that may have been re-ordered and which has comfortable chairs, modern lighting and fashionable furniture. This style of worship has evolved over the years as the organ has been replaced by a band of musicians who sing the latest worship songs. Over the years this new worship style has been identified with a number of well-known musicians and worship leaders, such as Graham

Kendrick, Darlene Zscech and more recently Matt Redman, Tim Hughes and Stuart Townend.

A feature of contemporary worship is usually its informality. Here, ministers do not usually wear clerical robes and the congregation tends to dress casually. This informality may well aim to reflect the intimacy in relationship with the Lord that this spirituality espouses, and on having a personal relationship with God, Christ and the Holy Spirit. In contrast to many traditional churches where this intimacy is not expressed so explicitly, this is a real strength of this style of worship. While the leadership style and atmosphere is likely to be informal, and aims for the immanence of God in worship, it may well result in the loss of his transcendence.

Another attractive aspect of contemporary worship is that it is usually joyful and lively. Also, drama or the visual arts are likely to be included in it. This genre of worship is also associated with a regular stream of new songs and can include those that are 20–30 years old. A normal Anglican service can have a cluster of songs or perhaps clusters of sung worship. This is often called a *'time of worship'* and can be seen as the place where the real worship takes place. In this context as sung worship along with the preaching are the main events, there is little that the worshipper has to know about the content, the dynamics, the flow, the liturgy and the theology of worship. This genre of worship probably does not claim to be intellectually demanding except perhaps for the preaching. No longer is the sanctuary-stage likely to be defined as a 'sacred space.' It may well resemble a concert stage which musicians and their instruments dominate.

Contemporary worship can refer to a 'movement and a style of worship that focuses on the culturally accessible and relevant, on the new and innovative, on the use of recent technologies of communication...At its heart is the attempt to relate to God and praise God in the language of the people. As that language changes so does the style, but not the substance and centre of worship.'[73] This may well reflect the Seeker Services similar to those Willow Creek initiated to attract non-church goers. T. & R. Wright believe the Contemporary Worship Movement, uses the style and language of secular people to communicate the truth of the gospel to them. It seeks to remove the barriers of religious language that keeps people from church.[74]

Contemporary worship can include the latest presentational technologies to project still or moving images from song lyrics to
video clips on a screen. 'High-tech worship relies extensively
on computer-based presentational technologies, from still and
animated slides created in programs like Power-Point to video
recordings and live video projection piped to screens in the
sanctuary.'[75] Q. J. Schultze also perceives the key to the wise use
of presentational technologies is not use for their own sake. He
believes technology tends to create hearts and minds bent on
control and manufactures worship in tune with mere human
desires. In contrast worship calls us to remember ultimately who is
in control, as worship is a God-sanctioned activity.

> When we fail to see technology within the context of the
> power, majesty and glory of God, we can become more
> enchanted with our technological ability than we are
> humbled by God's grace. We wrongly focus on our
> liturgical accomplishments, on our technological skills
> and apparent power, rather than on what God has done
> for us and is doing.[76]

In 'Discerning The Spirit,' Plantinga Jr. & Rozeboom share that
to more classically minded Christians, contemporary worship
represents the blowing not of the Spirit of God but of the spirit of
the age. These Christians believe the church has sold its soul and
worship seems less like the company of the saints and martyrs than
like a nightclub that forgot to close. So they wonder: 'Why present
the Gospel in an ethos that clashes with it? Why stand for worldly
entertainment rather than against it?'[77] Such worshippers are likely
to resonate with E. Farley's observation:

> To attend a typical Protestant Sunday morning worship
> service is to experience something odd…Lacking is a
> sense of the terrible mystery of God…If the Seraphim
> assumed this Sunday morning mood, they would be
> addressing God not as *'holy, holy, holy'* but as *'nice,
> nice, nice.'*[78]

While this may sound somewhat like a caricature it forces us to
reflect on whether the ethos of contemporary worship reduces God
to the immediacy of cultural convenience and fashionable trends
and divests him of his *'otherness'* as God.

It is interesting to note that there are three books that give the stories behind well known praise and worship songs. 'I Could Sing Of Your Love Forever,' are stories, reflections and devotions by the well known band Delirious – Regal Books 2007. 'Celebrate Jesus,' is edited by Phil Christensen and Shari Macdonald, Kregel Publications 2003, and 'The Sacrifice Of Praise,' is edited by Lindsay Terry, Integrity Publishers 2002. It is on occasions very moving to read about the circumstances that gave birth to some of these well known and loved contemporary songs.

We should not be defensive about Christian songs when there are critics whose perceptions challenge us to think about their quality. One such writer is Nick Page who has written a provocative little book called, 'And Now Let's Move Into A Time Of Nonsense.' Here are a couple of quotes from his work: 'Deep truths create deep worship. Shallow words create shallow worship. Banal meaningless lyrics, badly crafted and expressed in confusing language, will not lead us into the deep worship that our world and our church need to see…But the fact is that so many of the songs we sing today are instantly forgettable and instantly disposable. They are disposable because they are not the product of skill and craft. Too often the words to our worship songs feel like a kind of added extra to the music. If they have a telling phrase or a striking image that's a rare bonus'[79] One way to improve the quality of songs is to have an index in songbooks where each writer shares the inspiration of their song and how it evolved.

Resoundworship.org has been formed as a means of improving song writing. This is an exciting free resource for churches worldwide. Resound is a new project of the Jubilate Group. For many years this group of writers and composers has helped churches voice their praise to God, through radical projects like Youth Praise. This is a group of eight British based worship songwriters, seeking to resource the church with heartfelt, crafted accessible worship songs. Their aim is to provide local churches with fresh worship songs containing strong, biblical lyrics supported by singable, contemporary music. The group meets on a regular basis to critique each other's songs and this continues through a web forum, where they post and refine material. Once they have been through this process, and the songs have been tested on home-churches, they send the lyrics to an external theological critique group. Their songs can be downloaded for free.

Dan Lucani who was for many years a praise and worship leader in the Christian Contemporary Music Movement shares his understanding of worship. He perceives that the phrase the 'heart of worship' originates from the truth that God looks at the inward heart of man. But, he became disillusioned with this movement because he found that this phrase was used to justify any style or choice of music. He also came to see the very meaning of the word 'worship' changed.

> It no longer refers to the biblical practice of bowing in reverence and humility before a holy God. The word itself has been expanded beyond this basic meaning to include all the forms used for worship, any style of music played by any musician, dancing, drama and art. It can mean the service itself and anything that occurs within it.[80]

He also observes that in the Old Testament the Hebrew word translated as worship is *'shacach'* – to prostrate (especially in homage to God): to bow oneself down, to crouch, to fall down flat, to humbly beseech. In the New Testament the Greek word most commonly translated as worship is *proskuneo*, which means to kiss like a dog licking his master's hand: to prostrate oneself in homage. He says: 'The true heart of worship is when the attitude of our heart is in complete submission to God. We have nothing to offer God except our total devotion and obedience.'[81] He believes that a major problem with the contemporary notion of worship, is that we want God to affirm us through worship and make us feel good about ourselves. He implies that at the heart of this style of worship is the *'feel good factor.'* Whereas for him to achieve a good personal feeling is not an aspect of biblical worship.

> Worship is about bowing down and feeling lowly. True worship is about producing a sense of the fear of the Lord. The true heart of worship is the heart that bows before God and submits to his Word – no more and no less.[82]

Tim Hughes on the Worship Central website at Holy Trinity Brompton, where he is the Worship Director, speaks about writing songs with substance and simplicity. He quotes Brian Doerkson: 'The most enduring songs are virtually without exception the simple ones.' Tim expresses his concern that writing songs filled with content and doctrine can go too far and can be impossible to sing and remember. He feels that the aim has to be substance with simplicity and to convey a profound mystery in a simple lyric takes great skill and thought. He also has this to say about songwriting: 'Clarity – does the song have a focus? Is there a clear theme running through the song? A good test is whether you could summarise the theme of the song in a short sentence. Singability – does the song have a simple and memorable melody or hook? If it's hard to remember and pick up the tune, then it kills the whole point of it being a simple song.' On this issue Tim also quotes Sandy Millar who says: 'I would like to see a renewed energy going into writing simple, heartfelt intimate expression of love …we need songs that are simpler songs that can be learned very easily, and sung from the heart.' Here, Matt Redman has some wise words about songwriting. He speaks about having so much love in our hearts for God that we can hardly keep it in.

> That's the starting point with songwriting. Make sure it's not just some clever words put together with a nice tune. A meaningful song will always be the passionate expression of your heart towards God.
>
> Sometimes you hear a song and it's got a lot of heart, but doesn't sound like it's been worked on at all. It's meaningful but doesn't feel like it's been finished and made ready for congregations to use…Other times you'll hear a song and it has lots of words, perfect rhymes and a singable tune yet not much heart, it's missing that inspiration factor. The best songs have both. A mixture of heartfelt inspiration that has been carefully crafted for congregational use.[83]

Graham Kendrick on the Worship Academy website, points out that Matt Redman asked some prominent theologians which theological topics they think need to be written about. Here is a selection of some of their comments. 'We need a new genre of contemporary songs in the form of ballads that tell the biblical stories' – Eddie Gibbs. 'We need songs about God's intervention in our lives. The song of Moses in Exodus 15 serves as a model for theologising through song. I believe we need songs that follow this model: songs that arise out of the pain and difficulty confronting our lives and declare God's specific ways in which he meets us' – Roberta King. 'Writers like Watts and Wesley managed again and again to write songs that taught the entire

Gospel – from creation to the consummation of the ages – without putting us, or even what we gain, at the centre of the story' – Tricia Rhodes. 'It is time to pay attention to the times of God's saving actions, so my challenge is to write songs for the Christian year' *(for example Lent, Pentecost – italics mine)* – Robert Webber. 'First, the topic I have the hardest time finding new songs for is 'pressing on' in the Christian life. When people come to worship they come with emotions and struggles. Songs that acknowledge the hard work and the promise of the Christian life can be a great help in our pilgrimages. Second, I could use more songs that are recongisable settings of Scripture. Singing is a profound way of 'laying up' God's Word in our hearts. In college we sang Scripture that ran the gamut from ditties to moving meditations of the Psalms or other passages. I would love to help my congregation sing Scripture into their hearts, wedding profound texts to a meaningful musical idiom' – R. Kidd.

When we consider the content of sung worship there are those who feel the mood of intimacy and immediacy is endemic and this is a cause for concern by some critics. The proliferation of these songs can marginalise aspects of God's character such as his discipline and judgment. G. Kendrick says, 'The disproportionate number of 'subjective experience' songs being written begs the question of how much the world's agenda of placing existential experience and individual fulfillment at the centre of things has influenced our worship?....My own view is that the proportion of personal songs is far too high and is at the expense of songs that are actually about God, who he is and what he has done.'[84] In the introduction to his album 'What Grace' – 2001, Kendrick shares his concern about the excessively experiential focus of charismatic worship. 'It is too easy for our praise and worship to become experience centred...we need a lot more songs that look to the Lord and his qualities and then we can respond to that...If we continually expect people to sing about experiences and feelings they are not necessarily having, we will empty the act of worship of reality and devalue its content to the level of borrowed personal perspective. What is left is a certain blandness.'[85]

Stuart Townend has made his mark as a successful songwriter and worship leader. His outstanding compositions include: 'In Christ Alone,' 'How Deep The Father's Love,' 'Beautiful Saviour' and 'The Power Of The Cross.' He has worked in collaboration with

Keith Getty on 'In Christ Alone,' with Keith initially writing the melody. Both of them are motivated by capturing biblical truth in songs that not only enable people to express their worship but also build them up in their faith. The uniqueness of Townend's composition lies in his lyrical content that embraces a theological depth and poetic expression that is rare. His content is vitally important to him in our corporate worship and he believes that sometimes great melodies are let down by poor lyrics. He says, 'It's the writer's job to dig deep into the meaning of Scripture and express in poetic and memorable ways the truth he or she finds there.' Alongside the importance of Scripture and its poetic expression, he also advocates combining objective truth and subjective response to it in songwriting. Because the best hymns powerfully express the emotions of the worshipper in response to objective Christian truth. He echoes what others have emphasised, namely that we need more songs that are about God: more songs that declare the truth about God, his character, his actions, as well as songs about who we are in him.

The Rev Peter Moger, the National Worship Development Officer, for The Church of England, perceives that worship songs are markedly different from hymns and require different criteria of assessment. One might differentiate between hymns sung about God and songs addressed to God. This is sometimes a false distinction but it does highlight a major difference between the two. 'Much renewal music transmits a message of joy without tears, glory without suffering, resurrection without crucifixion. Human weakness is seldom acknowledged, sin and suffering are often dismissed. Church music must avoid the temptation to stay with the cosy and familiar, and if it is to be prophetic, it must disturb as well as console. Good church music will display theological integrity and musical quality. Important too, is the integrity of the act of worship as a whole, for church music is only one amongst many vehicles for the worship of God's people.'[86]

While all Christian songwriters may well claim their inspiration is scriptural, the amount of biblical truth their songs contain might not be very high. This can raise a question mark about their effectiveness. John 4: 23-24 shows the importance Jesus placed on worshipping God in spirit and truth.

But the hour is coming and now is, when true worshippers will worship the Father in spirit and truth, for such the Father seeks to worship him. God is spirit and those who worship him must worship in spirit and truth.

L. Morris has this to say about John 4: 23-24: 'Notice the word 'must' Jesus is not speaking of merely a desirable element in worship. He is speaking of something that is absolutely necessary...People cannot dictate the 'how' or the 'where' of worship. They must come only in the way that the Spirit of God opens for them.'[87] R. E. Brown draws our attention in these verses to worshipping the Father in the Spirit, 'God can only be worshipped as Father by those who possess the Spirit that makes them God's children...In John 17: 7-9, we shall hear that the truth is an agent of consecration and sanctification, and thus truth also enables man to worship God properly.'[88]

We cannot speak too strongly about the centrality of truth in sung worship or in our Services, because the depth and substance of our corporate worship is to a large extent determined by the biblical content of its component parts. The centrality of the truth is also of great importance because those who long to deepen their corporate worship, may find they can do this by ensuring it is immersed in biblical truth. The aim of truth in our sung worship is to enable us to be responsive in our hearts, minds and spirits on a deep level to the Trinity, and for the truth to have an impact in our lives throughout the week. Christian truth and revelation enable us to encounter God, Christ and the Holy Spirit, so that our response is not only on the level of feelings but one that has a profound impact in our hearts and lives. J. M. Boice emphasises we must worship on the basis of biblical revelation. 'If we are to worship in truth as God commands, we must do so in accordance with the principles of Scripture.' For him the essence of worship is to approach God in truth and this means we must approach Christo-centrically.[89] At the same time we should ask for the help and inspiration of the Holy Spirit in our worship. Stuart Townend also believes truth in worship is very important because as Jesus pointed out truth brings revelation. It is important to put truth into people's mouths and pray it will come as revelation into their hearts. He suspects people learn theology through songs, so truth is important in our worship. But we also need Christian truth to be empowered by the Holy Spirit to have an impact in peoples' lives.

Christians know that Jesus is the one *by* whom and *in* whom and *through* whom and *with* whom we are able to worship God. We do not come to worship God through the strength of our love, nor do we come through the excellence of our music or sung worship. In essence we do not come on our own merit. We come through Christ as he is the way to the Father. These truths are particularly important because some Christians may feel their love for the Lord is really strong and want to express this in sung worship, whereas other Christians may feel their love for the Lord is inconsistent and nowhere as strong. For them their confidence in worshipping God lies not in their love or in themselves – but in Christ who makes it possible. Those whose love for the Lord is strong still need to hold onto the truth that they too come to worship through Christ, and are also reliant on the help and inspiration of the Holy Spirit. Therefore, those who lead sung worship would do well to remember that songs that speak about the believer's love for the Lord may be difficult for some Christians to join in early on in sung worship. In the first part of a Service it is important to take time to prepare believers' hearts to worship God and also to reassure them of God's love and Christ's cleansing: and to ask the Holy Spirit to help them respond in gratitude and love to the Lord.

As we reflect on of truth in worship, what we sing also has to reflect the truth about God, Christ and ourselves. As ransomed children of God we come to sing about the truths of the Gospel and the truths about who God is, who Christ is and who the Spirit is. So care should be taken to ensure that what we sing about is the truth contained in Scripture and our response to it. This enables us to be objective about the emotional content and subjective feelings in our songs. It allows us to ask, what truths does this song contain that the lyrics are a response to? Asking such questions also helps us to ensure that what we sing is a response to biblical truth.

G. Kendrick writes about the theology of worship songs on the Worship Academy website. He points out that theology is simply the study of God and anyone who sings is expressing an idea about God, a theology, and that every song sung in Christian worship has a theology, for better or worse…So the role of songwriters and song selectors is that of local theologians. It is not that our songs are full of grievous errors though issues pop up from time to time.

In my view the pressing issue is to a large degree one of balance, or rather a lack of it. It is about what we are missing, the subjects we never sing about because the songs are not being written or not being chosen. And it's about the growing dominance of a *'default'* worship culture that only allows certain kinds of expression, a limited range of mood and style that edits out certain subject matter. Wrong theology robs God of his glory and as a result fails to represent him as He actually is. A large part of the purpose of worship is to lovingly and accurately, richly and comprehensively describe God's nature and qualities.

One aspect of contemporary songs is the focus on intimacy with the Lord. But, as the believer can often be the focus of these lyrics, how much are they reflecting a *'spiritual adolescence'* - as they focus on the believers' feelings so much? Clearly, from the perspective of some songwriters the answer is an emphatic 'no' because they are expressing their love to the Lord. At the same time not everyone shares this perception. David Stancliffe, the Bishop of Salisbury echoes his concern about the content of worship songs.

> They can give the impression of concentrating on the worshipper's feelings rather than on celebrating what God has done for us and inviting a response. Greater experience of co-operation between songwriters, liturgists and theologians will be important if we are to create the kind of liturgy in which people can both articulate their usual patterns of worship, and also find a way in which the beliefs held in the authorised liturgy of the Church of England can actually be made to work in a variety of different contexts.[90]

Yet the desire for intimacy is a legitimate one as Jesus spoke of the closeness between himself and the Father that his followers could expect to enjoy. But, it is important to be aware that intimacy is not only the prerogative of worship. It is also an integral part of fellowship with God and Christ in our lives. To have intimacy with Christ and the Father is something that Jesus himself promised in John 14: 18, 20: 'I will not leave you desolate: I will come to you. In that day you will know that I am in my Father, and you in me and I in you.' Moreover, Jesus also alludes to this intimacy in John 14: 23: 'If a man loves me he will keep my word and my Father will love him and we will come to him and make our home with him.' This indicates there is no dichotomy between intimacy in corporate worship and in our union with Christ and God. As a young teenage Christian and adult I found tremendous fulfillment through the friendship of Christ. His presence in my heart was as real as that of my best friends. In those days we didn't refer to this as intimacy but that is exactly what it was. Later, I also experienced this closeness with God as Father. Over 25 years ago I wrote a few lines to describe this intimacy.

> I love you. Though you are unseen
> Yet you dwell inside my being.
> Exactly what does my love mean
> To you – that you are receiving?
>
> You have become the intimacy
> My soul has constantly yearned for.
> Through all my life's changes I see
> You're more to me than I had before.

One feature of contemporary songs is that they often sing to *'Him'* or *'You.'* Although Christians know this refers either to Christ or God is there any reason why the name Lord, Jesus or God is not used instead? The names of God and Christ, like our names, are important as they represent who we are. Contemporary songs by various writers often focus on the individual singing to the Lord or receiving from him. It would reinforce being part of the body of Christ if the *'I'* on occasions was substituted by *'we.'*

As I thought about the psalmist calling on the 'name of the Lord' and personally declaring 'I love the Lord' in Psalm 116 - my mind focused on contemporary sung worship that often does not address the Lord by name. Instead, the lyrics of many songs simply use the word 'you' throughout when speaking about Christ, God or the Lord, or to them. On the one hand, the worshipper knows that 'you' refers to God or Christ. But, at the same time many of these songs could be addressed to anyone. As you look through The Psalms it is clear that the name God or Lord is used throughout in every single one of them. Also in just over 20 psalms (as in Psalm 116) the 'name of the Lord' is referred to.

The Psalms challenge us to think about the significance of addressing God personally by name as opposed to calling him 'you' - that is the tendency in sung worship. By addressing the 'Lord' or 'God' or 'Christ' or calling on the 'name of the Lord' - we are specifically identifying who we are speaking to. The name God or Lord in The Psalms speak about who God is. He is the God of Abraham, Isaac and Jacob - the God who saved the Hebrews and established Israel as his people. He is the God and Father of our Lord Jesus Christ. So to use the name of God, Christ or Lord, specifically reminds us of their character and what they have done for us and is a sign of reverence and respect. It also reminds us of their authority in heaven and earth and their salvation in our lives. When we use the names of God, Christ and Lord, they remind us of their character in a personal manner. Just as you would never refer to someone you were talking to as 'you' as this would be extremely rude and a derogatory term, so too The Psalms question contemporary practice that refers to God and Christ as 'you.' God and Christ have innumerable names that portray their character and personality and activity that are more appropriate to use. On those occasions when we are introduced to someone for the first time we might comment on how beautiful or lovely their name sounds and we may well ask them what it means. So too the names of God, Christ and Lord and all the other names in Scripture that refer to them, have a beauty about them because of their meaning and significance. It is time we stopped using 'you' for God and Christ as it is inappropriate.

Overtly loud sung worship runs the risk of making worshippers feel they are spectators at a Christian rock concert, rather than taking part in worship. Paul Oakley echoes this: 'Building a style of worship meeting that relies heavily on the band and the worship leader up front to lead us, can if we are not careful, bring about a spectator mentality.'[91] The worship in our church in Cambridge used to be led by the pianist on a grand piano. But about twelve years ago this was replaced by a band that reflected the direction of contemporary sung worship. Naturally, the volume of the music increased substantially and reflects the model of sung worship at charismatic Christian holidays and conferences. Jarrod Cooper on the Worship Academy website says: 'One of the great, yet subtle pressures on church leaders today comes from our church culture of camps and conferences. Once a year many in our churches exodus to wonderful camps where thousands congregate. The greatest preachers preach and the worship (especially the music) is often outstanding...the subtle errors that such conferences may teach us is that we need to re-create all aspects of the conference culture at home in our local church meeting.' Similarly, what musicians tend to overlook is they can lead sung worship as if there are 3,000 people present, when in reality there may only be between 100-300. Clearly, you do not play at the same volume for this number of people as you do for ten times that many! Flutes and violins are also drowned out when the volume of other instruments such as the drums, guitar or keyboard is too loud.

The volume of sung worship does not have to be overtly loud for it to be worshipful. Songs accompanied by a moderate volume create a more intimate, worshipful atmosphere. Although making a joyful noise to the Lord is scriptural, the volume of the band can be set at a level that is comfortable for everyone. The danger of having consistently loud sung worship is that it can be too triumphalistic and clearly unpastoral. Ian Stackhouse, Pastor of Guildford Baptist Church, echoes a similar concern on a blog discussing his book 'Gospel Driven Church.' 'As a pastor I know that many of my congregation arrive on a Sunday in a state of disrepair and to serve up week, after week, a diet of unreflective, unmediated, ahistorical worship is not only uncaring, it is also un-Christian.' I have experienced sung worship where the volume of the band wasn't too loud and this allowed the beautiful harmonies and melodies of the congregation to be heard above the music. Darlene Szschech has some wise insights about music and worship.

> True worship is not about the songs being sung: it is not about the size of the band: it is not about the size of the choir. Although music is a wonderful expression of worship, it is not in itself the essence of it. The core of worship is when one's heart and soul and all that is within, adores and connects with the Spirit of God. In fact regardless of how magnificent the musical moments are, unless one's heart is fully engaged in the worship being expressed – it is still only music.[92]

Whenever I preach or lead worship I pray that the Lord would point people to himself. This ensures that my motivation is right. This principle is important when a band leads the sung worship. Such issues as motivation, the style of the worship, the loudness of the music and how it is led, should be guided by the desire to point people to the Lord. The temptation to perform may also lead to 'hyping-up' the worship. This can lead to pressure to manipulate peoples' emotions and as a result the worship can lack integrity. Tim Hughes shares an example of Mike Pilavachi writing to the worship leaders at his church about this. He adds that Mike being Greek is prone to making the point somewhat strongly but says he is right! 'Do not only prepare your choice of songs but also how you will lead them. Never repeat a song for no reason. We are singing songs for too long at the moment. It is boring and pointless. If you are going to repeat a song then think what you meant to emphasise the second time. You can change the emphasis by changing the instrumentation. To repeat a song with the same musical backing, tempo and vocal emphasis is just laziness. Don't do it any more.'[93]

From some of the lyrics of contemporary songs one might reasonably conclude they are *more about me than Jesus.*' Pete Ward a lecturer at Kings College, London, and author of 'Selling Worship' (How what we sing has changed the Church) – shares his perception. He says: 'Matt Redman is clear in, 'When The Music Fades' that the heart of worship is all about you Jesus. This is a crucial insight but it could be observed that very few songs are really all about Jesus. In fact many of the songs including 'When The Music Fades' are not really all about Jesus at all: rather they are all about the worshipper and their experiences in worship. In other words the songs leave themselves open to the criticism that they have replaced the content of the Christian gospel with human experience. Instead of worshipping Jesus they give the impression that we are worshipping worship…it could be said that this trend in contemporary worship is in danger of being accused of a kind of idolatry.'[94]

From my observation of contemporary and charismatic worship there is a lack of liturgical content in it. C. Cocksworth echoes his concern about this aspect of worship and clearly emphasises the importance of Spirit-led liturgy.

> I propose a confident, grateful Spirit led use of the church's liturgy. In my own church tradition I worry about the passing of the older generation of evangelicals who though they might have been architects of all-age worship, or the trail-blazers of charismatic worship, knew their

prayer books and could draw on deep wells of liturgical formation. I grieve the two (false) choices that seem to be on offer in so many places I visit: 'traditional churches' with a lifeless form of liturgical worship or 'modern evangelical' churches with a reductionist, liturgy-less form of worship. I long to see planners and presiders of worship so understanding the structures of worship, they can move freely within them. I crave to see the classic texts of worship, which the Spirit of truth has given to the church, resting in the hearts and minds of evangelicals and rising to their lips in worship. I yearn for sustained periods of sung worship, glossolalia, prophecy, healing, woven into the movement of liturgical worship by Spirit-led leaders.[95]

Cocksworth believes that authentic Catholic-Evangelical worship is necessarily charismatic and his vision is clearly comprehensive. For him, evangelical worship refuses to reduce these intensive moments of worship to solely exaltation and adoration – the 'sacrifice of praise' – still less to particular feelings of worship experienced by the emotions of the spirit. 'Evangelical worship, worship according to the Gospel is heard and seen, celebrated and received, expressed, embodied and enacted: the reading and preaching of Scripture, the gathering, praying, singing and dismissal of the people…More specifically Catholic-Evangelical worship in the Spirit will have the capacities to hold together that which the flawed history of Christian worship and spirituality has forced apart: word and sacrament, prophetic and mystical, personal and communal, simple and ceremonial, ordered and spontaneous, exaltation and edification.'[96]

In Robin Parry's book 'Worshipping Trinity,' for him the heart of worship is all about God the Father, Son and the Holy Spirit. As a mild mannered charismatic he wondered how Trinitarian contemporary charismatic worship really is. One Sunday morning after returning home from worship he was disturbed because neither the Father nor the Spirit had received even a passing glance. The leader opened the meeting with a call to worship: 'We've come together this morning to meet with Jesus.' We then sang numerous songs all directed to Jesus or 'You Lord' who was also Jesus. There were also numerous prayers all directed to Jesus. The sermon waxed eloquent about Jesus, but his Father and the Spirit didn't get a look in. When he went home he randomly selected one of the best selling worship music CDs over the last few years and looked at the contents. Reading the lyrics was an eye-opener for him as there was no mention of either God the Father or the Holy Spirit. All the songs were addressed either to Jesus or to an anonymous god or lord. There was no mention of the incarnation of Jesus, the ministry of Jesus, the resurrection or the ascension. Only one song mentioned the cross. But there was a great balance on intimacy.[97] Parry also echoes his concerns about Trinitarian worship when some songs proclaim it's all about you Jesus. 'However, taken in a fairly straightforward sense the claim is simply false. *It is not all about Jesus.* It is all about God, Father, Son and Holy Spirit. My concern about songs like that is the ordinary person in the congregation, probably doesn't interpret the song in a suitably qualified way and simply runs with the straightforward (false) meaning, perhaps undermining little by little, the place of the Father and Spirit in their own spirituality. I want to suggest that the worship of Jesus is central to Christianity, and that it is honouring to both Father and Spirit. But, that it must not move towards an exclusive focus on worshipping Jesus, that denies the reality of the Trinity by pushing the Father and the Spirit to the margins. Trinitarian spirituality requires a balance, that some are in danger of losing.'[98]

A CRITIQUE OF CHARISMATIC WORSHIP

James Steven in 'Worship In The Spirit'– Charismatic worship in the Church of England, carried out a study of worship in six charismatic churches between 1993-1995. Three churches were Evangelical, one was Anglo-Catholic, another church was modern Catholic and the other was in an urban priority area. His research provides important insights that merit serious consideration. He perceives that the cultural backdrop to charismatic worship is the popular culture which evolved from the 1960s counter-culture. This had the emphasis of individual participation, expressiveness and impatience with formality and institutional life. He believes the romantic songs of pop culture are seen as a type of the intimate style of songs in charismatic worship. He makes a comparison with the disco culture that moves from songs with an upbeat dance rhythm to slower songs of romantic intimacy. He believes that traditional liturgies and symbols do not have the complexity to engage congregations with society, tradition and history. *These are sweeping claims to make as charismatic worship can hardly claim the sophistication to enable Christians to engage with tradition*

*and history. In reality does this genre of worship essentially appeal
to Christians rather than outsiders)* Consequently, spirituality is
redefined.

> Christians identify their deepest religious experiences 'not
> with public ritual and worship, but with private, personal
> experiences of intimacy and relationship' and so live with
> a model of the sacred that is based on intimacy, not
> liturgy.[99]

Steven suggests that liturgy is more readily judged according to
its therapeutic capacity to meet the needs of the individual.
Worshippers now 'look for the holy to reveal itself not in the awe
inspiring rite of Baptism and Eucharist, but in the awesome
precincts of the self.'[100] *While these are perceptive comments,
being familiar with liturgical worship I am inclined to think this
reflects a lack of exposure by charismatics to this style of worship.
Yet, his telling phrase the 'awesome precincts of the self' seems to
capture the focus of a great deal of contemporary sung worship.*

Steven also noted that charismatic worship tends to focus on the
dominant metaphor of Christ the Lord as the ascended, glorified,
majestic King so that his divinity is powerfully celebrated. He
expresses his concern that this concentration on the exalted Christ
obscured his humanity in charismatic worship and has almost
completely overshadowed the Gospel accounts of the Jesus of
Nazareth. 'Instead of singing to a Jesus who in his humanity faced
temptation, conflict and suffering, we sing to a triumphant Christ
who in his majesty and power defeats the powers of evil.'[101] He
also noted while the songs celebrated Christian joy, victory and
confidence they did not embrace other areas of the believer's life,
such as the cost of discipleship, or suffering and patient endurance
in the face of opposition and lament for human sinfulness.[102] He
astutely observes that another important omission is any reference
to Christ as our great high priest and his continuing priesthood in
his risen humanity in the heavenly sanctuary. Instead, Christ is
located in the past in his atoning death on the cross.

> The result of this was an experience of worship that had its
> entire centre of gravity located with the worshippers, who
> invite the Spirit to join them in their worship. In contrast to
> worship that is offered with its centre of gravity located *in,
> with* and *through* the priestly Christ in his offering to the
> Father.[103]

This centre of gravity in worship can be found in many of the lyrics of contemporary songs that tend to focus on the believer. One unspoken inference is that Christians *in* and *of* themselves can offer their worship to God. This can lead to a wrong approach and wrong attitudes in worship. The inherent danger of this approach is that it bypasses the truth, that it is only *in* and *through* Christ that we have *access to the Father*. For it is only in and through Christ our great high priest that we can *offer acceptable worship to God* – with the help and inspiration of the Holy Spirit.

Steven also identifies another feature of charismatic worship, its estrangement from a dynamic relationship with Christ's offering of worship, in the way that it draws attention to itself. Here song lyrics tend to celebrate the act of worship itself as much as the object of worship and the worshipping assembly believing itself to be the only subject of true worship, appears to have fallen into the temptation of gazing upon itself as it worships 'in the Spirit.' He quotes Tom Torrance:

> If there is no consciousness of our offering of worship being in, with and through Christ, then we are inevitably thrown back upon ourselves to offer worship to the Father: worship of our own devising, although it may be worship for the sake of Christ, motivated by him.[104]

On a different note, confession in contemporary worship tends to be brief and lacks Scriptural content. It is the responsibility of the leader to ensure that the content is biblically substantial. Tom Smail echoes a similar concern when in the 90s he spoke about the failure of charismatics to find a central and regular place in their worship, for the confession of sins and deep repentance that God's free forgiveness evokes from us and creates in us.

> It is often remarked that every great renewal in the Spirit begins when he convicts Christ's people of their sins and leads them to repentance (John 16: 8-11). This has not so far been characteristic of the charismatic renewal and the lack of it explains the impression of superficiality and even unreality, that the renewal and its worship can sometimes convey.[105]

For Smail the beginning of charismatic renewal in the 70s was marked by a new release of praise, intimacy and freedom and its distinctive feature was the corporate and spontaneous singing in tongues often called *'singing in the Spirit.'* 'Those of us who have actually participated in charismatic renewal worship, especially in its early days and our own early days in it, can bear witness that we have been carried not into some vague mystic ecstasies without Christian content, but into the kind of worship of the Ancient of Days and of the Lamb, who is in the midst of his throne that the book of Revelation describes. This added to our corporate worship of God, a dimension of immediacy, directness, depth, freedom and joy to an extent that we did not know.'[106]

Smail also highlights the shortcomings of charismatic renewal that may be a prophetic warning to those involved in it today.

> Nevertheless, while we have every reason to speak with great gratitude of charismatic worship, we have at the same time to recognise that at the moment all is not well with it. Often in the seminars out of which this book emerged (1993) we heard ministers and other leaders who had been deeply involved in renewal and its worship over long periods, expressing perplexity and dismay that somehow or other the glory had departed from it: that the high praises of God had degenerated into endless repetitive chorus singing that was in danger of becoming a bore and a burden rather than a release and a joy: that the celebration of the saving acts of God has been replaced by pious self-indulgence in religious sentiment for its own sake: that people were sometimes being worked up or manipulated into a strained and artificial worship, that concealed God's absence more than it responded to his presence.[107]

In retrospect it is possible that their worship may have reached a plateau. Although many Christians may have felt immersed in the ocean depths of worship, they were probably paddling at the water's edge. The dismay of the ministers may indicate an underlying factor that was never articulated. Namely, that they didn't know how to lead God's people deeper into charismatic renewal, or deeper in their worship. As a result their charismatic renewal and worship failed to mature and was predictable. Should we be asking whether these things are true of contemporary and charismatic worship today?

Ian Stackhouse, the Pastoral Leader of the Millmead Centre, at the Guildford Baptist Church, describes himself as a 'card carrying

Evangelical and charismatic to boot.' He expresses a number of concerns about charismatic worship and contributes important insights about its development. He points out it is in worship that all the tensions between form and freedom are seen fully at work. A reference to structure and spontaneity that represents liturgical and spontaneous free flowing worship, and formal and charismatic worship. He implies that charismatic worship requires greater depth and involves embracing aspects of historical and traditional sacramental worship. He says, 'The epitome of worship within charismatic Christianity, is to be in a place of corporate singing where the power of the Spirit is so tangible that there is no sermon, no Communion, no readings, but simply people prostrate in the presence of the Lord. Indeed, whole tracts of recent revivalist literature endorse this ideal, where, finally, because of the presence of the Spirit, we can do away with the sacramental apparatus of the church altogether. Who needs the encumbrance of a sermon, or a Communion table, when you have the immediate presence of God? Or so the argument runs.'[108]

Stackhouse also thinks that it is a mistake to see the Holy Spirit as only the irrational side of God, or as a synonym for the immediate presence of God, or as an excuse for a particular style of worship.

> Rather, the Spirit is as transcendent as the Father and the Son and works through the given means of the Church – preaching, Communion, prayer, the laying on of hands, etc – in order to accomplish his purpose. Nevertheless, there remains a popular perception that openness to the Spirit means a commitment to a specifically loose form of worship, and a euphemistic for a spirituality of perpetual surprises.[109]

He shares his perception of how charismatics have arrived at this position. He points out that the Charismatic Renewal Movement is itself a reaction to sacramental and liturgical formalism, leaving in its wake a legacy of suspicion towards the practices of the church that it is as deep today as it has ever been. And despite recent attempts to forge a marriage between liturgy and freedom in the Spirit, such a relationship is still something of an oxymoron for many charismatics – because to be free in the Spirit is by definition to be unrestrained by ecclesiastical formulations. He reflects that it is hard to see how charismatics in the mainstream denominations in the sixties could have avoided the dichotomy that now exists between sacraments and the Spirit.[110]

Stackhouse now perceives the opposite problem exists – 'namely, that a Spirit movement too long detached from the given means of grace, will simply engender its own brand of legalism, driven by the need for ever more, and ever new, immediate experiences of the Spirit. And any spirituality of immediacy will be through the experience of worship itself, rather than by receiving the given means of grace of the church through word and sacrament.

> Our point is that unmediated immediacy of the kind found within charismatic singing, meaning music, which in reality is often the only means of grace available within the charismatic worship, presents its own conundrums. For as well as providing huge amounts of energy and space with which to express genuine and heart-felt worship to God, it also has the capacity to foster its own brand of predictability as we move from one song to the next in search of the existential moment. As with all of these things its strength becomes its source of weakness. Bereft of the givenness of tradition, contemporary worship if we are not careful, degenerates into a non-Trinitarian act, as worshippers seek to access the divine either through the repetitiveness of the lyrics, or the rhythm of the beat...'[111]

I wonder to what extent ministers and Christians are aware of the deeper issues that Stackhouse raises concerning worship? Just as ministers in Tom Smail's day were dismayed that charismatic worship failed to progress beyond the repetitive singing of songs, in time will ministers also conclude the same thing is happening today? One way of avoiding this is for ministers to teach their churches about the comprehensive nature of Christian worship and to challenge the assumptions that pervade contemporary and charismatic worship.

A. Walker points out that the Charismatic Renewal Movement embraced a genuine spirituality but was at times a reaction to formal liturgies and rational evangelicalism, around the middle of the 20th century. Although renewal epitomised freedom in the Holy Spirit this did not embrace the theological and liturgical depths of deep church. (Deep church, as its name implies, is spiritual reality down in the depths – the foundations and deep structures of the Faith – which feed, sustain and equip us to be disciples of Christ). Had this taken place it would have challenged the widespread conviction in charismatic circles that routine liturgies, set prayers, regular collects and widely used lectionaries were spiritually dead precisely because they were structured, routinised and familiar. But, to limit knowing God to a mode that stressed the experiential over the intellectual, the intuitive over the rational, improvisation over sensible planning, the novel over the familiar...left the renewal movement living of its nerves.[112]

Stackhouse adds that what charismatic renewal has brought largely through its songs is a real sense of expectation where this was lacking. But, unless this is followed by sacramental renewal which places music within a wider framework, then all we can predict is descent into a peculiarly unchristian anxiety – for whatever else sacraments do they bind us to the revelation of God in Christ, relieving us of the burden of having to constantly prove our worth. In charismatic worship there is a sense that the real action is taking place other than in the sacramental life of the Church.[113]

CHAPTER SEVEN

BALANCED WORSHIP

INTRODUCTION

Any minister seeking to deepen the worship of their church can plan a preaching series to teach their congregation more about this topic. Having a resource library of books on worship is also an invaluable tool for the church to learn from, and to complement this home groups can devote a term or two to studying Christian worship. In large churches alongside the clergy there may also be a number of lay people leading the Sunday Services, and this involves being open to what the Lord is doing among his people. One advantage for ministers is that they are likely to have more experience in leading worship. Another advantage is that one aspect of their call is to devote time to plan, prepare and pray about the worship of the church and the way it develops. It is common knowledge amongst clergy that to preach a 20 minute sermon requires around 8 hours of preparation/study, possibly longer. Creative, interesting, stimulating worship that glorifies God, also requires a considerable amount of time for thought, preparation and planning and probably involves a number of people. Ministers should unashamedly build time into their schedule to ensure their corporate worship has depth.

The person likely to lead God's people deeper in worship is the one who regularly spends time in prayer, studying the Scriptures and in worship. Only as we are habitually in God's presence on our own as leaders, are we be able to lead others into his presence on a more profound level. The responsibility for doing this should not necessarily be with the musicians, but with the minister who is leading the service. Jarrod Cooper says 'You cannot lead people in rapturous worship when you have no personal worship life. You cannot obey the Spirit in a meeting when you are rebellious to him outside the walls of the church. You cannot exemplify intimacy and tenderness of heart before the congregation when you haven't spoken to God all week. The only way God's presence is going to move in and around you, is if you live a life soaked in his presence. Then you will be like a broken jar of perfume, with a presence flowing out of your heart. Everyone will see that you have been with Jesus.'[1]

On leading worship C. Cocksworth, Bishop of Coventry has this to
say:

> Good presiders *'feel the freedom'* of their role. They know
> their way around the liturgy. They feel the pulse of the
> people. They listen for the breath of God. They can move
> with the dynamics of worship giving space for spontaneity,
> room for silence and are trusted by their people to lead
> them towards moments of encounter with Christ, the head
> of the body.[2]

PENTECOSTAL WORSHIP

Chris Bowater on the Worship Academy archive makes some
astute comments that may well be relevant to contemporary and
charismatic worship. Pentecostal worship must instruct the mind
as well as the heart. Worship has both cognitive/intellectual and
emotional/experiential dimensions. These are not contradictory but
complementary emphases. We must not take complementary ideas
and transform them into opposites. This creates a false dichotomy
– we are not forced to choose between the two. It is not 'either/or'
but 'both/and.' To posit tension between the mind and heart
amounts to a deep distortion of both and is in the end a phoney
issue. Or to put it more positively, serious, responsible worship
attends to both mind and heart.

In recent years Pentecostal worship has frequently featured theologically deficient music. We are today, suffering the consequences
of the loss of theological substance in contemporary worship.
Content deprived worship is leading to an emaciated, weakened
church – exposed to the threat of doctrinal error and false teaching.
Worshippers are becoming increasingly concerned that worship
music is being emptied of sold lyrical content. It is time to restore
more good content into the songs we write and sing.

Pentecostal leaders having a 'celebration only' concept of worship
music, need to move to an understanding that more faithfully
reflects the biblical teaching that worship is a powerful didactic
tool. In an era when enrolment in Sunday Schools, children's
ministry and other forms of Christian education has dwindled
(contributing to an increase in biblical illiteracy), and pastoral
preaching often begins with the perceived needs of unbelieving
visitors (resulting in a decline in expository preaching and

teaching), the need for instruction in sound doctrine has never been greater.

Worship should be solid in its content. Many songs currently being used are theologically superficial and lyrically weak. Music that does not challenge worshippers is nothing more than sacred brain candy, giving the participants a nice feeling at the time the song is sung, but leaving a feeling of emptiness when finished. In a time when Christians are 'lazy and hazy' about their faith, it is especially important that leaders be vigilant in identifying and eliminating shallow worship music. Worship should not be 'dumbed down but smartened up.'

Balanced worship will also contain a healthy mix of objective and subjective music. Some of our music should reflect the objective doctrines of the Christian faith. These songs help us to understand truth in relation to Scripture. Other songs will be more subjective, providing the testimonial side of our faith. Objective songs tell his story: subjective songs tell our story. A constant diet of objective songs can cause worship to be detached and cerebral. On the other hand, a constant diet of subjective music can cause worship to become self-absorbed and sentimental. Objective worship needs the warmth provided by subjective songs: subjective worship needs the grounding provided by objective songs.

TRANSCENDENCE & IMMANENCE

Philip Greenslade in 'Worship In The Best Of Both Worlds'– explores the charismatic and liturgical dimensions of worship. In this he makes some very perceptive and profound insights about the transcendence and immanence of God – which challenge our understanding of these attributes in contemporary worship. He points out that the theologians S. Grenz and R. Olsen, argue that Christian theology has always sought a balance between these twin biblical truths.

> Because the Bible presents God as both beyond the world and present to the world, theologians in every era are confronted with the challenge of articulating the Christian understanding of the nature of God in a manner that balances, affirms and holds in creative tension the truths of the divine transcendence and the divine immanence.[3]

Greenslade argues confusion can occur when in practice we dissolve this *'creative tension'* by choosing between the transcendence and immanence of God as if they were opposites. The result is polarised worship: in transcendence we emphasise God's majesty or remoteness, whereas God's immanence suggests warmth and intimacy. In the former God is worshipped as distant and aloof best served by long-distance respect. Whereas in the latter God is rendered indistinguishable from us and courted with over-sentimental love-songs.[4] In effect when God's immanence - his closeness and presence amongst us has been interpreted primarily as intimacy - this is a distortion. Because, if God truly came amongst us as he did in 2 Chron. ch. 5, we are more likely to be flung onto our faces, as we would not be able to behold God's glory. We would be extolling God with 'holy, holy, holy' – not 'intimacy, intimacy, intimacy.'

Two texts which are usually associated with the polarities in God's transcendence and immanence are Isaiah 57: 15 and Jeremiah 23: 23-24. In the first the Lord says: 'I live in a high and holy place but also with him who is contrite and lowly in spirit.' But, the second in a critique of false prophets moves in the other direction stressing the transcendence of God. 'Am I a God nearby' declares the Lord, 'and not a God far away? Can anyone hide in secret places so that I cannot see him? 'Do I not fill heaven and earth?' – Jer. 23: 23-24. Brueggemann in his incisive manner says:

> God is not near and available. God is unavoidable (23-24). That God should be 'near' is a promise from the Temple cult. The assertion that God is distant thus stands over against the Temple ideology which seeks to draw God too near to favourite arrangements and to minimise God's sovereign freedom. Such worship is fed by false prophets whose cosy reassurances bring God too 'near,' hollow out his name, dumb down his word, and make his presence insubstantial and his blessings 'lite' – Jer. 23: 25-32.[5]

Greenslade says, 'Here is a recognition that misuse can go either way. Worship can either push God to the margins of effectiveness by making him remote from everyday life, or it can serve to control or tame God by containing him within familiar patterns of response. The real God can not only be lost in a flight into transcendence away from reality, but can be dissolved into comfortable cultic regularity that does not disturb the status quo. This God retains his sovereign freedom and is not accessible on our easy terms. In Freithem's words, 'God enters deeply "into the fray" but not in such a way that he ceases to be God.'[6] This challenges those who are involved in contemporary worship to accurately and faithfully do justice to God's transcendence and immanence – and it is also a challenge for our songwriters. Brueggemann suggests that we can end up relating to God in two separate ways concerning these attributes of his which results in polarised worship.

> God remains the transcendent one even when he is immanent. It might be better to speak of his otherness and his immediacy. God remains the transcendent God of majesty and greatness when precisely he manifests his immediate presence, his holy love, as it were, close up.[7]

What we should take care to avoid in our worship is dumbing-down God's transcendence and immanence, diluting his attributes and re-imagining God. When this happens our worship becomes theologically fragmented – and disturbingly we are unlikely to be aware of this.

CREATIVE LITURGICAL WORSHIP

The term liturgy sounds old-fashioned and is often linked with traditional worship, but, it is relevant to understand its proper meaning. 'Liturgy comes from the Greek word *leitourgia* and is made up of words for work (*ergon*) and people (*laos*). In ancient Greece a liturgy was public work performed for the benefit of the city or state. Similarly, liturgy in worship is a work performed by the people for the benefit of others…To call a service *liturgical* is to indicate that it was conceived so that all worshippers take an active part in offering their worship together. The word liturgy is used in the specific sense of the Eucharist, but Western Christians use *liturgical* to apply to all forms of public worship of a participatory nature.'[8] In the report 'Transforming Worship,' the Liturgical Commission of the Church of England, reminds us liturgy is also the work of God. God addresses us through the readings of Scripture and in our prayers of invocation we ask the Lord to be present and active among. There is a two-fold aspect of liturgy. It is both human construction and divine gift.[9]

I believe one of the outstanding weaknesses of contemporary and charismatic worship is the omission of *'liturgical texts.'* *'Liturgical texts'* help the congregation to connect with the Lord and to encounter him, interact and respond to him. Liturgical worship involves participation by all the people of God and includes *'liturgical texts.'* For example, the Lord's Prayer and Scripture readings are *'liturgical texts.'* In Anglican worship the Creed and the Gloria in Communion are *'liturgical texts'* as is the Eucharistic prayer of thanksgiving. Also, in the Communion Service, the striking thing about the Collect for Purity, the Creed, the Gloria and prayer of thanksgiving, is that they can all be sung. In 'Alternative Worship – 2003' for Pentecost some creative liturgy resulted in the following version of the creed:

> We believe in one God
> the creator of all things,
> who loves the whole creation
> with a father's tenderness
> and a mother's strength.
>
> We believe in one God
> our liberator Jesus Christ
> the Word of God made flesh
> true God and truly human:
> born among the poor he lived
> as bringer of God's Kingdom:
> a teacher and a healer
> a lover of life and a prophet of justice,
> forgiver of sins and friend of sinners,
> who welcomed the outcasts
> and challenged the powerful.
> Whose death on the cross
> defeated sin and death,
> who rose from the dead
> and is alive forever
> in power and glory.
>
> We believe in one God
> the Holy Spirit, the giver of life
> the breath of life in all life
> the gift of God to the people of God
> Disturber and our Comforter.

The fire and the dove,
who makes us one community
in peace and love.
We believe in one God
a community of love
a Trinity of holiness
the beginning and the end
of all life, Amen.[10]

In some Anglican churches even the Eucharistic prayer is sung which reminds me of the liturgy of the Greek Orthodox Church. Between 1992-1994 I worked with The Revd. Dr. Fraser Watts, a Catholic priest and in one of the rural churches, All Saints, Harston in Ely Diocese, he used to sing the Eucharistic prayer from the Rite B Communion Service. I found this very beautiful and moving and a spiritual dimension was added to this prayer of thanksgiving as it was sung. The Anglican Common Prayer Book – 2000 has a choice of eight Eucharistic prayers (prayers of thanksgiving). Although most of the new ones lack the poetic beauty of the established ones. The following is an example of a Eucharistic prayer from the Grace Fellowship in Ealing where Jonny Baker worships. It is called: **'Wounded Eucharistic Prayer.'**

Lift up your hearts
we lift them up to God
lift up your heads
we lift them up to God
lift up your voices
we lift them up to God
lift up your hearts
we lift them up to God

We praise you Lord for your unswerving love for us
though we are fragile
though we are wounded
though we are broken
you have never stopped loving us
and you have never forsaken us
greater love has no one than this that they lay down
their life for their friends

You take what is broken and transform it through
your death and love
what was once hurt
what was once friction
what left a mark
no longer stings
because grace makes beauty
out of ugly things

So we join with the angels singing
holy holy holy
holy holy holy
Lord God Almighty
Lord God Almighty
heaven and earth are full of your glory
heaven and earth are full of your glory
hosanna in the highest
hosanna in the highest

In your last meal with your friends
before your betrayal
you took the bread and gave thanks
you broke it and shared it saying
'take eat this is my body broken for you'
Christ's body is broken
we are Christ's body, we are broken
may Christ's broken body nourish you
in all the right places

you took the cup of wine, gave thanks and shared it saying
'drink this, my blood shed for you'
Christ's body is wounded
we are Christ's body, we are wounded
may the blood that flowed from Christ's wounds
heal you in all the right places

Send your Holy Spirit on us
heal our brokenness
by showing us our place in your community of faith
great is the mystery of faith

Christ has died
Christ is risen
Christ will come again

This is the table of Christ
today it is literally made of our brokenness
a sign that Christ welcomes us all as we are
there is no need to pretend and no need to hide
so gather at this table of Christ
not because you are whole
but because you recognise your need for healing
not because you are good enough
but because you recognise these gifts of God.

In the Anglican Communion service the prayers of penitence can also be introduced with a *'liturgical text,'* beginning with a summary of God's commandments and include verses of Scripture, that exhort us to search our hearts before we actually say the confession. Confession is dealt with later in this chapter, but here is an example from Celtic worship of a corporate confession with depth, which is usually lacking in contemporary worship.

Jesus forgive my sins.
Forgive the sins I can remember
and also the sins I have forgotten.
Forgive the wrong actions I have committed
and the right actions I have omitted.
Forgive the times I have been weak in the face
of temptation, and those when I have been
stubborn in the face of correction.
Forgive the times I have been proud of my
own achievements, and those when I have
failed to boast of your works.
Forgive the harsh judgments I have made of
others, and the leniency I have shown to myself.
Forgive the lies I have told to others
and the truths I have avoided.
Forgive me the pain I have caused to others
and the indulgence I have shown to myself.
Jesus have pity on me and make me whole.[11]

The intercessions in Communion also have a liturgical element to them because public prayer actively involves the worshippers, as in the refrain and response: 'Lord in your mercy' – 'hear our prayer.' The intercessions can begin with prayers of thanksgiving before we make our request for the wider church, the world and our fellowship and community. Yet often there is one long informal prayer that lacks creativity and imagination. There are many written sources that can inspire us to prepare meaningful corporate intercessions. Here are three examples from Celtic Daily Prayer.

> *One thing I have asked of the Lord*
> *this is what I seek:*
> *that I may dwell in the house of*
> *the Lord all the days of my life:*
> *to behold the beauty of the Lord*
> *and to seek him in his temple.*

Who is it that you seek?
We seek the Lord our God.

Do you seek him with all your heart?
Amen. Lord have mercy.

Do you seek him with all your soul?
Amen. Lord have mercy.

Do you seek him with all your mind?
Amen. Lord have mercy.

Do you seek him with all your strength?
Amen. Lord have mercy.

A PRAYER OF HOPE IN BROKENESS
O God I cannot undo the past
or make it never have happen.
I ask you humbly
and from the bottom of my heart:
Please, God
would you write straight
with my crooked lines?
Out of the serious mistakes of my life
will you make something beautiful for you?

Teach me to live at peace with You.
To make peace with others
and even with myself.

Give me fresh vision. Let me
experience Your love so deeply
that I am free to face the future,
forgiven and strong in hope.

A BIDDING PRAYER

Come Lord, come down
Come in, come among us.
Come as the wind to move us:
Come as the light to prove us:
Come as the night to rest us:
Come as the storm to test us:
Come as the sun to warm us:
Come as the stillness to calm us:
Come Lord, come down,
Come in, come among us.
To God the Father, who created the world:
To God the Son, who redeemed the world:
To God the Holy Spirit, who sustains the world:
Be all praise and glory, now and for ever. Amen.[12]

When we begin our Services with a welcome and notices and then move straight into a cluster of sung worship, we have not had time to properly prepare our hearts to worship the Lord. But, *'liturgical texts'* at the beginning of a service can help the congregation to connect with the Lord and respond to him and can also be used by the Holy Spirit to help prepare our hearts – and the set prayer or Scripture reading they include enable us to corporately tune in to the Lord. This is important because it reminds us that we need God's help to worship him – and just as importantly need his help to respond to him. Using established *'liturgical texts'* expresses our reliance on the Lord to come and worship him. Failure to include these *'liturgical texts'* impoverishes our worship and we may inadvertently be relying on ourselves. In the summer of 2008 I attended a Christian holiday conference. I went to the main evening celebrations having arrived somewhat down in my spirit. To get a decent seat you had to get there about half an hour early. This meant the sung worship lasted for up to an hour or more which I found it difficult to emotionally connect with. There was no use of *'liturgical texts of prayer,'* or *'liturgical texts of truth'* from Scripture, to uplift and warm my heart or to help God's people to worship the Lord and respond to him.

How we begin our Services should help focus peoples' attention onto the Lord and look to the Lord to help us to worship him. People should be made aware that the beginning of the service is where the worship really does begin (not when we get to the sung worship): and the beginning is the place where we invoke the help of the Holy Spirit through *'liturgical texts'* and extempore prayer to help us in our worship. This is a time to quieten our hearts, to focus on the Lord and get ready to listen to him and respond to him. But, in contemporary worship people may not be aware of the importance of the concept of the gathering. Yet, people of all ages come to church and some will come with joyful, thankful hearts. Others will come burdened and yet others may have been hassled getting their children ready. Michael Perham points out that people arrive with their personal needs and are expected to be part of a congregation with people they may not know and possibly with people they have not seen since last Sunday.

> The gathering is a recognition we need binding together with our neighbours, if we are genuinely to be a congregation and the body of Christ. We need gathering time to prepare. We need to get ready for communication with God. We need to begin to understand what it is that we are specifically gathering to celebrate. In some churches today people prepare for worship by the singing of songs and choruses for a time before the 'service proper begins.' It is a recognition of the same thing that liturgy has always nearly seen, that we need time to warm up to God, to each other and to what we are to celebrate.[13]

The words of the gathering at the start of the Anglican Communion Service are also *'liturgical texts'* when the minister addresses the congregation saying, 'The Lord be with you' – to which the people reply 'and also with you.' A sentence or verses of Scripture can be included in the gathering, along with an extempore prayer invoking God's blessing on the worship. The Collect for purity is also a *'liturgical text'* included in the gathering. I love this prayer because it reminds us that we need the help of the Holy Spirit to renew our hearts and minds and also to help us in our worship.

> Almighty God
> to whom all hearts are open
> all desires are known
> and from whom no secrets are hidden:
> cleanse the thoughts of our hearts
> by the inspiration of your Holy Spirit
> that we may perfectly love you
> and worthily magnify your holy name
> through Jesus Christ our Lord. Amen.

Contemporary songs often have a limited life span but *'liturgical texts'* are far more enduring and connect us with our Christian roots. An appreciation of liturgy can help us not just to rediscover lost riches from the past, but to see ourselves in continuity with our Christian roots, because the liturgy is the culmination of a long process stretching back for centuries. Liturgy also connects us with the body of Christ throughout the world. It can give us a sense of belonging to the universal Church down the ages.[14] Our approach to liturgical texts as Anglicans is influenced by our being part of the one, holy, catholic and apostolic Church. One important aspect of worship is our response to God's revelation of himself and in historical texts of liturgy there is a response to revealed truth. 'The liturgy announces who we are and who we are to become in Christ. Liturgy, therefore, is the bedrock upon which we build our theologies of God, Church and salvation.' This teaching in effect was one of Cranmer's prime concerns and explains why so much of the liturgy in the Book of Common Prayer is in the form of exhortations. One of the great strengths of having a fixed liturgical form is this link with doctrine. It safeguards the doctrine by its incorporation in the worshipping heart of the Church and nurtures the worshippers in their faith.'[15]

Caroline Headley in 'Liturgy and Spiritual Formation' points out her concern about the changing liturgical forms of our present age: 'The danger is that both the quality of some of our modern liturgical writing and even the sheer variety of it, mean that generations are growing up that have no texts, new or old, in their memory to feed their souls.'[16] One of the great strengths of the diversity of *'liturgical texts'* in the Anglican Communion Service, is that they provide a structure in which preaching and sung worship are an integral part of the liturgy, instead of dominating a service on their own. I would suggest that one of the main weaknesses of contemporary worship is the content – because essentially it consists of preaching and clusters of sung worship. Consequently, the biblical content contained in these services can be low. In comparison, a well balanced and unabridged liturgical service of Holy Communion, can also include clusters of sung worship and has much more biblical content. C. Cocksworth, in a lecture at the Oase Conference in Norway (Feb. 2007), emphasises the importance of liturgy in worship.

> Liturgy is essential to orthodoxy. Without an insistence on the use of certain Spirit-proved texts and on the necessity, not just advisability, of patterns and structures made credible by common use, worship will all too easily slide into the syrup of the surrounding culture, mirroring contemporary assumptions and attitudes, rather than facing people with the transcendent and transforming themes of the gospel. The liturgy is not the enemy of the Spirit. Of course, it is not the master of the Spirit either. But, it is the Spirit's servant.[17]

He also believes that Common Worship (the Anglican Service Book), maintains the historic Anglican commitment to authorised texts and shapes of worship used in common throughout the Church, receiving them as historic gifts of the Spirit to the church. He believes this recognises that the context counts and worship leaders need both variety of texts and optionality in the way they use them. This puts an enormous responsibility on leaders to devise forms of worship that are appropriate for the context. He says: 'I am convinced that what churches need is a form of worship that *holds together* the classical liturgical preferences and weaves them together into one holistic culture of Christian worship, that is at the same time charismatic, evangelical and catholic. Or to put it another way, a form of worship that is *one* (in the sense of integrated and whole): *holy* (in the sense of being inspired and guided by the Holy Spirit): *catholic* (in the sense of being tangibly connected with the worship of the whole body, receiving the deep historical wisdom of the whole body on how to worship): and *apostolic* (in the sense of carrying the apostolic mission into this age and beyond to the ages of ages).'[18]

In 'Holding Together' – 2008, Cocksworth with acute perception puts his finger on the attitude Evangelicals have towards liturgy and how they lead worship. 'For some Evangelicals – especially Anglicans, often of the older sort – liturgy is an honourable feature that should be respected. It is kept on in the service – more so in situations where a certain dignity and formality seems to be more appropriate, such as the Lord's Supper or funerals – but it is not used for worship. The words, and a minimum of the action, are retained perhaps out of deference to the past or because of obedience to present authorities, or perhaps out of a nebulous sense that they might do us some good at some point. But the worship itself – the personal and corporate engagement with God – is positioned to happen at another level. The introductions and connections made by whoever may be steering the service, the songs of worship and the prompts of the 'worship leader,' the words of the intercessor…shape and stimulate the worship rather than the movement and words of the Liturgy.'[19]

I believe these observations are also true of much younger Anglican evangelicals and charismatics. For them leading worship also relies extensively on personality. Whereas, in an unabridged Communion Service – *(Evangelicals have the habit of omitting parts of the liturgy of H. C.)* the minister aims to be self-effacing, allowing the worship to naturally flow with the liturgical texts, and trusts the Holy Spirit to animate the worship. Leading this style of worship requires being acquainted with and at home with the liturgy, so that it becomes an integral part of you. Cocksworth also expounds the history and use of the liturgy in Evangelicalism in an insightful way that is both scholarly and spiritual. He does not think Evangelicalism's rejection of the deep wisdom of the liturgical tradition is sustainable. Yet, in my experience of the past thirty years or so, I seriously doubt whether Evangelicals are likely to embrace liturgical worship in any meaningful way, because their services essentially revolve around preaching and hymns/songs. This tradition is so thoroughly ingrained in the movement that it is difficult to see the liturgical tradition being embraced by Evangelicalism. Moreover, Anglican Evangelicals and charismatics, do not associate their identity and spirituality with this tradition. The other stumbling block is that it is extremely unlikely that their older and younger clergy, or those ordained in recent years, will want to embrace the liturgical tradition. Their spirituality is not consciously immersed in the liturgy. It has not shaped them. And it is not a conscious expression of their worship.

Cocksworth also challenges both Evangelicals and charismatics about their sacramental theology. He says, 'While they welcome the power of the Holy Spirit in 'extraordinary' mediations they are forgetful of the pledged promise through the 'ordinary' gifts of broken bread and poured out wine. Because of this there remain serious tendencies towards reductionalism in Evangelical and charismatic sacramental practice – a way of doing the Eucharist that implies the real locus of God's activity is to be found elsewhere.'[20] I believe the stumbling block for Evangelicals and charismatics to have Communion as their regular Sunday Service, is because for the former their worship has an established tradition that focuses on preaching, whereas for the latter their worship has an established tradition that focuses on the Holy Spirit. I have found it is extremely rare to find Communion as the main Sunday Service within these traditions. Their lack of familiarity with the liturgy of Communion, essentially means that its meaning has not penetrated the core of Evangelicalism and the Charismatic Movement. As a result they have not been deeply exposed to, and immersed in, the truths its liturgy embraces – in a way that has had a formative impact on their spirituality. As an analogy it is like being familiar with Shakespear's plays without ever having been immersed in them in any depth, as a result you are not drawn into their deeper meaning. It is the reluctance to regularly celebrate Communion that needs to be addressed by Evangelicals and charismatics. Only as a student of Shakespeare immerses himself in his plays, his plots and his characters, will they become deeply meaningful. The same truth applies to Holy Communion for these two strident movements.

BIBLICAL OR ROMANTIC INTIMACY?

Many Christians value singing worship love songs to Jesus or the Lord while there are others who are more reticent about this. It is instructive to look at the model of '*biblical intimacy*' with the Lord from the Psalms, and compare this to the model of '*romantic intimacy*' that we often come across in our sung worship. Before looking at these models it is relevant to see what guidelines in Scripture there are to express our love for God and Christ.

One of the most important spiritual truths to be aware of is that God and Christ through the Holy Spirit take the initiative and reach out to us to reveal their love for us. So when we declare our love for them in sung worship this is a response to their initiative of love which is clearly stated in 1 John 4. 19: we love because he first loved us. In John's Gospel Jesus also clearly says in 14: 15: 'If you love me you will obey my commandments' and in 14: 21 he says this again: 'He who has my commandments and keeps them, he it is who loves me.' This clearly dovetails and resonates with what God asked of his people in Deut. ch. 4 - 8 which was to 'love the Lord your God, with all your heart, soul, mind and strength' and to obey all his commandments. Clearly, love for God and Christ is expressed in obeying their commandments and keeping their Word. As we know from Jeremiah's temple sermon in Jer. ch. 7 God's people were neglecting the issues of justice, obedience and righteousness, but still came to worship with their religious mantra: 'the temple of the Lord, the temple of the Lord.' But the Lord saw through it and it was unacceptable to him.

Our love for the Lord is revealed by the way we live, so if we are being obedient to the Lord and walking in his commandments we can authentically say: 'I love you Lord.' For intimate sung worship to have integrity, it has to flow from an obedient walk with the Lord. Otherwise, if the songs that express our love for the Lord or a desire for intimacy with him are not undergirded with holy and obedient lives that express our delight and love for the Lord, they can end up being no more than a romantic ideal. A desire for an existential intimacy of the moment to make us feel better. I would suggest that one of the most extraordinary features about contemporary worship, is that the ten commandments are never included in an act of confession, or as a prelude to introducing our intimate sung worship. It is as if we have 'jettisoned' them and made them obsolete in our 'memory bank of Scripture.' This is clearly an astonishing omission. We are singing intimate love songs to the Lord, but in the process, we may be overlooking the practical expression of that love in them.

What is striking about many Psalms is that the author expresses his intimacy with the Lord or his love for him by focusing on God's character in some detail or specifically sharing what the Lord has done for him and by saying how he has been faithful and obedient to the Lord. But, in contemporary songs of 'romantic *intimacy'* this does not tend to happen very much. Psalm 18 is an example of *'biblical intimacy.'* In this psalm which is one of thanksgiving for answered prayer David declares in v. 1-3, 'I love you O Lord, my strength. The Lord is my rock and my fortress and my deliverer, my God, my rock, in whom I take refuge, my shield and the horn of my salvation, my stronghold.' We have solid content as to why David loves the Lord. In v. 4-15 we find an imaginative description of how the Lord in his power rescued David when he called out to him in distress. Verses 16-25 then clearly testify that the Lord has rescued him and that he has rewarded him because of his obedience-righteousness which reveals his love for the Lord. One would have thought that this psalm could have naturally ended at v. 24, but David continues to elaborate on God's help that not only rescued him, but, gave victory over his enemies, concluding in v. 46-50 with him extolling and praising the Lord.

Another striking thing about The Psalms is that they assume an underlying intimacy and close walk with the Lord. In some psalms when this closeness has been interrupted, the psalmist declares why this has happened and looks to the Lord to restore it. For example in Psalm 42 the author is depressed and his soul downcast, so he declares in v. 1-2, 'As a hart longs for flowing streams, so longs my soul for you O God. My soul thirsts for God, for the living God.' He wanted to experience once again the close fellowship and intimacy with the Lord that would restore his soul and bring equilibrium to his innermost being. Similarly, in Psalm 63, when David is pursued by Saul and his men in the wilderness and feels somewhat worn out by this, he says in v. 1: 'O God, you are my God, I seek you, my soul thirsts for you: my flesh faints for you, as in a dry and weary land where there is no water.' His heart's desire in the wilderness reflects the dryness of his soul, and he longs for a fresh touch from the Lord to renew his communion and intimacy with him. In v. 2-7 as David meditates on the Lord, his steadfast love and his presence and power and glory, his soul is satisfied and he sings for joy, as the Lord has answered his prayer in v. 1 for renewed communion with him.

It is informative to look at some of the songs of *'romantic intimacy'* beginning with those of T. Hughes and M. Redman to see how they expresses their love for the Lord. These love songs do not go along the same lines as the model of *'biblical intimacy'* with the Lord that is also explained in depth later from Psalm 119. Instead, they remain at the level of *'romantic intimacy'* that usually does not go beyond focusing on one's feelings. As the Lord calls and commands us to love him and to praise and worship him, we know he delights to hear us express our love for him in our sung worship. On the other hand, the subliminal message songs of *'romantic intimacy'* may give, is that it is sufficient to declare our feelings of love for the Lord. But, biblical love is not only all about feelings: it also involves our soul, mind, will and strength. Are these songs in danger of reflecting a genre that has become enamoured primarily with feelings? Are we deflecting our attention away from the challenge of obeying God's commandments by an excessive focus on our feelings? The following are some examples of the songs of 'romantic intimacy' by T. Hughes and M. Redman.

'If there's one thing' - Tim Hughes 2001.

You called us first to love Your name, to worship You
To please Your heart, our one desire O Lord
If there's one thing we are called to do
It's to love You, to adore You
We will bring our all and worship You
Bow before You, as we love You
Your honour Lord, Your name's renown
We long to see
So let the glory of your name be praised
I will celebrate this love
Jesus you are everything to me
For what more Lord can I do?
I will give this heart, this life to You

In this song there is clearly a genuine desire by Tim to express his love for the Lord. The song begins with statements of truth followed by a response. This song is like a thank you prayer to the Lord for his love and saying that we love you too. This is something that is actually rare in our intercessions. It is also a song of commitment, but, to take this song beyond the level of 'romantic intimacy' the line 'for what more Lord can I do?' could have been elaborated on.

'Jesus You alone' - Tim Hughes 1999.

    Jesus you alone
    Shall be my first love
    My first love
    The secret place and highest
    Praise shall be yours

    To Your throne I'll bring devotion
    May it be the sweetest sound
    Lord this heart is reaching for You now
    So I'll set my sights upon You
    Set my life upon Your praise
    Never looking to another way
    You alone will be my passion
    Jesus, You will be my song

    You will find me longing
    After You
    Day and night I'll lift my eyes
    To seek You
    To seek you
    Hungry for a glimpse of You
    In glory, in glory

This is a lovely song that enables the believer to tell Jesus how much they love him. In it there is a delightful note of intimacy that captures Tim's commitment to the Lord. This is the sort of song that has lyrics that demand to be sung prayerfully. But, does the longing of romantic intimacy in the last verse really add anything to the song?

'Beautiful One' - Tim Hughes 2002.

    Wonderful, so wonderful is Your unfailing love
    Your cross has spoken mercy over me
    No eye has seen, no ear has heard
    No heart can fully know
    How glorious, how beautiful You are

        Beautiful one I love You
        Beautiful one I adore
        Beautiful one my soul must sing

Powerful, so powerful Your glory fills the sky
Your mighty works displayed for all to see
The beauty of Your majesty awakes my heart to sing
How marvellous, how wonderful You are
You've opened my eyes to Your wonders anew
Captured my heart with this love
Cause nothing on this earth is as beautiful as You
    My soul must sing
    Beautiful one I love you X3

This is a love song to Jesus as the 'beautiful' one that has a feeling of romantic intimacy about it. 'Your cross has spoken mercy over me' demands more than just being a statement. The remainder of the verse and chorus about Jesus being so beautiful is presumably a reflection on the cross, but in what ways is not at all obvious because Tim has not spelt out why. To simply say 'Jesus I love you, Jesus I adore you' - I would suggest is more meaningful rather than 'beautiful one.' If Tim's main theme was the unfailing love of Jesus shown by the mercy of the cross and that his heart has been captured by this love - the song would have been much stronger if he had elaborated on these themes, instead of using the word 'beauty' and beautiful.

'Let my words be few' - Matt Redman 2004.

You are God in heaven
And here I am on earth.
So I'll let my words be few.
Jesus I am so in love with You.
And I'll stand in awe of You
Yes I'll stand in awe of You
And I'll let my words be few.
Jesus I am so in love with You.
The simplest of all love songs
I want to bring to you
So I'll let my words be few
Jesus I am so in love with You.

There is something delightful about songs that help the believer to tell the Lord that thy love him. My feeling is that they are best sung prayerfully as they are like thank you songs to Jesus. Clearly, there is a romantic element in telling Jesus I love you a number of times in this song. Any believer singing this would be

curious to know exactly why Matt is so in love with Jesus? To
have gone into some detail about this would have made the
content much stronger and much nearer to the model of *'biblical
intimacy.'*

'Intimacy' - Matt Redman 2005.

> One thing my heart is set upon
> One thing that I would ask
> To know You, Lord, as close as one
> Could hope to be on this earth

>> Intimacy
>> O Jesus, intimacy
>> My treasure will be, O Jesus
>> Your intimacy

> To look upon your beauty, Lord
> Your glory and your heart
> To know You close, and closer still
> With each day upon this earth
> Lord, since the day I saw You first
> My soul was satisfied
> And yet because I see in part
> I'm searching more to find

This song fits the genre of *'romantic intimacy'* as Matt expresses
his desire to know the closeness and intimacy of Jesus in his life.
Yet, it is also a prayer to know the Lord in this way. I would
suggest the answer to this intimacy is given by Jesus in John 14:
21, 23: 'He who has my commandments and keeps them, he it is
who loves me: and he who loves me will be loved by my Father:
and I will love him and manifest myself to him. If a man loves me
he will keep my word and my father will love him, and we will
come to him and make our home with him.' For this song to
beyond the level of romantic intimacy it has to focus in its content
on these words of Jesus.

John Buckeridge, the Editor of Christianity, interviewed Matt
Redman on Premier Radio in 2006 on the topic: 'Worship songs
aren't for the blokes.' This is a slightly shortened version of the
interview that involves one of the most influential artists in
contemporary worship. John said 'I was chatting to someone at

church the other week. He was a blokish sort of bloke who said: 'What is it with worship leaders? Why do they come up with songs that make me feel so uncomfortable?' I said, 'What do you mean?' 'Well I can't just stand there and close my eyes and sing *'how much I love you, I just so love you, oh I love you Jesus.''* I can't sing a love song to Jesus - as a bloke it just doesn't do anything for me.'

'What do you make of that Matt? Do you feel he has a point?' 'I do feel he has a point. I'm definitely revisiting a couple of things I've written. A blokey-bloke who comes in is he going to connect with what's going on? Some of the romantic imagery used in worship, the more I think about it, the more I study Scripture, I'm not so sure about some of this. I am still on a learning curve. I don't have all the answers. 'Beautiful' is a lovely song. I grew up on the Vineyard song and it effected a lot of change in my life. If I revisit that song now, people do not come up to Jesus in the Bible saying 'you are beautiful'- not even in Revelation. The writer is trying to talk about the splendour, radiance and brightness of God. Beautiful in our language has lots of other connotations.

I wouldn't too often use the words 'you are beautiful God,' although Psalm 27:4 talks about the 'beauty of the Lord.' We need to make sure things are water tight Scripturally and also culturally they mean what we think they mean. For blokey-blokes in church these songs can have a whole baggage. Let me give an example. In 'Let my words be few' - if I am totally honest, I regret a little bit ending the song with the line - 'I am so in love with you.' The reason is I know what I mean by that. But if you put a song out there, there are other people who might think that's a bit weird and romantic. That's not what was in my heart. Maybe I should have said 'I am so in awe of you.' It's a learning process and I don't know if I am being too candid.'

In many of the songs of *'romantic intimacy'* the build-up and climax of the lyrics is an intimate encounter between the Lord and the believer that reflects the romantic ideal of total fulfillment between lovers. These songs can be seen to encourage in the believer the expectation God will give them an experience of emotional fulfillment with him. In Scripture God's relationship with people like Moses, Jeremiah or Isaiah, while very intimate, were primarily to empower them to serve the Lord, rather than for an emotional encounter.[1] Many of the songs of *'romantic intimacy'* also suggest that the high point of being a Christian is personal fulfillment in our relationship with God and Christ. The danger this can present is that our faith can become very personal and narrow in outlook - as opposed to engaging with the world.[22]

Many of the songs of *'romantic intimacy'* often refer to God and Christ as 'You' or 'Your,' although on occasions they also refer to them by name. Are we being disrespectful to God and Christ by predominantly referring to them as 'you or your' instead of using their names? Would it not be considered rude and disrespectful to constantly speak to someone we know well and address them by saying 'you' rather than using their name? Clearly, there is only one answer. In every single psalm the name God or Lord or variations of God in Hebrew are used when speaking to God or the Lord or addressing them. There is something lovely in sung worship when we sing to Jesus or to Christ or to God or to the Lord. I would suggest that using 'you' instead devalues what we are saying to them and is in fact very disrespectful. When we only relate to the Trinity by using 'you' or 'your' this prevents Christians cultivating a rich scriptural imagination as Scripture offers many names for God and metaphors about what He is like. There are hundreds of metaphorical references, names, descriptions and allusions to what God, Jesus and the Holy Spirit are like.[23] Romantic worship songs can be helpful in encouraging an intimate, heartfelt relationship with God and Christ, but they should also express loving the Lord with our heart, soul, mind, will and strength. While, the romantic motif is a sound biblical theme when alluding to the Church as the bride of Christ, with Christ as the lover - it is the body of Christ, the Church that is betrothed to Christ not the individual. So, it is appropriate to have songs that express the Church's love for Christ, with lyrics that focus on 'we' and 'our.'

A very large number of contemporary songs are free style in composition and few rhyme. Although an index in songbooks may list pages with biblical references for the songs it is often difficult to identify these references in them. Very few songs are in fact based on a passage of Scripture that unfolds as the song progresses even if they were inspired by a Bible passage. One feature of this genre of songs that clearly stands out is that the overwhelming majority of lyrics are not aesthetically worshipful on their own - they are heavily reliant on the music. Another feature that also clearly stands out is that there is a much greater focus in them on the believer as the object than on God or Christ. Here the believer's focus often remains on them as they attempt to express their feelings for the Lord and ask the Lord to minister to them in some way or another. At the same time there is often an intimacy expressed in the songs in the believer's relationship with the Lord. The following are also songs of 'romantic intimacy.'

'In moments like these' - David Graham 1980.
>In moments like these I sing out a song
>I sing out a love song to Jesus
>In moments like these I lift up my hands
>I lift up my hands to the Lord
>Singing I love you Lord X 3
>I love you.

We do not have an explanation of what these moments signify. Is the author thankful for what Jesus has done for him on a special occasion? Is he praising him because he has had a memorable experience of his love? Why is he singing a love song to Jesus? In keeping with the model of *'biblical intimacy'* with the Lord he could have provided more content in his song to explain the inspiration behind its composition. Then we would have known why he wanted to sing a love song to Jesus.

'Hallelujah'- B. Brown and B. Doerksen 2000 Vineyard.
>Your love is amazing, steady and unchanging
>Your love is a mountain, firm beneath my feet
>Your love is a mystery, how you gently lift me
>When I am surrounded, Your love carries me.
>Hallelujah, hallelujah,
>Hallelujah, Your love makes me sing X 2

>Your love is surprising, I can feel it rising
>All the joy that's growing deep inside of me
>Every time I see you, all your goodness shines through
>And I can feel this God song rising up in me

>Yes you make me sing
>Lord you make me sing, sing, sing
>How you make me sing.

As we read in between the lines of the first verse, it sounds as if the authors are referring to a specific occasion or times when the Lord's love lifted them and carried them through their difficulties. Although, on the other hand, they might be referring in general to the Lord's love. But, in keeping with the model of *biblical intimacy'* with the Lord they could have elaborated more fully as to why the Lord's love is, or was, so amazing to them. How did the Lord express his love for them in concrete ways that led them to be joyful and sing about it?

'Over the mountains and the sea' - Martin Smith 1994.

  Over the mountains and the sea
  Your river runs with love for me
  So I will open up my heart
  And let the healer set me free
  I'm happy to be in the truth
  So I will daily lift my hands
  For I will always sing of
  When Your love came down.

  I could sing
  I could sing of Your love forever
  I will sing
  I could sing of Your love forever X 3

  And O I feel like dancing
  It's foolishness I know
  But when the world has seen the light
  They will dance with joy
  Like we're dancing now

What is immediately apparent is there is no specific mention of the Lord, God or Christ in this song, although 'Your' presumably refers to them. The first verse feels very cryptic. We do not know if the reference to love is general or whether it refers to a specific experience of the Lord's love. The chorus with the heightened refrain on 'Your love' gives the impression of a memorable encounter, but what this is, is never explained. We must assume this is so clear to the author he presumes it will also be clear to the world who will join in his celebrations, although he gives no hint as to how they are going to have such an epiphany. This song would have definitely benefited from following the model of *'biblical intimacy'* with the Lord by clearly explaining the cryptic nature of verse one and also explaining how the world would be enlightened about this love.

Some of the intimate love songs in sung worship can almost be seen to have a subliminal erotic interpretation that likens the relationship with the Lord to that of a human lover. Also, some songs that do not mention God, Christ or the Lord by name can easily be addressed to a person. The genre of *'romantic intimacy'* in worship love songs can be compared to Jesus' words: 'If you keep my commandments you will abide in my love' and 'this is my commandment that you love one another as I have loved you. Greater love has no man than this, that a man lay down his life for his friends' - John 15:11-12. We should not be surprised if some Christians find these songs difficult to relate to as they do not call for a rugged discipleship or a costly love but a sentimental romanticism. Perhaps, we should also sing about how we can serve one another and how we can lay down our lives for one another to express our love for Jesus.

'I give you my heart' - Reuben Morgan 1995
> This is my desire to honour you
> Lord with all my heart I worship you
> All I have within me I give you praise
> All that I adore is in you.
> Lord I give you my heart
> I give you my soul
> I live for you alone
> Every breath that I take
> Every moment I'm awake
> Lord have your way in me.

'Draw me close' - Kelly Carpenter 1994.
> Draw me close to you
> Never let me go
> I lay it all down again
> To hear you say I'm your friend
> You are my desire
> No one else will do
> Cos nothing else could take your place
> To feel the warmth of your embrace
> Help me find the way, bring me back to you

You're all I want
You're all I ever needed
You're all I want
Help me to know you are near.

These two songs also adhere to the model of *'romantic intimacy'* although they can be interpreted as having an erotic slant to them as they have a very personal edge. One has to wonder to what extent songwriters are aware or familiar with The Psalms that express a hunger and a longing for closeness and intimacy with the Lord. It is informative to compare these songs with the model of *'biblical intimacy'* from one of the psalms, Psalm 84. In v. 1-2 the author identifies the Temple with the presence of the Lord. In effect when he says how 'lovely' is your dwelling place O Lord of hosts, he is not praising the architecture of the building. He is delighting in the Lord and extolling how lovely he is. When he says in v. 2, 'My soul longs for, yes faints for the courts of the Lord' again he is not praising the architecture. He is consumed with a longing and passion for the Lord to encounter him in the Temple as it is synonymous with His presence. In v. 3 the psalmist says, 'my heart and flesh sing for joy to the living God.' The anticipation of encountering God's presence to experience an intimacy with him fills the psalmist with great joy and delight. There is a hint in v. 5 that those who will encounter the Lord are those who have obedient hearts. In v. 8 the psalmist hints that the desire and longing for intimacy with the Lord is in fact a prayer. It is a desire that the Holy Spirit has inspired that he has given voice to. So sweet is his close experience of communion and fellowship with the Lord that in v. 10 he extols dwelling in the courts of the temple and being a doorkeeper in the house of God. Not because he is captivated by the Temple and how wonderful it is - but because his heart and soul have been captivated by the Lord.

INTIMACY WITH THE LORD
PSALM 119

The model of *'biblical intimacy'* with the Lord is far richer and more comprehensive and imaginative than the model of *'romantic intimacy'* which is prevalent in our sung worship. This is clearly seen in Psalm 119 as this is the model par excellence of *'biblical intimacy.'* This complex psalm embraces a number of themes. Brueggemann calls this 'a massive intellectual achievement.'[24] It is then somewhat surprising to find that biblical commentators do not tend to devote a great deal of space to it, even though it is the longest psalm with 176 verses. That is apart from J. M. Boice with 100 pages and John Goldingay 2008 with 67 pages. But, they do tell us that this is an acrostic psalm. This means that for each letter of the Hebrew alphabet there is a stanza of eight verses which implies it is carefully constructed. 'Psalm 119 is structured with delicate sophistication about the life of the Spirit. On the one hand, the psalm understands that life with Yahweh is a two-way-street. Torah-Law keepers have a right to expect something from Yahweh. Obedience gives entry to seek God's attention and God's gift…This is the speech of one who has access not because of arrogance, but because of submission. The speech is not unduly deferential and certainly not strident. It is an articulation of legitimate expectation between partners who have learned to trust each other.'[25] Of all the biblical commentators I looked at not one suggested who the author of this complex psalm might be. However, I am inclined to think that it is David for a number of reasons. The intimate knowledge and relationship with the Lord the author of Psalm 119 describes and aspires to is reminiscent of David. Only a man anointed with the Holy Spirit and who had known the Lord closely could have composed a psalm that is resplendent with such emotional intensity. In this psalm David openly shares his love for Lord and his delight in his ways.

We can perceive that the Holy Spirit inspired David to write this psalm although we do not know the circumstances that led to it. We can sum up the essence of this psalm by saying it is about David's love for the Lord and also about his delight in his laws – Word. The psalm describes a single minded determination to keep God's laws. It seems as if the writer is obsessed with God's commandments, his laws, his ordinances, his precepts, his statutes, his truth and his Word. But, his passionate concern is not at all a legalistic one. At the heart of Psalm 119 is David's delight in the Lord and his love for him. Although the Holy Spirit inspired David to write about these things, we should note that it is the Lord who drew him into an intimate relationship with himself.

To delight in the Lord invariably results in delighting in his laws and Word. The converse is also true. To delight in keeping God's laws and Word is a reflection of David's delight in the Lord. The Law was a gift from God and it led him to the Lord: and he knew that his closeness with the Lord depended on keeping his commandments. The Spirit inspired David to write this psalm to show us the closeness we can also aspire to in our relationship with the Lord. An intimacy the Lord desires us to have with him as we learn to delight in him and his Word. As we read Psalm 119 we can perceive in David evidence of an artistic, creative and sensitive temperament. At the same time we discern a tenderness towards the Lord. In v. 10 he says, 'with my whole heart I seek you.' In v. 4 he says, 'In the way of your testimonies I delight as much as in all riches.' In v. 35 he says, 'Lead me in the path of your commandments for I delight in it.' In v. 57 he says, 'The Lord is my portion: I promise to keep your word.'

This passionate '*biblical intimacy*' with the Lord clearly demands a wholehearted commitment to love the Lord and to keep his Word. It also demands diligence to live in submission to the Lord and to his Word. In v. 10 David sums up the desire the Lord put into his heart through the inspiration of the Holy Spirit – 'With my whole heart I seek you, let me not wander from your commandments.' The first sixteen verses of Psalm 119 give an indication of the tenacity required 'to walk in the law of the Lord,' in response to the promptings of the Spirit. This tenacity is described in these verses and is seen by David's actions: to walk in the law: to keep his testimonies: to seek him: to diligently keep: to steadfastly keep: to be fixed on: to learn: to observe: to guard: to not wander: to lay up your word: to declare: to delight: to meditate.

The Lord calls us to be in a close relationship with him and have an intimate walk with him – but it does not come easily. What is demanded is similar to the desire required to acquire wisdom in Proverbs 2: 1–10. Here, the author points out to the young man that to gain wisdom is a demanding and a very strenuous task. To achieve this in v. 2 he has to be attentive to wisdom and incline his heart to understanding. In v. 3 he has to cry out for insight and raise his voice for understanding. In v. 4 he has to seek it like silver and search for it as for hidden treasure. Verse 5 indicates that only then will he understand the fear of the Lord and find the knowledge of God. Verse 6 says 'the Lord gives wisdom and from his mouth come knowledge and understanding.' On the one hand, they are gifts of God's grace. But, these verses also imply the Lord will only give them to the person who wholeheartedly longs for them and seeks them.

Having read the opening verses of Psalm 119: 1-16, one might be led to believe that David enjoyed a carefree life, without any difficulties or troubles full of God's blessings. But, as the psalm progresses this is clearly not true. Interspersed throughout is the allusion to his enemies and their persecution. This theme is representative of many of David's psalms and strongly indicates he is the author of Psalm 119. We see evidence of his enemies in the following verses: 21-23, 42, 51, 61, 69, 78, 84-87, 95, 98, 110, 121, 157 and 161. What is striking about these verses is that while they refer to David's persecution, in every instance he declares his commitment and faithfulness to the Lord. The following verses describe the impact of his enemies upon him. He says in v. 15 'they utterly deride me'– v. 22 'their scorn and contempt of me'– v. 42 'those who taunt me'– v. 69 'they besmear me' – v. 78 'they subvert me' – v. 110 'a snare has been laid for me.' Moreover, on three occasions there comes an appeal for life in the midst of danger, as in verses 169-176. Unsurprisingly, prayer for deliverance is linked to these occasions. We first get a glimpse of David's prayer interspersed in this psalm in v. 25, 'My soul cleaves to the dust: revive me according to your word.' His prayer is repeated in verses 81, 88, 134 and in v. 173, 'Let your hand be ready to help me, for I have chosen your precepts.'

For David who on occasions was involved in battles against Israel's enemies and against Saul, their opposition during his life was a cause of concern for him. This was the reality he faced alongside the reality of knowing the Lord intimately. His faith and love for the Lord was refined and tested in the circumstantial events he was caught up in. Yet he believed that the Lord was involved in his life and caught up in protecting and rescuing him from his enemies. Rather than turn him away from the Lord their persecution taught him to rely on the Lord and trust hjim to save him. (Although on occasions, he failed to turn to the Lord for help, as in 1 Sam. 27 when he turned to Achish and stayed in the land of the Philistines). One of the themes that is interwoven into Psalm 119, alongside that of his enemies and the danger they pose to his life and future, is the theme of 'promise.' This is recorded in verses: 38, 41, 49-50, 58, 76, 82, 116, 123, 133, 140 and 144.

There are two different types of promise David is referring to. The first is a conditional promise which means that God will bless those who keep his laws as stated in Exodus. Failure to keep God's

laws means you forfeit the promised blessing. A conditional
promise is one that David refers to at the beginning of Psalm 119:
1-2. 'Blessed are those whose way is blameless, who walk in the
law of the Lord. Blessed are those who keep his testimonies, who
seek him with their whole heart.' This blessing is in keeping with
God's promises in Exodus. It is also a promise of knowing God's
steadfast love and faithfulness. Having his life threatened by his
enemies and possibly being killed by them is seen by David as a
violation of this promise of blessing. So he claims this promise of
deliverance, protection and salvation. But, there is also another
very important promise that David alludes to as he considers the
possible threat to his life. This is an unconditional promise from
the Lord and does not depend at all on him keeping God's laws. In
effect God has promised to bless David regardless of his obedience
or failure. This unconditional promise can be found in Psalm 89:
3-4 and in 2 Samuel 7: 8-29.

Psalm 89: 3-4:
I have made a covenant with my chosen one,
I have sworn to my servant David:
I will establish your descendents for ever,
and build your throne for all generations.

2 Samuel 7: 11-16:
Moreover the Lord declares to you that the Lord will make
you a house. When your days are fulfilled and you lie
down with your fathers, I will raise up your offspring after
you, who shall come forth from your body and I will
establish his kingdom. He shall build a house for my name
and I will establish the throne of his kingdom for ever.
I will be his father and he shall be my son. When he
commits iniquity I will chasten him with the rod of men,
with the stripes of the sons of men: but I will not take my
steadfast love from him, as I took it from Saul whom I put
away before you. *And your house and your kingdom shall*
be made sure for ever before me: your throne shall be
established for ever.

Even in the context of his intimate walk with the Lord and the
demands this makes on David, he tenaciously reminds God of his
promise and in prayer asks him to fulfill it. Bearing in mind
David's experience of the Lord and the declaration of his love for

him and his delight in his ways, it does seem an extraordinary failure by him that led to his sin with Bathsheba, which in turn resulted in God's punishments upon his own family. But despite this God kept his promise to David and Solomon inherited the kingdom, although later in his life it was divided due to his sin with his concubines and foreign wives. As David was a direct ancestor of Christ, God fulfilled his promise to him about having a direct descendent on his throne.

The other prayer that David offered to the Lord was for help to keep his commandments and to love him. This is seen in v. 10, 'With my whole heart I seek you, let me not wander from your commandments.' Verses 32-36 are also a good example of this.

> I will run in the way of your commandments when you enlarge my understanding. Teach me O Lord the way of your statutes and I will keep it to the end. Give me understanding that I may keep your law and observe it with my whole heart. Lead me in the path of your commandments for I delight in it. Incline my heart to your testimonies and not to gain.

Psalm 119 epitomises what '*biblical intimacy*' with the Lord is at its best. It represents the Lord's desire for us to have a intimate walk with him. It also symbolises the reality of our lives alongside our own particular difficulties and trials. It presents us with the challenge to nurture a tender relationship with the Lord, and it reminds us that we prayerfully need his help to fulfill the potential of a '*biblical intimacy*' with the Lord.

PREACHING, PRAYER & SILENCE

In contemporary and charismatic worship the lectern may be a music stand that is also used as a pulpit. Yet liturgically there is a symbolic significance attached to it. A proper lectern is more than just a place to put our notes on especially if it also doubles as a pulpit. It speaks to us about the importance of Scripture, along with the central place of preaching the Word of God. For instance, to have a solid oak or ash lectern/pulpit signifies the authority of God's Word, as it is read and expounded. One of the most surprising things about Evangelical worship in both traditional and contemporary services is that there is often only one Scripture reading. The impact of God's Word is not solely confined to preaching. This can be just as powerful when read out aloud as this allows the Lord to speak directly through his Word to his people. Is it time to elevate the reading of God's Word and to have three Scripture readings: one from the O. T., one from the N. T. and also a Psalm? Alternatively, one from the O. T., one from the N. T. and a Gospel reading? A Eucharistic church would invariably include three readings. God's Word has an intrinsic authority as it is read out aloud and it enhances the biblical content of our worship when we include more Scripture readings.

In contemporary worship public prayer can fall into the pattern of a personal informal style. One long informal prayer often embraces all the topics without any response for the congregation to participate in. The traditional manner of leading public prayer as is found in Common Worship – the Anglican Service book, is a more suitable model. This begins with prayers of thanksgiving followed by the intercessions for the wider church, the world and the local church and community. This allows many different topics to be introduced and invites the congregation's participation using the refrain and response: 'Lord in your mercy – Hear our prayer.' Yet, I am constantly surprised, by how rare it is to hear prayers in public begin with thanksgiving to God and Christ.

The Lord's Prayer is rarely used in contemporary worship. This omission is highlighted by Stephen Croft, Bishop of Sheffield. He reported in the Church of England Newspaper on 3rd Aug. 2007, a fascinating but worrying conversation over supper with a group at a clergy conference. 'I asked how the Lord's Prayer was being used in churches with an informal liturgy and a charismatic tradition. They admitted it wasn't being used much at all. But then a couple went on to tell me that the whole tradition of intercessory prayer no longer had a place in their informal worship...Our worship is focused around a time of praise then the sermon and then personal ministry time.' Croft expressed his concern in response to this when he replied: 'As a regular habit, it would be a sign to me that our worship is becoming very introverted and centred on ourselves...I leave on one side the strange situation we have been led to by liturgical revision where no group of Christians can say the Lord's prayer in an identical way. We need to make sure in our existing churches and new communities that the Lord's Prayer is understood and prayed and taught – that it forms and shapes our discipleship.'

In our worship we may find we are bombarded with stressful levels of loud music. This reminds us that silence is an essential and integral aspect of worship. Silence can help us to gather our thoughts at the beginning of a Service to be aware of God's presence. Silence before the confession and after the absolution can help us to take in God's forgiveness. Silence after the Scripture readings and the sermon is also helpful as we respond to hearing God speak to us through his Word. Silence can also be appropriate when we have sung our worship songs and sensed the stillness of God's presence amongst us.

INFORMALITY

A characteristic of contemporary and charismatic worship is the informal atmosphere and the casual dress of the leaders. This has become more common in the past 20-30 years. It would not be surprising if this style was identified with John Wimber at the beginning of the 80s when he came to this country. Carol Wimber in her book about her husband mentions the background of how the Vineyard Fellowship was established. Originally, they were Quakers, but after they started moving in the realm of the gifts of the Holy Spirit they were asked to leave the denomination. A group of 60, twenty or so adults and young people aged 16-25 not counting young children, were invited to be affiliated to the Calvary Chapel and as a fellowship to be based in Yorba. Carol says of their first meeting: 'What has come to be synonymous with the Vineyard, the causal dress code, was certainly evident that morning. Most of them wouldn't have even worn shoes except that it was raining. Some of us sat on chairs but just as many sat on the floor like they were used to doing.'[26]

Causal dress and informality were introduced before Wimber and have been around in Anglican Family Services designed to appeal to non-church goers. Those who embrace this style probably do so as it is appeals to young people and young adults and is seen to be cool. As a minister who was formerly in fashion, I am inclined to think that those who lead public worship should dress up rather than down. On occasions I have observed that the person leading the service is not that smartly dressed. It may be timely to reflect on whether we have gone too far with this informal style and casual dress and ask exactly what this is saying about God, our faith and our worship? Is it time to question the philosophy and theology behind this model and think about its implications more carefully? Mark Ashton the Vicar of the Round Church in Cambridge, that meets at St. Andrew the Great, highlights the impression of superficiality that may be communicated when leading services in an informal manner.

> The person leading the service must seek to achieve a balance between gripping the interest and attention of the congregation and communicating the seriousness of what is happening. Some service leading is good at holding attention but communicates a sense of superficiality.[27]

In this informal style of worship on occasions the manner of leading can feel like a compere fronting a show that borders on entertainment. But there is nothing novel in this approach. Just under thirty years ago an Anglican minister I knew well discarded his clerical robes and collar and led services in a suit. At the time this was a radical approach. But this felt more like entertainment than worship. David Stancliffe, Bishop of Salisbury, echoes his concern about the way worship is often led:

> I mind a lot about worship and wonder at the quality of what is offered in some places in this most important area of the Church's life. In an age when the standards of public performance are so high, how do worshippers manage to keep on going to church faithfully when the way the worship is prepared and offered is often so dire: when it is frequently confused with entertainment, and when it is led by those who apparently have no idea about what they are doing, or professional competence in doing it?[28]

Those accustomed to an informal style of worship may feel this is somewhat of a caricature and overlooks the fact it may be considered to be culturally relevant. But, there can be a downside to this, as it can feel as if our worship is *'lite'* and has been *'dumbed down.'* If the theology behind the informal approach is a desire to embrace the immanence of God, we have to ask ourselves to what extent it cloaks his transcendence?' We may be *'chummy'* with God in our colloquial chats with him, but leading worship in this way can seem too casual and lead to complacency: and perhaps inadvertently lead to a lack of reverence for the Lord and detract from our worship.

This may well be a timely reminder that the Church is called to be separate from the world in its character as it is holy. And the Church at worship is radically different because it is subversive and counter-cultural as it challenges many of the values of the world. We may well ask whether Christian worship should be led with reverence and a godly fear for the Lord? Bearing in mind the attention to detail God required of worship in the Old Testament, (see ch.1), is it time to question the ethos our informal style of worship embraces? Is it time to concede that a more formal manner of leading Services, albeit in an informal setting, may reflect a more reverent approach and atmosphere in our worship of the Lord? Might this also be more evangelistic in appealing to outsiders and their perception of God and Christian worship?

CONFESSION

In contemporary worship the confession tends to be over quickly and often does not have much biblical content. Equally, when a confession is used that someone has composed this can also lack substance. Having a corporate confession without any Scriptural introduction and time to reflect on what we are coming to confess to the Lord, does not help the congregation to deal with their sin. The confession has three component parts and it is helpful to bear these in mind when leading others in this act of worship. '1. The biblical injunction to confess. 2. The right attitude of confession, humble, penitent, obedient, honest. 3. The character of God, he is Almighty seated on a royal throne: but is also a heavenly Father, of infinite goodness and mercy, gracious and ready to forgive.'[29] It may be helpful to those leading worship to use these principles as a guideline for choosing or writing a corporate confession and to ensure that it is biblically substantial.

If the confession comes near the beginning of a Service time has to be given to prepare peoples' hearts so they can meaningfully participate. For Anglicans the confession from the Communion Service can be used. The 'Collect for Purity' from Communion can also be used as a preparation for confession in other Services. For instance, this can be sung 2-3 times before the confession and can be followed by verses of Scripture that remind us of God's forgiveness. Alternatively, 'Your Blood Speaks' by Matt Redman (No: 150 Soul Survivor 2006), or 'By Your Blood' (Hosanna Music 1991) can be sung. After this silence allows the Holy Spirit to search peoples' hearts. Equally, Scripture can be read as part of the preparation before the confession. The opportunity can be taken to vary where the confession comes. Sometimes it may be appropriate to have this as part of the intercessions or after the sermon. On occasions after the absolution a song can express the gratitude in peoples' hearts for God's forgiveness. Ensuring that the confession is a substantial act of worship, allows the Lord to minister to those whose hearts are burdened by the guilt of sin.

In the Anglican Communion Service a weakness of the corporate confession lies in the fact it is general rather than specific. Should we be taking into account in the confession, not only the sins we have committed, but also sins of the imagination and the sins of omission? Here it is particularly interesting to note what Sigmund Mowinckel says about the Penitential Psalms.

> It is part of old Israelite mentality and of the way of feeling and thinking in The Psalms, that the poet will try to give as strong expression as possible in the confession of sins…there can be no doubt at all that in The Psalms we do find evidences of a really deep and spiritualised consciousness of sin.[30]

Living in a culture where the notion of sin is weak, it may well be timely to use the Penitential Psalms that were acknowledged by the Ancient Church – 6: 32: 38: 51: 130 and 143, on which to base our models of confession. We can learn not to be embarrassed to specifically name the sins we have committed, along with sins of the imagination and the sins of omission, so that we may have assurance of the Lord's forgiveness. James 5: 18 says: 'Therefore confess your sins to one another and pray for one another that you may be healed.' General or superficial confessions can result in our not being thoroughly cleansed from our sins – because we have not thoroughly confessed them. It would be beneficial to any Christian community to teach its members about confession from these Penitential Psalms – not only for their benefit but as a means of outreach, in a society permeated by sinful practices with no means of absolution.

Having spent time thinking about confession, I have been struck by the importance of *'confessing and naming'* our sins to God in worship. John Goldingay highlights this aspect from Psalm 32. He points out that to keep quiet is not a mark of Old Testament piety and gives the impression, and raises the suspicion, a person is concealing something. He says: 'If the worshipper covered over wrongdoing instead of acknowledging it – then Yahwh would not cover it over. Because the worshipper did not cover it over or stopped doing so, Yahwh has done so' – Psalm 32: 5.[31]

Similarly, J. Mays also emphasises that confession of sin must be said to God, as secret remorse or intimations of guilt are not confession. He believes that such silence must be broken in God's presence and also when we have wronged someone. Because silence can negatively affect relationships and can reflect stubborn pride or the fear of being found out. Confession of sin to God, is also confession of faith in God. He also points out that confession of sin must be made with integrity which Psalm 32: 1 refers to by the phrase: 'in whose spirit there is no deceit.' Because, although God is not deceived, the sinner may deceive himself and others too.[32] The apostle John in his first letter also echoes the importance of confessing sin when he says in ch. 1: 8-9: 'If we say we have no sin we deceive ourselves and the truth is not in us. If we confess our sin God is faithful and just and will forgive us our sin and cleanse us from all unrighteousness.'

When there is a Healing Service people can come forward and kneel to receive prayer. I am inclined to think there should also be the opportunity for people to come forward and kneel as an act of penitence. This may be valued when they are burdened by the guilt of their sin or have been through a phase when they have struggled with temptation. There may also be those who would value this because their failure in the past still troubles them. In the silence of their hearts as they kneel they can confess their sin to the Lord, as the minister then pronounces God's forgiveness. Alternatively, they may wish to read out a prayer of confession and then receive God's forgiveness. This can be very meaningful if the corporate confession and absolution is not dealing with their feelings of failure or guilt. To include this act of public penitence allows a corporate identify with those who go forward. It is also a sign the Christian community acknowledges Christ's forgiveness to them. This has the potential to be a very meaningful and powerful aspect of our worship. I myself as a minister would value the opportunity to go forward in such an act of public penitence.

MUSIC

In 'Resounding Truth' – Christian wisdom in the world of music, J. Begbie reminds us of the role of music in the Hebrews Scriptures, especially in relation to praise. 'Liturgical music is reported to have become a regular institution in Israel in the era of David and Solomon, along with the establishment of professional musicians drawn from the Levites. In 1 and 2 Chronicles, David's founding of the Temple choir and its patronage by his successors, the organisation of the musicians, the instruments used and the place of music in temple worship are all described.

In an important dissertation John Kleining has sketched the key dynamics of the way music in worship is presented in Chronicles. He traces a twofold movement from God to worshippers and from the worshippers to God. On the one hand, *singing is announced, and became a vehicle of, the presence of the Lord and his people* (e.g. 1 Chron. 16: 10-11).

> Through the ritual performance of choral music during the oblation of the burnt offering, the singers presented the Lord to his assembled people. They evoked the Lord and announced his presence to the congregation…they spoke for God to his people. As they sang their songs of praise, they announced the Lord's acceptance of his people, and declared his favourable disposition to them: they also proclaimed the Lord's deliverance of his people and secured his intervention against their enemies.'[33]

Begbie also points out that instruments seem to have been caught up in the movement from God to his people and from the people to God. Three groups of instruments were used in Temple worship, trumpets, symbols and strings. The trumpets proclaimed the presence of the Lord, were closely associated with the divine presence and were regarded as 'holy vessels' and could only be played by the priests. They also announced the presentation of the burnt offering and called the people to prostrate themselves. Similarly, the symbols proclaimed God's gracious presence and announced his acceptance of the burnt offering. They were also used to introduce the singing, to call the congregation to attend to the performance of sacred song. Lyres and harps and stringed instruments could announce the Lord's presence and accompany songs of praise.[34] It was important to be aware the Levites offered song on *behalf* of the congregation not *instead* of them. And they could be invited to sing along with them –1 Chron.16: 8-13, 16: 36b. The congregation became an active partner in praise.[35]

We are all impacted by music in different ways. When we go shopping in spacious arcades we have soothing classical music in the background. When we go to a movie half the sound track is likely to be classical music. When youngsters use video games they are likely to be accompanied by music too. 'And on Sundays we go to church and a great deal of the service may include music…Yet many of us rarely if ever stop to think about what music is, how it works, what it might be doing to us, and what we might be doing with it. Christians are no exceptions…one needs to be honest and admit that what is going on musically outside of the church is often far more interesting and boundary breaking than what goes on inside it.'[36]

In church life a great deal of music in contemporary sung worship sounds pretty much the same, yet we can be far more selective in our choice of music. For example on Easter Sunday in 2007, I led the 9am Communion Service in my church without any hymns. Attendance is usually around 20 and it seemed appropriate to have some music so I played a track from Handel's Messiah – 'I know that my Redeemer liveth.' There was a profound stillness amongst us as this captured the joy and wonder of Christ's resurrection. R. Kidd an American Professor in worship recalls how shortly after he became a Christian that he was introduced to Handel's Messiah at Christmas time. 'I was completely unprepared for the experience. It's not that I had never heard any of the music before. But I had never heard it in context, all at once, or, more importantly, from the inside, from a posture of faith. Minutes into the program I was weeping. I was overwhelmed by the beauty, the majesty, the poetry, the melding of the passion and thoughtfulness, of loveliness and truth – the things that make Handel's *Messiah* the special phenomenon it is. I felt bathed in a new existential awareness.'[37]

Having a marvellous piece of music like Handel's Messiah is a reminder of the sacramental dimension of music which can bring a tangible sense of God's presence. In his essay, 'Real Presences,' Steiner refers to sacramental as his conviction that music puts our being in touch with that which transcends the sayable and that which outstrips the analysable.'[38] Rudolph Otto also attempts to capture the sacramental dimension in music. He observes, 'that worship has a natural affinity with music. The object of religious awe or reverence cannot be fully determined conceptually: it is non-rational, as is the beauty of a musical composition, which no less eludes complete conceptual analysis.'[39]

R. Kidd speaks about classical music in worship. He believes Christ inspires people from all walks of life, including the wealthy and privileged, the educated and powerful.

> Out of their training and resources, 'classical' or 'high art' musicians create music that answers to important dimensions of Christ's own person...Because he is the very Logos of God and agent of creation, Jesus is deserving of the most elegant, the most intellectually rigorous and challenging – and the most passionately romantic – aesthetic expressions of worship imaginable. Christ merits majestic worship. For many people, and for good reason, the attraction of a classical aesthetic is that it connotes transcendence, elegance and excellence – and is therefore especially apposite to worship of the exalted Christ.[40]

Kidd is struck by the fact that Johann Sebastian Bach crafted music which adorns the nobility of our Saviour and it has been rightly said that Western music is pre-Bach and post-Bach. His nearly 300 church cantatas, of which 200 survive, define what it is to wed the biblical story to musical craftsmanship – the cantatas are, to borrow a term...'sermons in music.' Singer and writer Jane Stuart Smith likens them to Rembrandt paintings:

> The cantatas join the Bible, music and history into a unified whole – the same thing Rembrandt did in his etchings and paintings, expressing scriptural truth by means of great art.

> Bach brought to their pinnacle two musical genres that are largely the province of the church: the cantata and the passion. His Passion According to St. Matthew and his Passion according to St. John are masterpieces of classical musicianship, as they weave together challenging music with contemporary congregational hymns.[41]

Kidd is attracted to Bach because he believes that he embodies the voice of Christ as the One who sings in the City of God and because his work is a rich testament to the power of Christ to wed head and heart. 'The glory of Bach lies in the way he places disciplined musical craftsmanship in service of God's great romance...His music incarnates impeccable orthodoxy and indescribable passion and his theology is entirely submitted to Scripture and the creeds.'[42]

He also thinks, 'Christ is fond of classical music and wants his people to explore it. This kind of artistic expression is true to majesty, it embodies his grandeur. At every turn, classical music presents us with another Christian masterpiece to be reckoned with – from just about anything by Bach...and from Handel's Messiah to Paul Hindemith's Mathis der Maler and his Noblissima Visone. Also classical music puts us on the stage where the great conversation about the relationship between the 'true' and the 'beautiful' is carried out. Christ sings through Bach and kin: there is an expansiveness of spirit Christ would inculcate in us and which art of this kind fosters.'[43]

Clearly, music in the Christian church has an influential role in our worship. Depending on the make-up of a congregation there may well be a number of gifted musicians in their midst who have played in an orchestra or in a band of some sort. At the same time members of the congregation are likely to appreciate a wide range of music even if they are not musicians. Yet, in worship, music is not something we think about in isolation. Music, whether it is an organ, a piano, a band or an orchestra, along with the hymns and songs, can provide a unity to the component parts of our worship and enhance it. Charlotte Kroeker believes the 'nature of church music is interdisciplinary.'[44] She justifies this by saying:

> Church music is in the service of the liturgy, so liturgy matters. Church music at its best is a way to understand theology, so theology matters. When worship is crafted well it ministers, so the ministry and pastoral aspects of church music matter. Music in Christian worship is participatory, so the knowledge and experience of the congregation matter.[45]

Music in relation to these other disciplines matters precisely because it is connected to them. Music is important because of the influence it can have on these other aspects of Christian worship. The music along with what we sing can either enhance or detract from these other disciplines. This inter-relatedness allows us to question our choice of music and hymns/songs. For example, what theology do our hymns/songs contain or express? How does the choice and style of the music enhance our liturgy and our worship? What pastoral impact does the music and what we sing have? How are they building our corporate faith and identity as a community? Bob Kauflin a worship leader thinks that we can be tempted to choose songs because of the music rather than the theological content. He believes we need to realise that when words are combined with music we can be deceived. Music can make shallow lyrics sound deep. A great rhythm section can make drivel sound profound and make you want to sing it again. If the words are theologically shallow or vague music won't add anything. It will only give the illusion that the words are substantive. It's not that music is irrelevant. If great words are being sung to terrible music no one will remember them or want to sing them. But according to the Lord's command, what should be dwelling in us richly is the Word of Christ not musical experiences. The bottom line is: 'Sing God's Word. Lyrics matter more than music. Truth transcends tunes.'[46]

Harold Best in 'Unceasing Worship' speaks about music and its unique role. He comments on Eph. 5: 19-2- and Col. 3: 16. 'But, be filled with the Spirit, addressing one another in psalms and hymns and spiritual songs, singing and making melody to the Lord with all your heart, always and for everything giving thanks in the name of our Lord Jesus Christ to God the Father.' 'Let the Word of Christ dwell in you richly, as you teach and admonish one another in all wisdom, and as you sing psalms and hymns and spiritual songs, with thankfulness in your hearts to the Lord.' He believes Paul showed remarkable intellectual thoroughness and conceptual accuracy in these two passages because the importance of them is twofold. One is concerned with the role of the text and the other with the role of music, as two completely separate but coordinated actions, fulfilling two functions and going in two separate directions.

First, we are told that we are to teach and admonish with psalms, hymns and spiritual songs. What do we teach? We teach truth and music cannot teach truth. Only truth can teach truth. Therefore, we can assume that it is the text, the Word, that teaches and admonishes.[47]

Best also says, 'Excellent church music…must be embedded, not primarily in the nature of music and musical types, standards, practices and scholarly excellence, but in a bed-rock of theological perspective.'[48] As we experience a revolution in contemporary Christian music around the world, we should have an intellectual and theological rationale to answer questions about the role of music in worship. Without a biblically informed model we run the risk of producing worship music that is inarticulate and driven by the latest cultural musical trends. Concerning the function of worship music, David Pass, a worship scholar believes that we should begin with the nature of the church. He says: 'The nature of church music is determined by the nature of the church, and the nature of the church is determined by its mission.' In other words, as we understand the nature of the church, we understand how worship, and worship music should function.[49]

According to New Testament scholars the nature of the Church has a triangular base derived from Acts 2:42. This embraces the three foundational aspects of the church: *kerygma (proclamation), koinonia (fellowship) and leitourgia (service, ministry, worship).* D. Pass sees these three aspects as inter-connected and necessary for the church to fulfill its mission in the world. Therefore, if the mission of the church dictates its nature, and by implication the nature of church music, then balanced worship music should reflect these three aspects *'regularly, creatively, systematically and carefully.'*[50] Problems can occur in worship when there is a lack of balance among these three aspects. Because they are inextricably intertwined, changes or deficiencies in one will, affect the others. If there is too much *koinonia* for example, worship may lose its moorings in the *kerygma* since the community depends on the gracious acts of God in Christ (1 Cor. 1: 18-25). If *koinonia* loses touch with its *kerygmatic* basis, then it has no option but to depend more on its own resources whether those be cultural, political, aesthetic, or social, rather than biblical. In effect, worship that represents the mission and communication of the church will have a balance of *kerygmatic, koinonia and leitourgic* expression.[51]

HYMNS

As you look through well known hymns, a theme evolves through the verses and you often sense the writer has penned them from a profound experience of God and Christ. On occasions you can sense this is also true of contemporary songs. There are books written that share the stories behind the composition of well-known hymns. These testify to the authors' spiritual experiences that led to their inspiration to write them. See 'An Annotated Anthology Of Hymns' by J. R. Watson, Oxford University Press and preaching on hymns by F. Colquhoun, Mowbray.

Redman in 'The Heart Of The Worship Files' mentions that a friend gave him a copy of an old Methodist Hymnbook published in Baltimore in 1849. As he looked through this he was struck by the tremendous diversity of biblical themes it contained. The attributes of God included his wisdom, holiness, justice, goodness, truth, faithfulness, trinity, love, eternity, omnipresence and omnipotence. He indicates the extraordinary breadth of topics these hymns covered and concluded that it inspires and encourages him in his songwriting. He says: 'Let us build a greater vocabulary of songs, that we might more worthily magnify His name and more capably serve God's church as lead worshippers.'[52]

It is no surprise to learn that Isaac Watts who wrote over 400 hymns, was an educated man and a prolific author who wrote sixty books and who had studied several languages.[53] It is also not surprising to learn that Charles Wesley's hymns:

> ...are controlled by a craftsmanship which came from his classical education and by a natural poetic skill. Again and again a line or a verse of his hymns seems to be exactly right, to say what it wants to say with a richness of vocabulary and an economy of diction, and instantly recognisable as the work of a master.[54]

It is interesting to note that traditional hymns are not that old. Isaac Watts the most famous early father of English hymns had them published in the 18th Century. His hymns include: 'O God, Our Help In Ages Past,' 'When I Survey The Wondrous Cross' and 'Joy To The World.' His hymns were written to tie in with the meanings of his sermons. He believed they had to be more than just the repetition of Scripture and that authentic Christian worship had to include original personal expressions of faith. It is Watts more than any other man who established the model for hymns we sing today. He saw his task as writing for ordinary people and hymns were intended to be read as poetry. By the end of the 19th Century there were around 400,000 hymns in use and it is reckoned that out of these there are only about 200 really fine hymns.[55] A salutary lesson for today's song-writers.

Hymns can unite a congregation with wonderful harmonies and meaningful lyrics and they can also be profoundly moving when sung by choirs. Hymns such as 'Abide with me' which is sung on occasions at rugby international matches in Britain can still evoke powerful religious feelings. Hymns can teach biblical truths and convey the essence of Christian discipleship. They can also tell the narrative of God's stories from the Bible. The hymnbook Common Praise – 2000 contains some modern hymns along with traditional ones. Many of these former remind me of the fellowship I grew up in as a boy and I find the Lord still speaks to me and touches me through them.

As we trace the history of hymns from the medieval era (600-1400 C.E.) we find that in the West the Office hymns evolved in the monastic tradition by writers such as Bernard of Cluny, Bernard of Clairvaux, Abelard and Hildegard. They all produced Greek and Latin hymns and Benedictine monks systematically worked their way through The Psalter. The great majority of these hymns were sung by clergy or clergy dominated choirs and very little if anything was sung by ordinary Christians, so there was a lack of congregational participation. By the time of the Reformation in the early 16th century this process was reversed. People like Martin Luther and John Knox gave rise to a new wave of hymns and new psalm translations for congregational use. On the other hand Calvin insisted congregations only sang The Psalms.[56] In the 18th century in England, Isaac Watts paraphrased most of The Psalms, omitting the ones that called for vengeance on one's enemies. The Wesleys were Anglican priests in the high church tradition and were influenced by the spirituality of the Moravian missionaries. They founded the Methodist societies that in time became the Methodist Church and wrote around 7,000 hymns. Charles wrote many Eucharistic hymns that were published in 1745 as 'Hymns on the Lord's Supper.' This hymnbook was the most circulated and continuously used of all Methodist hymn books.[57] In the second half of the 19th century an important hymnbook, 'Hymns Ancient

& Modern' 1860-61, was produced and edited by Henry Baker and William Monk. At the same time in America the Gospel hymn tradition evolved along with black spirituals hymns which included some powerful laments.[58]

The second half of the 20th century spawned a new wave of song writers such as Graham Kendrick, Stuart Townend, Matt Redman and Tim Hughes. Since the 60s this resulted in a constant stream of new songs played on the guitar and then more latterly by a band. As a result for many congregations towards the end of the 20th century, worship songs have often been closely aligned with contemporary forms of worship. In turn, music in this genre reflects the pop, rock model led by a band. Here traditional hymns have taken a backseat and often have a low profile and in my experience are not included very often. What is striking about this genre of music is that it does not necessarily reflect the range of music congregations might listen to. They are likely to come across well known classical musical scores when they see the latest movies, such as the Lord of The Rings. Shopping arcades and supermarkets may also subtly provide soothing background classical music as we shop. Christians also listen to music on the radio and that too may be classical or middle of the road. It goes without saying that music impacts a considerable part of our lives. We may well ask to what extent do congregations actually listen to pop and rock music outside of corporate worship? The irony for many Christians is that the music they worship to on Sundays, may bear little resemblance to their taste in music. Bearing these things in mind, it is surprising that Christians do not actually demand a greater choice of music in their corporate worship!

TRANSFORMING WORSHIP

When Isaiah encountered God (Isaiah ch. 6), the Lord didn't reveal himself in all his holiness and glory to give him a feeling of intimacy. He came to cleanse, commission and transform him. Through encountering God in worship he had a new vision of God and a renewed vision to serve. Matt Redman says:

> Isaiah is broken, stunned and shaken in the presence of God. But this brokenness is not a destructive thing: God is stripping him apart in order to put him back as a stronger, purer worshipper – a worshipper whose heart cry is: 'Here am I Lord send me.' Of course there is a time to be joyful

in worship, content and even comfortable. But there are times when God will make us distinctly uncomfortable. He puts us under the spotlight of his holiness where we begin to search our hearts more closely.[59]

When Paul wrote to the Corinthian Christians he addressed a charismatic church that used spiritual gifts in their worship. Although this caused problems it is striking to note in 2 Cor. 3: 18, that he refers to a truly charismatic phenomenon when he says: 'And we all with unveiled face beholding the glory of the Lord are being changed from one degree of glory into another.' It is clear as you read this letter that this was not the case in this church. Nevertheless, Paul raises the possibility of spiritual transformation using Moses as an example of someone who used to stand in the presence of the Lord. Matt Redman perceives: 'Moses was ushered into an incredible level of revelation, so deep into the heart of God's glory that his face is actually shining. So radiant in fact that the people were afraid to look at him…That passage gives us insight into two things: the deep revelation of God and the change it brings to those who experience it. And the greater the revelation the greater the transformation.'[60]

If we see the ultimate aim of worship as the Lord coming among us and revealing his glory, the climax of our worship is not intimacy – but to be immersed in the overwhelming glory of the presence of the Lord. And to be transformed more into the likeness of Christ, so that our faces and personalities radiate his glory.

APPENDIX

Jarrod Cooper, author of 'King of Kings Majesty,' had the courage to step out in a new direction in worship after a ministry trip to Africa, where he experienced the glory of God moving through the Holy Spirit in a powerful way in signs and wonders. Although while he was there he was invited to lead worship he declined because he felt out of place. As the days passed by he realised that he was locked in a blueprint of worship that revolved around western culture.

> God wasn't readily available in his power. In reality he had to move within certain boundaries and cultural expectations. Perhaps that's why I had never experienced the dead raised, the ground shaken, or governments enlisting my opinions.[1]

Also, his time in Africa became a wake up call as he experienced what may be termed a *'divine discontent'* about worship. He wondered, 'Could there possibly be more to worship than the 'fast few songs, few slow songs' worship time? Is there some way we can go beyond this current culture of worship, a design that, apart from some new songs, seems little changed since the 1970s? Is it possible for the church to become a place of prayer and power? Can we really be overwhelmed by the power and glory of God week after week?'[2]

Jarrod saw three weaknesses in the contemporary worship culture. The first he saw as being one of predictability where we can almost tell exactly what is going happen in our worship. As he travelled, ministered and spoke to people, he perceived the second sign was one of prayerlessness and the third as 'worship leader dependency' 'Have we become so dependent on music rather than mature Christianity and Spirit-filled leadership that we have bred a weak, entertainment-orientated version of Christianity? These and other signs were apparent through my own early years of worship-leading in the 1980s and early 1990s. Numerous questions brought enough frustrations to my life to cause me to step out on a journey seeking more.'[3]

In his search for a new blueprint of worship Jarrod was rather radical in his response, although he believed the solution was a simple one. He believed it was necessary to remove the musicians for a time and learn to be church without them and re-establish a true following of the Spirit. As a result the church stopped all music and began a journey discovering what prayer, corporate worship and public gatherings may have been like for the early church. 'For three months it was Hell! We taught and taught: how to meet God, how to pray fervently, how to hear God's voice, sing in tongues, overcome the feelings of the flesh and how to be an initiator instead of a spectator in worship...Congregation members begged me, on their knees, to play some music, "Please – just one little note to help us feel like worshipping!" they said. My resolve complete, we struggled on through the pain barriers to reach a new place in worship – and it was worth it.

After three months of painful growth we arrived at our first mountain top. We could now pray in the Spirit, crying out in intercessions for half an hour at a time on a Sunday morning. I remember seeing young children weeping, crying out to God for the lost. At times we had to shout out to guide the enthusiastic prayers, they were so fervent! I saw people saved right in the middle of our praying in tongues. I recall seeing a visiting leader's wife refuse to come into our building, kneeling in the entrance saying, 'The holiness of God is so strong in there – I can't go in!' I remember the congregation, children included, singing in tongues for over an hour with no musical backing...I remember seeing people healed as we sang and people walking to the front in tears, overcome by God's presence – we had simply sung in tongues.

As far as we knew how we let God lead our services. Although they were now led by experienced ministers full of the Spirit who were sensitive to God's leading. You never knew what would happen next: prayer, listening to God, team ministry, preaching, prophetic action, quietness, spontaneous song, teaching, dancing. Some meetings were all teaching, some all worship, others were family services or fun times. We made many mistakes but that was covered in love and the fruit was well worth it...The amazing thing was that for months not a note of music was played...After several months we restored music to our *new worship.* The music ministry had become what I believe God intended it to be. A tool to enhance and accompany the worship of a powerful, prophetic, self-initiating body of believers.'[4]

FOOTNOTES

INTRODUCTION

1. B. Kauflin Worship Matters Crossway 2008 250
2. Ibid 251
3. Liturgy And Liberty J. Leach Marc 1993 22
4. Living Liturgy J. Leach Kingsway 1997 14
5. Ibid 14
6. J. Pritchard The Life & Work of A Priest SPCK 2007 11-12
7. J. Gledhill Leading A Local Church – In The Age
    Of The Spirit SPCK 2003 38
8. G. Kendrick Worship Kingsway 1984 23
9. D. Peterson Engaging With God – A Biblical Theology Of
    Worship Apollos 1992 17
10. Ibid 19
11. Ibid 46
12. M. Dawn Reaching Out Without Dumbing Down quotes
    W. Temple Eerdmans 1995 80
13. C. Cocksworth Holy, Holy, Holy – Worshipping The Trinitarian
    God DLT 2004 32-33
14. J. F. White Christian Worship Abingdon 1986 17
15. Ibid 17
16. C. Cocksworth ibid 145, 163, 189-190
17. Ibid 191
18. T. A. Dearborn & S. Coll Worship At The Next Level
    Baker 2004 11-12
19. D. Ngien Gifted Response Paternoster 2008 xv, xvii
20. D. F. Ford & D. W. Hardy Living In Praise DLT 2005 8
21. Ibid 8-9
22. Ibid 64
23. Ibid 64-65
24. Ibid 65-66
25. R. Otto The Idea Of The Holy O. U. Press 1958 12
26. Ibid 13,17

CHAPTER ONE

1. D. Peterson ibid 23
2. A. Hill Enter His Courts With Praise Kingsway 1998 32
3. Ibid 32
4. Ibid 32-33
5. C. Westermann Genesis Ch. 12-36 Fortress Press 1995 356
6. W. Brueggemann Genesis J. Knox Press 1982 185
7. Ibid 187
8. V. P. Hamilton Genesis Ch. 18-50 Eerdmans 1995 99
9. Ibid 99-102
10. Ibid 103-104, 107

11. M. Redman Facedown Kingsway 2005 29
12. D. Peterson ibid 24
13. T. E. Fretheim Exodus J. Knox Press 1991 264-265
14. A. Motyer Exodus IVP 2005 250
15. M. Redman ibid 29
16. T. Hughes Holding Nothing Back Survivor 2007 24-25
17. A. Motyer ibid 267
18. T. E. Fretheim Ibid 315
19. C. Cocksworth Lecture on The Liturgy and the Spirit given at The Oase Conference – Norway in Feb 2007
20. R. E. Webber Worship Old & New Zondervann 1994 135
21. J. M. Boice Psalms Vol 3 Baker 1998 1064
22. G. Fee 1 Corinthians Eerdmans 1987 563-564
23. A. Thiselton 1 Corinthians Eerdmans 2000 890
24. A. Hill ibid 3-4, 13
25. D. Zscech Extravagant Worship Bethany House 2002 80
26. A. Hill ibid 121-122
27. Ibid 122-125
28. B. Childs Exodus SCM 1987 564
29. T. E. Fretheim ibid 281-282
30. B. Childs ibid 566
31. Ibid 542-543
32. Pope Benedict XV1 The Spirit of The Liturgy Ignatius 2000 22-23
33. T. E. Fretheim ibid 280-281
34. G. Wenham Leviticus Eerdmans 1979 129
35. D. Tidball The Message of The Cross IVP 2001 68
36. G. Wenham Ibid 26
37. Ibid 27
38. W. H. Bellinger Jr. Leviticus Paternoster 99
39. D. Tidball ibid 69
40. Ibid 70
41. Ibid 72
42. Ibid 78
43. W. H. Bellinger Ibid 101
44. S. R. Phifer Worship That Pleases God Trafford 2005 40
45. Ibid 43
46. Ibid 42

CHAPTER TWO

1. W. Brueggemann Jeremiah Eerdmans 1998 36
2. W. Brueggemann quoting A Welch ibid 36
3. Ibid 39
4. Ibid 78
5. Ibid 79-80

6. D. J. Simundson Amos Abingdon 2005 164
7. Ibid 188-189
8. J. L. Mays Amos SCM 1969 106-107
9. J. A. Motyer Amos BST 1974 131

CHAPTER THREE

1. M. Ashton in Worship By The Book Editor D. A. Carson
    Zondervann 2002 82
2. N. T. Wright Simply Christian SPCK 2006 131
3. B. F. Polman in Music In Christian Worship Liturgical Press
    2005 63
4. R. M. Kidd With One Voice Baker 2005 51,53, 63, 68
5. C. G. Broyles Psalms Paternoster 2002 2-3, 7-9, 11
6. P. Westermeyer Te Deum – The Church & Music Fortress
    Press 1998 34-35
7. J. L. Mays Psalms J Knox Press 1994 1
8. Ibid 1
9. Ibid 1
10. P. Westermeyer ibid 24
11. Ibid 7
12. S. R. Phifer ibid 147
13. H. Gunkel An Introduction To The Psalms Mercer University
    Press 1998 122-124, 127, 130-131
14. S. Mowinckel The Psalms In Israel's Worship 2004 Vol 2
    8-9, 15-17
15. W. Brueggemann The Message Of The Psalms Augsburgh
    1984 15
16. W. Brueggemann The Psalms – The Life Of Faith Fortress
    Press 1995 101-102
17. Ibid 102-103
18. Ibid 104
19. P. Ward Selling Worship Abingdon 2005 204
20. Brueggeman ibid 107
21. P. Westermeyer ibid 26
22. M. Pilavachi & L. Hoeksma Worship, Evangelism, Justice
    Survivor 2007 36
23. C. Croeker Music In Christian Worship Liturgical Press
    2005 77-78
24. R. Redman The Great Worship Awakening
    Jossey-Bass 2002 26
25. W. A. Bailey in Music In Christian Worship Liturgical Press
    2005 75
26. P. Westermeyer ibid 30
27. W. Brueggemann Israel's Praise Fortress Press 1988 4
28. Ibid 11
29. A. Weiser Psalms J. Knox Press 1962 219

30.   C. Westermann Praise & Lament In The Psalms J. Knox Press 1981 52

31.   J. L. Mays ibid 107

32.   Ibid 105-106

33.   J. Goldingay Psalms Vol 1 Eerdmans 2006 325-326

34.   D. Tidball The Cross IVP 2003 86-87

35.   Ibid 88

36.   Ibid 89

37.   A. Weiser ibid 224-225

38.   J. M. Kidd Ibid 78

CHAPTER FOUR

1.   Hawthorne: Martin: Reid Dictionary of Paul & His Letters IVP 1993 562

2.   P. O'Brien Philippians Eerdmans 1991 388-389

3.   M. Hooker Paul A Short Introduction Oneworld Oxford 2004 50-51

4.   J. D. G. Dunn The Theology Of Paul The Apostle Eerdmans 1998 251-254

5.   P. O'Brien ibid 232-233

6.   G. Fee ibid 222-223

7.   Ibid 224

8.   P. O'Brien ibid 238, 241

9.   D. Peterson Ibid 253

10.   F. F. Bruce Hebrews Eerdmans 1990 57-58

11.   Ibid 31

12.   Ibid 30-31

13.   R. Brown Hebrews IVP 1982 93-94

14.   Ibid quoting A. T. H. Robinson 96

15.   P. Ellingworth Hebrews Eerdmans 1993 268

16.   C. R. Koester Hebrews Anchor 2001 283, 293

17.   R. Brown ibid 100

18.   F. F. Bruce ibid 131

19.   C. R. Koester ibid 299

20.   F. F. Bruce ibid 185-186

21.   R. Brown ibid 152

22.   W. Nee The Normal Christian Life Kingsway 1989 13-14

23.   R. C. Moberly Ministerial Priesthood J. Murray 1899 245

24.   Ibid 246

25.   F. F. Bruce ibid 339

26.   C. Gray The Fire & The Clay Guiver et al SPCK 1999 48-49

27.   C. Cocksworth & R. Brown Being A Priest Today Canterbury Press 2002 6-7

28.   M. Ramsey The Christian Priest Today SPCK 1987 106-107

29.   P. H. Davids 1 Peter Eerdmans 1990 87

30. T. R. Schreiner 1& 2 Peter Broadman & Holman 2003 105
31 Ibid 106

CHAPTER FIVE

1. M. Redman Facedown Kingsway 2004 18-20
2. J. N. Oswalt Isaiah Ch. 1-39 Eerdmans 1986 180
3. B. S. Childs Isaiah J. Knox Press 2002 55
4. J. N. Oswalt ibid 176
5. Ibid 177
6. W. Brueggemann Isaiah Ch. 1-39 J. Knox Press 1998 58-59
7. J. N. Oswalt ibid 180
8. W. Brueggemann ibid 59-60
9. J. N. Oswalt ibid 185
10. B. Childs ibid 56
11. W. Eichrodt Ezekiel Westminster Press 1970 2, 4
12. D. L. Block Ezekiel Ch. 1-24 Eerdmans 1997 87
13. J. Blenkinsopp Ezekiel J. Knox Press 1990 16
14. C. J. H. Wright Ezekiel IVP 2001 22-23
15. W. Eichrodt ibid 53-54
16. C. J. H. Wright ibid 24-26
17. Ibid 51
18. Ibid 51-52
19. D. L. Block ibid 96
20. Ibid 97
21. Ibid 105
22. Ibid 109
23. G. E. Ladd Revelation Eerdman 1972 7-9
24. M. E. Boring Revelation J. Knox Press 1989 5-7
25. D. A. Carson ibid 23
26. I. Boxhall Revelation Continuum 2006 83-84
27. Ibid 85
28. Ibid 86
29. G. E. Ladd ibid 77
30. I. Boxall ibid 89
31. Ibid 99
32. Ibid 101-102
33. N. Due Created For Worship Mentor 2005 222
34. M. E. Boring ibid 193

CHAPTER SIX

1. P. Ward ibid 2005 70-72
2. J. Steven Worship In The Restoration Movement Grove Booklet 1989 3-4, 9-11
3. R. Redman ibid 34-35
4. Ibid 36

5.   V. Cooke Understanding Songs In Renewal Grove Booklet
          2001 17
6.   Ibid 18
7.   M. Bonnington Patterns In charismatic Spirituality Grove
          Booklet 2008 18-21
8.   Ibid 4
9.   Ibid 4
10.   P. Hocken Streams Of Renewal –The Origins & Early
          Development Of The Charismatic Movement Paternoster
          1997 148-149
11.   Ibid 149-150
12.   Ibid 159-165
13.   P. Hocken ibid 75
14   R. Cantalamessa Come, Creator Spirit The Liturgical
          Press 2003 9-10
15.   A. Park To Know You More Kingsway 2002 19-320
16.   Ibid 320-321
17.   Ibid 317
18.   Ibid 312-313
19.   Ibid 321-322
20.   V. Cooke ibid 8
21.   Ibid 11
22.   Ibid 12
23.   J. Leach Liturgy & Liberty ibid 152-153
24.   P. Oakley Soul Survivor Songbook 2001 Article in Index
25.   M. Pilavachi & L. Hoeksma ibid 2007 36
26.   This information about Soul Survivor and Mike Pilavachi can
          be found on their website.
27.   P. Ward ibid 152
28.   Ibid 16
29.   Ibid 17
30.   M. Pilavachi For The Audience Of One Hodder 1999 134-135
31.   M. Redman The Unquenchable Worshipper Kingsway 2001 29
32.   V. Cooke ibid 5
33.   Ibid 5-6
34.   Ibid 6
35.   Ibid 7
36.   Ibid 8
37.   P. Roberts Alternative Worship in the Church of England
          Grove Booklet 1999 14
38.   Ibid 3
39.   Ibid 9
40.   J. Baker: Gay: Brown Alternative Worship SPCK 2003 18-19
41.   P. Ward Editor Rite Stuff BRF 2004 38-39
42.   C. & J. Leach How to Plan and Lead All-Age Worship
          Grove Booklet 2008 4

43. Ibid 4
44. A. Barton All-Age Worship Grove Booklet 1997 10
45. R. Lamont Understanding Children Understanding God SPCK 2007 18
46. C. & J. Leach ibid 4-5
47. Ibid 5
48. Ibid 13
49. A. Barton ibid 25
50. S. M. Stewart & J. W. Berryman Young Children & Worship WJKnox 1989 18
51. N. Harding Young Children Can Worship Kevin Mayhew 1999 40-47
52. Ibid 48-49
53. J. Gardner Mind The Gap IVP 2008 118-119
54. C. & J. Leach ibid 17
55. General Synod Report Children In The Way Church House Publishing 1988 6
56. Ibid 39
57. M. Carter All God's Children SPCK 2007 71
58. General Synod Report ibid 40
59. Ibid 40
60. M. Carter ibid 71
61. General Synod Report ibid 40
62. M. Carter ibid 71
63. General Synod Report ibid 40
64. M. Carter ibid 71
65. General Synod Report ibid 40
66. M. Carter ibid 72, 75
67. General Synod Report ibid 58, 62-63
68. Ibid 114
69. CGOMC Core Skills In Working With Children Barnabas 2006 16
70 Ibid 18
71. M. Carter ibid 114
72. M. Withers Mission-shaped Children Church House Publishing 2007 35
73. T. & J. Wright Contemporary Worship Abingdon 1997 21
74. Ibid 23-24
75. Q. J. Schultze High-Tech Worship Baker 2000 20
76. Ibid 23, 26-27
77. C. Plantinga Jr. & S. A. Rozeboom Discerning The Spirits Eerdmans 2003 3
78. C. Kroeker Editor Music In Christian Worship F. B. Brown Liturgical Press 2005 151-152
79. N. Page And Now Let's Move Into A Time Of Nonsense Continuum 2005 30-31

80. D. Lucarni Why I Left The Contemporary Christian Music Movement Evangelical Press 2002 52
81. Ibid 53-55
82. Ibid 58-59
83. M. Redman S. S. Songbook 2001 Article in Index
84. I. Stackhouse Gospel Driven Church Paternoster 2004 55
85. Ibid 46, 57
86. P. Moger Music & Worship: Principles To Practice Grove 1994 14, 18-19
87. L. Morris John Eerdmans 1995 240
88. R. E. Brown John Ch. 1-12 Anchor 1966 180
89. J. M. Boice John Vol 1 Ch. 1-4 Baker 2000 298
90. D. Stancliffe God's Pattern – Shaping Our Worship, Ministry & Life SPCK 2003 40
91. P. Oakley S. S. Songbook 2001 Article in Index
92. D. Zscech ibid 26
93. T. Hughes Passion For Your Name Kingsway 2003 84
94. P. Ward ibid 209-210
95. C. Cocksworth in Remembering Our Future 2007 Edited by A. Walker & L. Bretherton Paternoster 2007 142-143
96. C. Cocksworth Holding Together Catholic Evangelical Worship In The Spirit – Lecture in Anvil 2005 7,13
97. R. Parry Worshipping Trinity Continuum 2005 1-2
98. Ibid 109
99. J. H. S. Steven Worship In The Spirit – Charismatic Worship in the Church of England Paternoster 2002 132-133
100. Ibid 133
101. Ibid 188-189
102. Ibid 192
103. Ibid 199
104. Ibid 193-194
105. T. Smail, Walker, Wright Charismatic Renewal SPCK 1993 112
106. Ibid 111
107. Ibid 110
108. I. Stackhouse in Remembering Our future ibid 153
109. Ibid 153-154
110. Ibid 154
111. Ibid 154-155
112. A. Walker in Remembering Our Future ibid 8-9
113. I. Stackhouse ibid 156-157

CHAPTER SEVEN

1. J. Cooper ibid 118
2. C. Cocksworth & R. Brown ibid 75

3.   P. Greenslade Worship In The Best Of Both Worlds
      Paternoster 2008 51
4.   Ibid 51
5.   Ibid 53
6.   Ibid 53
7.   Ibid 56
8.   T. A. Dearborn & S. Coil ibid 25
9.   Liturgical Commission Transforming Worship Church House
      Publishing 2007 8-9
10.   Alternative Worship ibid 112
11.   B. O' Malley A Celtic Primer Canterbury Press 2002 95-96
12.   The Northumbria Community Celtic Daily Prayer Collins
      2005 7, 223, 293
13.   M. Perham ibid 40, 43
14.   J. leach Liturgy & Liberty ibid 1989 51, 55
15.   C. Headley Liturgy & Spiritual Formation Grove Booklet
      1999 18
16.   Ibid 22
17.   C. Cocksworth Lecture given at the Oase Conference ibid
18.   Ibid
19.   C. Cocksworth Holding Together Canterbury Press 2008 157
20.   C. Cocksworth in Remembering Our future ibid 147
21.   R. Woods & B. Walrath The Message In The Music Abingdon
      2007 47-48
22.   Ibid 48-51
23.   Ibid 48-49
24.   W. Brueggemann The Message Of The Psalms Augsburh
      1984 39
25.   Ibid 41
26.   C. Wimber John Wimber – The Way It Was Hodder 1999
      121, 123
27.   M. Asthon ibid 96
28.   D. Stancliffe ibid xiii
29.   A. Atherstone Confesing Our Sins Grove 2004 11
30.   S. Mowinckel ibid 13-14
31.   J. Goldingay ibid 455-456
32.   J. Mays Psalms ibid 147
33.   J. S. Begbie Resounding Truth – Christian Wisdom in the
      World of Music Baker 2007 65
34.   Ibid 66
35   Ibid 67
36.   Ibid 13, 24
37.   R. M. Kidd ibid 37
38.   A. L Blackwell The Sacred In Music Lutterworth Press 1999 29
39.   Ibid 221-222
40.   R. M. Kidd ibid 133-134

41.   Ibid 134-135
42.   Ibid 140
43.   Ibid 140-141
44.   C. Kroeker Music In Christian Worship ix
45.   Ibid x
46.   B. Kauflin ibid 93
47.   H. M. Best Unceasing Worship IVP 2003 146-147
48.   R. Woods & B. Walrath ibid 92
49.   Ibid 93
50.   Ibid 93
51.   Ibid 96
52.   M. Redman The Heart Of The Worship Files Kingsway 2003 42-43
53.   P. Westermeyer ibid 202
54.   J. R. Watson Hymns OUP 2003 164
55.   Ibid 12,15
56.   B. F. Polman in Music In Christian Worship ibid 66
57.   J. R. Watson ibid 205-208
59.   B. F. Polman ibid 67-69
59.   M. Redman ibid 22
60.   Ibid 45

APPENDIX

1.   J. Cooper Glory In The Church Authentic 2003 xvii-xviii
2.   Ibid 16
3.   Ibid 13-15
4.   Ibid 18-24

BIBLIOGRAPHY

P. Atherstone Confessing Our Sins Grove Booklet 2004

J. Baker: G. Gay: J. Brown Alternative Worship SPCK 2003

A. Barton All-Age Wroship Grove Booklet 1997

J. S. Begbie Resounding Truth Baker 2007

H. M. Best Unceasing Worship IVP 2003

J. Blenkinsopp Ezekiel John Knox Press 1990

D. L. Block Ezekiel Ch. 1-24 Eerdmans 1997

J. M. Boice John Vol 1 Ch. 1-4 Baker 2000

M. Bonnington Patterns In Charismatic Spirituality Grove Booklet 2007

M. E. Boring Revelation John Knox Press 1989

I. Boxall Revelation Continuum 2006

P. O'Brien Philippians Eerdmans 1991

C. G. Broyles Psalms Paternoster 2002

R. Brown How Hymns Shape Our Lives Grove Booklet 2001

R. E. Brown John Ch. 1-12 Anchor 1966

F. F. Bruce Hebrews Eerdmans 1990

W. Brueggemann Israel's Praise Fortress Press 1988

W. Brueggemann The Message Of The Psalms Augsburg 1984

W. Brueggemann The Psalms Fortress Press 1995

W. Brueggemann Isaiah Ch. 1-39 John Knox 1998

W. Brueggemann Jeremiah Eerdmans 1998

D. A. Carson John IVP 1991

M. Carter All God's Children SPCK 2008
Church House Publishing Children In The Way 1988

S. Christou The Priest & The People Of God Phoenix Books 2003

E. P. Clowney 1 Peter IVP 1988

Consultative Group On Ministry Amongst Children B. R. F. 2006

C. Cocksworth & R. Brown Being A Priest Today Canterbury Press 2002

C. Cocksworth Evangelical Eucharistic Thought In the Church of England CUP 2002

C. Cocksworth Holy, Holy, Holy DLT 2004

C. Cocksworth Holding Together – Catholic Evangelical Worship In The Spirit Lecture in Anvil Vol 22 NO 1 2005

C. Cocksworth Lecture on The Liturgy & The Spirit – given at The Oase Conference in Norway in February 2007

C. Cocksworth Holding Together Canterbury Press 2008

V. Cooke Understanding Songs In Renewal Grove Booklet 2001

J. Cooper Glory In The church Authentic 2003

P. H. Davids 1 Peter Eerdmans 1990

M. J. Dawn Reaching Out Without Dumbing Down Eerdmans 1995

T. Dearborn & S. Coll Worship At The Next Level Baker 2004

N. Due Created For Worship Mentor 2005

J. D. G. Dunn Theology Of Paul The Apostle Eerdmans 1998

W. Eichdrot Ezekiel Westminster Press 1970

P. Ellingworth Hebrews Eerdmans 1993

G. Fee 1 Corinthians Eerdmans 1987

G. Fee Philippians Eerdmans 1995

F. Ford & D. W. Hardy Living In Praise DLT 2005

J. Gardner Mend The Gap IVP 2008

J. Gledhill Leading A Local Church SPCK 2003

J. Goldingay Psalms Vol : 1-41 Eerdmans 2006

P. Greenslade Worship In The Best Of Both Worlds Paternoster 2008

H. Gunkel An Introduction To The Psalms Mercer U. Press 1998

V. P. Hamilton Genesis Ch. 18-50 Eerdmans 1995

N. Harding Children Can Worship Kevin Mayhew 1999

Hawthorne: Martin: Reid: Dictionary Of Paul & His Letters
IVP 1993

C. Headley Liturgy & Spiritual Formation Grove Booklet 1997

A. Hill Enter His Courts With Praise Kingsway 1998

P. Hocken Streams Of Renewal – The Origins & Development
Of The Charismatic Movement In Gt. Britain Paternoster 1997

M. Hooker Paul Oneworld Oxford 2004

G. Hughes Meaning as Worship C. U. Press 2003

T. Hughes Passion For Your Name Kingsway 2004

T. Hughes Holding Nothing Back Survivor 2007

E. James A Life Of Bishop J. A. T. Robinson Collins 1987

B. Kauflin Worship Matters Crossway 2008

G. Kendrick Worship Kingsway 1984

G. Kendrick Collection 150 Songs World Wide 2000

D. Kennedy Understanding Anglican Worship Grove Booklet 1997

C. R. Koester Hebrews Anchor 2001

C. Kroeker Music In Christian Worship Liturgical Press 2005

R. M. Kidd With One Voice Baker 2005

G. E. Ladd Revelation Eerdmans 1972

R. Lamont Understanding Children Understanding God SPCK 2007

C. & J. Leach How To Plan & Lead All-Age Worship Grove 2008

J. Leach Liturgy And Liberty Monarch 1989

J. Leach Living Liturgy Kingsway 1997

Liturgical Commission Transforming Worship 2007

J. Lucarni Why I Left The C. C. M. Movement Evangelical Press 2002

J. R. Lundbom Jeremiah Ch. 1-20 Anchor 1999

B. O' Malley A Celtic Primer Canterbury Press 2002

J. L. Mays Amos SCM 1969

J. L. Mays The Psalms J. Knox Press 1994

P. Moger Music & Worship Principles To Practice Grove Booklet 1994

L. Morris John Eerdmans 1995

J. A. Motyer Amos BST 1974

S. Mowinckel Psalms In Israel's Worship Eerdmans 2004

Northumbria Community Celtic Daily Prayer Collins 2005

D. Ngien Gifted Response Paternoster 2008

R. Otto The Idea Of The Holy C. U. Press 1958

J. N. Oswalt Isaiah Ch. 1-39 Eerdmans 1986

N. Page And Now Let's Move Into A Time Of Nonsense Continuum 2004

N. & C. Page Celebrations! All Age Worship Authentic 2007

A. Park To Know You More Kingsway 2003

R. Parry Worshipping Trinity Continuum 2005

M. Perham New Handbook Of Pastoral Liturgy SPCK 2000

D. Peterson Engaging With God IVP 1992

S. R. Phifer Worship That Pleases God Trafford Publishing 2005

M. Pilavachi For The Audience Of One Hodder 1999

M. Pilavachi & L. Hoeksma Worship: Evangelism: Justice
Soul Survivor 2006

C. Plantinga Jr. & S. A. Rozeboom Discerning The Spirits
Eerdmans 2003

Pope Bendict XV1 The Spirit Of The Liturgy Ignatius 2000

J. Pritchard The Life & Work Of A Priest SPCK 2007

M. Ramsey The Christian Priest SPCK 1985

M. Redman Facedown Kingsway 2005

M. Redman The Unquenchable Worshipper Kingsway 2001

R. Redman The Great Worship Awakening Jossey-Bass 2002

Q. J. Schultz High-Tech Worship Baker 2004

D. J. Simundson Amos Abingdon 2005

Smail, Walker, Wright Charismatic Renewal SPCK 1993

I. Stackhouse The Gospel Driven Church Peternoster 2004

D. Stancliffe God's Pattern, Shaping Our Worship SPCK 2003

J. H. Steven Worship In The Restoration Movement Grove
Booklet 1989

J. H. S. Steven Worship In The Spirit Paternoster 2002

S. M. Stewart & J. W. Berryman Young Children & Worship
John Knox 1989

A. Thiselton 1 Corinthians Eerdmans 2000

J. A. Thompson Jeremiah Eerdmans 1980

D. Tidball The Cross IVP 2003

A. Walker & L. Bretherton Editors Remembering Our Future -
Explorations In Deep Church Paternoster 2007

J. R. Walton Hymns OUP 2003

P. Ward Editor The Rite Stuff Bible Reading Fellowship 2004

P. Ward Selling Worship The Church Continuum 2005

R. E. Webber Worship Old & New Zondervann 1994

R. E. Webber Ancient –Future Worship Baker 2008

A. Weiser The Psalms SCM 1962

C. Westermann Praise & Lament In The Psalms John knox 1981

P. Westermeyer Te Deum – The Church & Music Fortress 1998

J. F. White Christian Worship Abingdon 1986

C. Wimber John Wimber – The Way It Was Hodder 1999

M. Withers Mission-Shaped Children Church House Pub 2007

R. Woods & B. Walrush The Message In The Music Abingdon 2007

C. J. Wright Ezekiel IVP 2001

N. T. Wright Simply Christian SPCK 2006

T. & R. Wright Contemporary Worship Abingdon 1997

D. Zscech Extravagant Worship Bethany 2003.